GOD'S ORDER AND NATURAL LAW

This book fills an important gap in the theological interpretation of the Laudian Divines. Iain MacKenzie presents the theology of the Anglican theologians of the early seventeenth century, exploring the concept of order first in God but then in creation in its relation to the Creator, and then examining the working out of this concept based in theology in civil and ecclesiastical structures and practice. Mapping the Laudian Divines' perceptions of how order primarily and necessarily resides in God existing as Father, Son and Holy Spirit, this book sets out the essential and necessarily practical application of theology as seen by seventeenth-century theologians, and traces the legacy which they have left. This theological, as opposed to a merely historical or literary, study of this important period for the development of society, will be of particular value to theologians, historians and those concerned with the intellectual history of the seventeenth century.

God's Order and Natural Law

The works of the Laudian Divines

IAIN M. MacKENZIE
Canon Residentiary of Worcester, UK

Ashgate

Published by
Ashgate Publishing Limited
Gower House, Croft Road
Aldershot, Hants
GU11 3HR
England

Ashgate Publishing Company
131 Main Street
Burlington
VT 05401–5600
USA

Ashgate website: http://www.ashgate.com

The author has asserted his moral right under the Copyright, Designs and Patents Act, 1988, to be identified as the author of this work.

British Library Cataloguing in Publication Data
MacKenzie, Iain M., 1937–
God's order and natural law: the works of the
Laudian Divines
1. Order – Religious aspects – Christianity
2. Natural law – Religious aspects – Christianity
I. Title
261.5

US Library of Congress Cataloging in Publication Data
MacKenzie, Iain M., 1937–
God's order and natural law: the works of the
Laudian Divines / Iain M. MacKenzie.
    p. cm.
Includes bibliographical references (p.).
1. Order – Religious aspects – Church of England – History
of doctrines – 17th century. 2. Natural law – Religious
aspects – Church of England – History of doctrines – 17th century.
3. Church of England – Doctrines – History – 17th century. I. Title.
BX5075.M29 2002
241'.2–dc21   2001053625

ISBN 0 7546 0841 7 (Hbk)
ISBN 0 7546 0843 3 (Pbk)

This book is printed on acid free paper.

Typeset in Times Roman by Manton Typesetters, Louth, Lincolnshire, UK.
Printed and bound in Great Britain by MPG Books Ltd, Bodmin, Cornwall.

Contents

Preface

This work on the concept of 'Order' in the works of the Laudian Divines, is the result of discussions and correspondence with the Very Reverend Professor T.F. Torrance on the more general concept of 'Order' as expressed particularly by the Pre-Nicene and Nicene Fathers and its unfolding thereafter in systematic theology. It holds an important place in many of his own recent works and in Karl Barth's *Church Dogmatics*. The recent, renewed interest in the doctrine of Creation in relation to the doctrine of the Incarnation, and the subsequent results for thinking about the realities of the created dimension in relation to the realities of God in His Self-revelation in Christ as attested in Scripture and Tradition, has brought this concept of 'Order' to the fore in theological thought.

Having already undertaken research on 'The Doctrine of the Holy Spirit in the Works of Lancelot Andrewes'[1] under Professor Torrance, it had become increasingly clear to me that, with the Anglican theological method as operated in the seventeenth century, of using Scripture, Tradition and Reason in a particular relationship, the concepts of the early Church underlay Anglican thought to a much greater extent than is apparent by a surface reading of the works of the Laudians. This is true of Patristic observations on the *oikonomia* of God, the order which God is in Himself in His Triune Being and the order which He bestows in His act of creation.

The particular circumstances of the seventeenth century, with the widening of scientific discovery on the one hand and the unsettlement of political and social stability on the other, gave rise as a matter of pressing necessity to an emphasis on the theological concept of 'Order' in the preaching and writings of these Divines.

To state the genius of the seventeenth-century Laudian Divines, is to admit the problem of analysing their works. They had no theological system whereby doctrine was neatly put into tidy compartments. Rather, they operated with a theological method and therefore any systematic way of thinking is difficult to elucidate and construct into a consistent pattern of theological statement.

There is a twofold character to the doctrine of the seventeenth-century divines. First, it is a statement of that Catholic faith which is scripturally founded, and clarified and safeguarded by the Fathers and Councils of the Church of the first five centuries. Second, it is applied by them, and given direction for their particular time and place. The first character is determined by the insistence on scripture and tradition, the second by reason.

The relation between scripture, tradition and reason will be set out later. For the moment it will suffice to note that this is the hallmark of these divines; it is their *modus operandi*. It is a theological method developed from the work of Richard Hooker – in which indeed theology is explicitly set out. But the difficulty comes in the fact that at no other time is this method so scrupulously applied to all manner of contemporary issues – political, social, legal, liturgical and so on. Reason, therefore, takes on a peculiarly seventeenth-century application. More often than not, that second character of their theology, reason, *seems* to assume a primary role, and this can lead to a distortion of interpretation of their works if it is not constantly held in mind that there is still an implicit primary place given to scripture and tradition – an acceptance of the determinative role of scripture and tradition which can only highlight the importance of these two categories.

It is of the utmost importance to realize that the method adopted by Richard Hooker of setting out Scripture, Tradition and Reason in separate categories – albeit related loosely – develops by the seventeenth century into a harmonious relation and interdependence between the three. For all the implicity of the role and place of scripture and tradition in the seventeenth-century divines, to the extent that they seem to be bent to fit reason's necessary approach to the addressing of certain problems and issues of the time, a careful examination of their theological method will indicate that reason is the handmaid of the first two, related to them by being shaped by them for its proper application.

One example of this is Andrewes's treatment of his texts in the *Sermons* preached on the anniversary of the Gunpowder Plot and the anniversary of the Conspiracy of the Gowries. The seemingly facile way in which the Jesuits or the Earl of Gowry and his brother (the respective villains of these two series of sermons) are identified with dissatisfied parties from the Old or New Testaments, would tend to indicate that scripture was being bent to suit contemporary purposes. But there is, as may become apparent when these sermons are noted later, a deeper and wider significance more universally applicable.

Any critique of the work of the Laudian Divines must take account of another problem. This concerns the selection of quotations. Such is the general style of the Laudians – though this has particular bearing on the writings of Lancelot Andrewes – that it is difficult, and indeed sometimes impossible, to use a brief quotation to illustrate a point. They tended to be masters of the short and pithy statement; but such statements can be artificially wrested from the matrix of their context to the detriment of their full meaning and significance. I have found it, therefore, more respectful to the propriety of their intent and thought, to quote from their works sometimes at length. Apart from this, lengthier quotations illustrate their direction and development of thought, and permit the writers to speak for themselves more eloquently and tellingly, it may be added, than any exposition of that thought. This has allowed, moreover, the appreciation in these quotations of the theological method using Scripture, Tradition and Reason in their relation one to the other, employed by the Laudian Divines, to be realized as the characteristic lying behind their way of thinking and expression. I have used quotations, therefore, not just as examples around a particular issue, but as vehicles of the ethos of these Divines.

The quotations from John Swan's, William Laud's works and Lancelot Andrewes's sermons, contain phrases and sentences in italics or capital letters. These are found in the original editions cited and are these authors' own emphases.

There were no masters of theology in the seventeenth century, at least among the Laudians. Lancelot Andrewes's complaint that there were those who supposed and claimed that they could read off the decrees of God at their fingertips,[2] exhibits the general attitude of these Divines to theology – that it was a safeguarding of the mystery which God is in His being and His acts. It was not a scheme of explanation to be mastered by man. There is, therefore, a reluctance to define a specific corpus of doctrine. Any work of systematically constructing a body of opinion about any particular issue or area of belief out of the writings of the Laudian Divines, is therefore a necessity of quarrying into their works and hewing out or picking up little hints, passing references, general statements and significant emphases from larger tracts of sermons, disputations and treatises on much wider themes.

The concept of 'Order', however, is a stratum of thought which emerges, again and again, in different forms owing to the different circumstances to which particular works were addressed.

This work on that concept of 'Order' within the works of the Laudian Divines, is an attempt to make a contribution from a particular area and time of theological endeavour and development, to the much larger debate concerning Creation, Incarnation and the 'Economy' of God. There is much that has been neglected in the matter of a doctrinal assessment of seventeenth-century Anglican thought. This is an attempt to redress part of that lack.

With regard to 'Order', and especially to God's ordering of creation, it is only part of the necessity of a much wider exercise. The interest in English theology in created order lies as yet dormant. But it is there. There is a vast sweep of significant thought as yet to be uncovered and brought to light in, for example, the English tradition of the Hexaemeron. This long tradition, in deposited instinct at least, lies within John Swan's *Hexaemeron* included in his work *Speculum Mundi*. Although he makes no reference directly to certain significant Hexaemeronic works within the English tradition, the general concepts are there which were laid out before by Bede and Grosseteste. The Hexaemeron of each of these is the ground on which this tradition has developed by the seventeenth century. By that time, Grosseteste's work had more or less been forgotten, but certainly not in substance. Swan's observations on light, its quality, nature and precedence in the created order, and its relation to uncreated Light, could have been lifted immediately from Grosseteste's *Hexaemeron* and *De Luce*.[3]

The tradition set by Basil's fourth-century *Hexaemeron*, Gregory of Nyssa's completion of that work by Basil in his *The Making of Man*, and all Jerome's works on creation, entered English theological development via Bede (*c*.673–735). Grosseteste (*c*.1170–1253) according to R. Southern,[4] took this up, and the undoubted emphases and influences remained, if not, for some time, the actual texts of the last named. These emphases and influences surface again in Swan's seventeenth-century work. This tradition deserves a long and deep scrutiny and assessment, and this work on 'Order' in the writings of the Laudian Divines is, I hope, a part of the necessary acknowledgement and reverence for that tradition and its English expression.

This English Tradition concerning 'Order', is, in turn, also part of an even wider context of theological concern. This wideness is expressed in much of T.F. Torrance's recent works.[5] This is an area of theological endeavour of vast importance as scientific advance, in its microscopic and macroscopic fields, penetrates farther to the boundaries of existence and time and space. In its thought forms, theology has much to say regarding the concept of 'Order' in dialogue with scientific endeavour. Any attempt, such as this within the particular historical context of the Laudian

Divines, can only be a very small contribution to a far greater understanding and clarification of theological thought in this respect.

I am indebted to T.F. Torrance for his encouragement in the matter.

Notes

1 I.M. MacKenzie: 'The Doctrine of the Holy Spirit in the Works of Lancelot Andrewes'. Unpublished thesis for M.Th., University of Edinburgh, 1970.
2 Lancelot Andrewes: cf. *Ninety-six Sermons*, Sermon 3 of the *Nativity*, 1635 edn, p.548.
3 Robert Grosseteste: cf. *Hexaemeron*: IV: text by Dales and Geiben, published for the British Academy by Oxford University Press, pp.88ff.
4 R. Southern: *Robert Grosseteste: The Growth of an English Mind in Medieval Europe*, Clarendon, 1988.
5 T.F. Torrance: e.g. *Divine and Contingent Order*, Oxford University Press, 1981; *Space, Time and Incarnation*, Oxford University Press, 1969; *Space, Time and Resurrection*, Handsel Press, 1976; *The Ground and Grammar of Theology*, Christian Journals, 1980.

Introduction

The use of the term 'Laudian' is often a matter of loose convenience to historians, being generally employed by them concerning the politics of the seventeenth century. In the same way, the use of 'Erastian' and 'Arminian' as prefixes to certain divines of the time, has been determined by an individual historian's point of view and decided aim. Whether the terms 'Laudian', 'Erastian' and 'Arminian' have been understood and applied in the context of seventeenth-century English theology is another matter.

Several issues underlying the disputes of the seventeenth-century have not been seen in their theological context by certain historians. When they have been so viewed, it is doubtful if the theological issues have been significantly grasped. This is partly due to the attitudes and aims with which respective historians operate. We may summarize generally out of the stances of some historians, by way of example, their varying historical interpretations of the causes of the Civil War.

R.H. Tawney claims that the root causes of the Civil War lay in the fact that the gentry were determined to take the political power to which their economic success entitled them. H. Trevor-Roper (Lord Dacre), on the other hand, takes the view that the cause for unrest lay in the poor and discontented gentry from the provinces rebelling against administrative and economic centralization. In this instance one historian views the cause of war as the gentry rising, the other as the gentry falling.

The traditional 'Whig' view of the Civil War as expressed by nineteenth- and early-twentieth-century historians such as Thomas Macaulay and G.M. Trevelyan, sees the struggle as being a clash of Liberty (Parliament and what it stood for) versus Despotism (the Monarchy), or the right of the individual seeking to protect fundamental liberties and overthrowing a tyrannical form of government. This contradicts the 'Tory' view as expressed by Clarendon in the seventeenth century, that the monarchy of Charles I was not tyrannical but sought to protect the ordinary people from exploitation by a small group of capitalists, people serving their own interests, who dominated the House of Commons and who were strongly Puritan in their religious interests.

The 'Whig' view also contradicts the 'Marxist' interpretation, as typified by Christopher Hill in his earlier writings, that Charles I's government represented an obsolete system, the feudal order, which the bourgeoisie sought to overthrow in order to create conditions suitable for a free capitalist development.[1]

The difficulty of historical interpretation is underlined here. When precise theological issues are dealt with by historians, the difficulties become sharper. One such issue which is a casualty of the historian's pen has been the concept of the Divine Right of Kings, and this generally again because of anachronistic aims and ends. Such attitudes on the Divine Right of Kings as those expressed variously by both 'Whig' and 'Socialist' historians, have also viewed the bishops of James VI and I and Charles I as sycophantic. Historians cannot be expected to be theologians.

Nevertheless, it is expected that due care is taken of contemporary sources. To cite but one source among many, the sermons of Lancelot Andrewes, particularly those preached on state occasions, are clear enough – even for the theologically untutored eye to see – that the Divine Right of Monarchs has an inseparable corollary, the Divine Responsibility of Kings. In any case, the concept of Divine Right has been held to mean, generally and simplistically, that the King is in place of God and therefore can do no wrong. A more careful reading of the texts of divines on the subject would reveal that this is a questionable interpretation of the matter.

One example where the question of failure to appreciate theological texts must be raised, is furnished by H. Trevor-Roper (Lord Dacre) in his *Archbishop Laud*, where he remarks that essentially Andrewes was 'a professor rather than a churchman, and politics he regarded as outside the Church, whose doctrines only he expounded and annotated' (1962:30). The very essence of Andrewes's awareness of the universal implications of doctrine was that God had entered and taken to Himself the realities of the world, including the affairs of Caesar, in the Incarnation. The failure here is to grasp the insistence by Andrewes that God is concerned with the physical, the corporeal, the 'secular', society and state, as much as with the spiritual and (in Trevor-Roper's limited view of the word) 'doctrinal'. Doctrine for Andrewes was something else, and this will be examined fully, later. Such careful appreciation is necessary when dealing with the subject of 'Divine Right of Kings'.

The particular subject of the Divine Right of Kings is complicated. Its interpretation depends on an appreciation first, of the order which God is in Himself eternally and the order by which He expresses the sort of God He is in creation and re-creation; secondly of that created order contingent upon the rationality of God and corresponding to that Divine rationality in its temporal and spatial limitations and nature, and thirdly, of the concept of Natural Law, which is seen to be a Christian society's response to the sort of creation which God, in His revelation in Jesus Christ, intends creation to be.

This last concept embodies, for the divines of the period, all true human identity and dignity. Its upholding is for the glory of God, the peace of the Church, the stability and true welfare of society and the regard of the individual. It is the estate and vocation of kings under God to uphold that Natural Law. Kingship is not outwith Natural Law nor can monarchy be exercised other than that Law's expression and as its guardian. Moreover, these divines constantly remind, while kings are worthy of the highest regard for their excellent and difficult office, yet they are to be aware that they are but mortal and must appear before the judgment seat of the King of Kings. God's vice-regents they are; that they are also stewards accountable to God is the obverse of that office.

The term 'Laudian' employed here is determined by that theological insistence on 'Order', common to many of the seventeenth-century divines. 'Order' and its upholding, is a continuous thread running through their works. Indeed, it is a fundamental concept upon which so much of their thought concerning all aspects of ecclesiastical and temporal life and concern is built.

Clearly, some of the divines which I have included in the heading 'Laudian', preceded Laud. 'Laudianism' I see as an insistence common not only to the seventeenth-century divines contemporary with Laud, but that which pervades the works of the divines of the Elizabethan, Jacobean and Caroline church. That is to say, I interpret 'Laudianism', not as a phenomenon within one generation, but as an emphasis within the Church of England – an ongoing trend – with an insistence on 'order' which finds its climax in Laud and his contemporaries. It takes its title from Laud as the martyr exponent of 'order', even if he were perhaps over-zealous and over-scrupulous in imposing order as he saw it. Hence the choice of those concerned with 'order' stretches from Richard Hooker – perhaps the first advocate of the Anglican assertion of the concept – through to Laud and his contemporaries. 'Laudian' therefore is applied to a wide theological emphasis rather than any narrow historical term of convenience or confined luturgical practice. In this sense is the term used to encompass the divines whose works are examined here.

If what is now called 'churchmanship' was the factor controlling the use of the term 'Laudian', some divines included here – Francis Mason, John Swan, for example – would not fall into this category. This is to determine the classification 'Laudian' by only surface liturgical considerations. By the same token, Lancelot Andrewes should be regarded as more 'Laudian' than Laud.

The selection of the divines cited here is determined by the theological concept of Order, on which there is remarkable consistency and agreement throughout their works. All of them would insist, whatever their 'churchmanship' on dignity and reverence in worship as an expression of Order, and all of them have an abhorrence of individual interpretations of Scripture and Liturgy. But that is not the only consideration and appreciation of Order which they shared. It goes deeper than that; it is the only true foundation and sure supply of both men and states – because it rests on that Order which the Triune God is and that Order which He has decreed in His creative and re-creative works as an expression of His Being.

The criticism may be offered that some of these divines were 'Calvinist' and therefore cannot possibly be classed as 'Laudian'. Such a charge rests on a fundamental failure to appreciate the nature of Calvinism in this period. English Puritanism was not the Calvinism of Geneva. Puritans, of whom Laud was the implacable foe, may have seized on some of Calvin's emphases, but other and distorting factors produced that phenomenon known as 'Puritanism'. The term 'Puritan' itself does not describe one heterogeneous body of opinion. Indeed sectarianism was the hallmark of Puritanism with its attendant division and dispute, as Cromwell was only too well aware, and which his army could alone hold in check.

England learned its Calvinism from the returned Marian exiles, and they, particularly those returning from Holland, had learned that brand of Calvinism which had emerged in the Low Countries and is called 'Federal Calvinism'. This had an overwhelming emphasis on double predestination which it hardened into a structure of legalistic proportions, accompanied by an insistence that the elect were observably known by their piety. This is far removed from the Calvinism of Geneva, with its insistence on a predestination in Christ, and such a doctrine used only to safeguard the mystery of the grace of God as over against all human attempts to explain and codify salvation.

It is necessary from the outset to clear that which appears distorted as in a mist in the works of both theologians and historians concerning the relation between the Anglican divines of the late sixteenth and early seventeenth centuries and Calvinism. This concerns the nature of Calvinism perceived or shunned, comprehended or misunderstood, embraced or dismissed, as the case may have been, in England.

What does not seem to be understood generally by those not completely familiar at first hand with the works of John Calvin, is that in that phenomenon labelled sweepingly as Calvinism, a distinction has to be appreciated and carefully observed. This concerns the very different doctrinal emphases between, on the one hand, Calvin and the orthodox Calvinists, and on the other, those influenced to a degree by his works, but, though claiming allegiance to him, departed from the mainstream of his thought, intermingling other considerations with his theological *modus operandi*. These latter are more properly called Federal Calvinists.

It has been mentioned already that England was taught its Calvinism through those who, in the main, were returned Marian exiles. Though few in number (about 500) they were from the landed gentry and clerical ranks and in a position to exercise much vocal and administrative influence. The sojourn of these exiles had been mainly in the Low Countries, and it was there that that distinct difference between the Calvinism of Geneva, and what went under the general nomenclature 'Calvinism' was apparent. For there, while appeal was made to the works of Calvin, other extraneous influences tempered the use of his thought and manipulated it for other ends. These influences require much research, but in general terms, the legacies of somewhat rogue Augustinians swayed vaguely by aspects of Lutheranism, and of humanists and of pietists, not to mention the echoes of Lollardy and various pre-Reformation attempts at reform, carrying over in their own respective ways the reverberations of severe scholasticism (from which none of these modes of thought freed itself, for they only, in their respective ways again, reinterpreted it) are evident. The 'Calvinism' of the returned Marian exiles was tempered by this radicalism. The state of affairs in the Low Countries is well set out by Alastair Duke.[2]

Moreover, it might be said that the whole history of theological thought in England previous to, and during, the English Reformation, indicates a particular tendency of mind directed to other considerations and, blinded by such considerations, unable to perceive in its fullness the breadth of Calvin's work and achievement.

In other words, the English theological background in the larger part had little scope for genius to cope with and appreciate what Calvin was truly proposing. That lack had a tendency which picked out of Calvinism, either positively or negatively, what it would for the furthering of rather insular objectives as opposing parties, aligned and determined by historical vicissitudes, variously saw them.

It is regrettable that McAdoo in his invaluable *The Spirit of Anglicanism*,[3] can accuse Calvin of having constructed a system, and as a systematizer the compulsive reducer of reality on reliance on one determinative factor. This factor McAdoo construes as *soli Deo gloria*. This he further sees as exemplified in the question of predestination as handled by Calvin, and accuses him of being scholastic in that his approach to the question is syllogistic to the extent that his system becomes the victim of the rigidity of its own logic and ultimately irrational in its conclusions.

The mistake lurking behind such assertions is an illusion caused by viewing Calvin through the lens of Federal Calvinist mechanics, and wrongly perceiving that *soli Deo gloria* must be reduced to predestination. It is perfectly true that Calvin's inspiration is the appreciation that all things are for the glory of God alone, and that predestination is part of this precept. But the God to whose glory all things live and move and have their being is, for Calvin, the God of grace, and not the God of static decrees. Moreover, his doctrine of predestination is Christocentric. Predestination is in Christ, who alone is the Elect and the Rejected. Indeed, Christ is predestination.

The confusion is amplified by the entirely false view that Calvin treats predestination as the decree by God of *double predestination* – that is, that God makes an eternal decree apportioning who shall be the elect and who shall be the reprobate, behind the back of Christ as it were, so that Christ is the mere agent of the decree. Predestination for Calvin is that which is on the circumference of the doctrine of salvation, safeguarding what is primary and on what redemption depends, namely the doctrine of the grace of God in Christ Jesus. Predestination for Calvin is supplementary to, and not determinative of, the doctrine of grace.

Double predestination is a hallmark of Federal Calvinism, and certainly this is arrived at by the rigidity of the same sort of logical process adopted by the schoolmen but here adapted to the particular question of the elect and the rejected. A careful reading of Calvin's view of predestination must cut through his involved arguments (dictated by his opponents' criticisms) in, for example, his *Concerning the Eternal Predestination of God*, published at Geneva in 1552, in answer to the criticism of his earlier work *Concerning Free Will* written in 1543. The argument in this work – as indeed in the passages on predestination in his *Institutio* – hardly fulfil the expectations of a precise and rigid system of thought which McAdoo would describe as *architectonic*.[4] In *Concerning the Eternal Predestination of God*, Calvin has to refute arguments to safeguard the assertion that God's grace does not find but makes people elect by, for example, having constant recourse to St Paul's 'O man, who art thou that repliest against God?'[5] – something which expressly forbids the erection of a satisfactorily rounded-off system. It is the very intrusion into the decrees of God, or their summary dismissal in favour of human decision of will, regarding redemption, to which Calvin is opposed.

Indeed the very thrust of Calvin's theology attacks any systematization. He criticizes the adamantine edifice of systematized compartments constructed schematically by 'the frigid doctors of the Sorbonne', for he perceived that theology, not only in the last resort but in awareness throughout its process, is dealing with the God who is lord over our thoughts and before whom our thoughts and statements can only dissolve in wonder and awe and worship. The *soli Deo gloria* of Calvin is to be recognized not as the motto of a theological system, but as the very epitaph of all attempts at systematization in theology.

The self-revelation of God, reconciling all creation to himself in Christ, and our union with that Christ in whom we are permitted to share in the knowledge which God has of himself and be embraced by the actuality of God as he exists as Father and Son bound in the divine bond of love the Holy Spirit, is the main, and indeed only, thrust of his theology. This is apparent certainly in the 1559 edition of Calvin's *Institutio*, particularly in the magnificent statement of Christocentricity in Book IV.

Predestination has not a central and controlling place except that Christ is the Head and Substance of election. It is not a doctrine in itself and is very much on the circumference of Calvin's theology, where it is the corollary to the mystery of our union with Christ and a safeguard against all human attempts to seize the primacy and the prerogative of God's grace and transform it into a work and natural possession either of the individual or of the institutionalized church.

Predestination was appropriated and systematized first in France but more radically in Holland where it became in Federal theology, with its similarity of working with the medieval schoolmen, an independent system determinative of all other doctrine. The doctrine of the Person and work of Christ became subservient to it, Christ becoming, as we have noted, merely the agent of the predestinated decrees.

It is unfortunate that as a result of this, Calvin has not been treated fairly in general in English history and theology, but has been regarded as the *éminence grise* of a supposed cardinal doctrine on which everything else depends of a God of legalistic severity administering the execution of a horrid decree to the debasement of humanity in its reduction to be the victim of fatalism. It is this view of Calvin, seen through the medium of the Federal Calvinists which so swayed, for example, Peter Heylyn (1600–62), who, making the mistake of regarding the articles passed by the Synod of Dort (1618–19) as the epitome of Calvin's theology. He could write of Calvin:

> Now this man goes to work like a logician, and frames his syllogism in this manner, viz. that whatsoever was in Adam, was in him by God's will and ordinance. But sin was in Adam, ergo, sin was in him by God's will and ordinance.[6]

He dismisses Calvin as the 'Master of the Sentences'[7] – the nomenclature used by Calvin himself[8] of Peter Lombard in the midst of a criticism of Lombard's *modus operandi*. This is a travesty of Calvin's view of the fall of Adam, nor can it stand up to the ability of Calvin's mind who, even if he had indulged in such syllogistic reasoning, would never have jumped to a conclusion through such an obvious unplaced middle in a syllogism. A close reading of the first chapter of the second book of the *Institutio* would bring about a realization of this. For example, Calvin notes:

> Let us have done then, with those who dare to inscribe to the name of God on their vices, because we say that men are born vicious. The divine workmanship, which they ought to look for in the nature of Adam, when still entire and uncorrupted, they absurdly expect to find in their depravity. The blame of our ruin rests with our own carnality, not with God, its only cause being our degeneracy from our original condition. And let no one here clamour that God might have provided better for our safety in preventing Adam's fall. This objection, which, from the daring presumption implied in it, is odious to every pious mind, relates to the mystery of predestination, which will afterwards be considered in its due place (Tertullian: De Praescript. Calvin: Lib. de Predest.). Meanwhile, let us remember that our ruin is attributable to our own depravity, that we may not insinuate a charge against God himself, the Author of nature. It is true that nature has received a mortal wound, but there is a great difference between a wound inflicted from without, and one inherent in our first condition. It is plain that this wound was inflicted by sin; and, therefore, we have no ground of complaint except against ourselves. This is carefully taught in Scripture. For the Preacher says 'Lo, this only have I found, that God made man upright; but they have sought out many inventions' (Eccl. VII:29). Since man, by the kindness of God, was made upright, but by his own infatuation fell away into vanity, his destruction is obviously attributable only to himself (Athanasius: in *Orat. Cont. Idola.*).[9]

Not only does this throw suspicion on Heylyn's assessment of Calvin, it also, even in the short compass of this quotation, pours doubt on such common simplistic assertions, repeated by McAdoo, that Calvin merely appeals to Scripture as of 'complete sufficiency . . . the only authoritative source for a system in terms of the transcendent'.[10] While it is true that the Scriptures are, for Calvin, the full sufficient source for the things of the faith, that does not preclude, as is implied in McAdoo by omission, that he does not appeal to the Fathers. Indeed his works are full of erudition concerning the Fathers, particularly Augustine, Bernard, Origen, Athanasius (whom he often disguises under quotations from Augustine in order to appeal to the western church's preoccupation with him as the patristic yardstick without whose authority no appeal was valid), and a general and generous spread of others. These Calvin regards as the best interpreters of Scripture. His appeal also consists to that of reason, illuminated by the objective knowledge of God gleaned from the Scriptures and attested to by the Fathers. This threefold appeal, in which the Scriptures hold the primacy, is of little difference to that of the Jacobean and Caroline divines such as Andrewes, Laud and Mason, in whom the development from Hooker, with his tendency to put Scripture, tradition and reason in separate compartments in a rather legalistic way, is made by seeing that they are linked by the same 'Scope' (in the Athanasian sense of skopos, the substance, goal and horizon) namely Christ as the objective determinative of knowledge to which the mind must be attuned. It is very much a case for Calvin that '*in thy light* we see *light*':

> Whithersoever the believer turns, however loftily he climbs, however far and wide his thoughts extend, he must not go farther than the love of Christ, but must be wholly occupied in meditating upon it, as including in itself all dimensions.[11]

It is also significant that Heylyn's criticism of Calvin is centred round his complaints of the returned Marian exiles. He notes that the first alteration in doctrine in England stems from their reinstatement. They,

> though otherwise men of good abilities in most parts of learning, returned so altered in their principles, as to points of doctrine, so disaffected to the government, forms of worship here by law established, that they seem'd not to be the same men at their coming home, as they had been at their going hence.[12]

The variety of religious opinion in the Low Countries is hinted at by Heylyn, but he sees this rather as disputes between Calvinists rather than an inclination away from, and a perversion of, Calvinism proper:

> the differences betwixt the Remonstrants and the Contra-Remonstrants in the Belgick Provinces . . . who published their discourses one against the other, [and] sharpened the appetite of many students.[13]

The confused medley of opinions and aims, religious or quasi-religious, informed or ignorant, which held in the Low Countries in the 1520s before persecution drove them underground and gave them an even more determined sharpness when they resurfaced, was the same theologically turbulent context in which the Marian exiles later found themselves. Mixed with political, sociological and economic upheavals, it is hardly surprising that the works of able theologians were plundered and their insights adapted to suit compelling ends. It is therefore also hardly surprising if Calvin's work did not suffer quarrying and reassembly of the pieces while appeal was still made to his authority. That a hard and fast Protestant scholasticism should emerge was more or less inevitable. The end product is perhaps best encapsulated in J. Wollebius's *Compendium Theologiae Christianae of 1626*. This work begins with a consideration of God's essence and being, and moves through pre-creation predestination, original sin, the work of Christ, the covenant of grace, sacraments as seals of that covenant, justification, sanctification and the last judgment, the last being linked to works accomplished in observation of the ten commandments. It is indebted to Calvin in bits, but its Calvinism inclines towards a legalistic and rigid Federal Theology and therein its departure from Calvin himself is obvious, as is the proximity of the theology of the Westminster divines to it. Its method is scholastic rather than that of Calvin. It is a post-Synod of Dort work. Yet this (and other disparate works far removed from Calvin's theology) is thoughtlessly but constantly gathered by many a theologian and historian under the nomenclature of 'Calvinism'.

Unhappily, through such generalizations, the prevailing Anglican view of Calvin, fostered by such as Peter Heylyn, tended to be composed of the consigning of the various and varied theological parties of the continent into one promiscuous heap labelled 'Calvinism', without recourse first of all to what Calvin wrote and taught. There, to a large extent, it has remained.

It must be pointed out that the Anglican divines use the term 'Calvinist' in an ambivalent fashion – sometimes deploring it, sometimes applauding it – but that this apparent contradiction is resolved when the distinction between Calvinism in its pure form and Federal Calvinism is appreciated. So, while Mason can appeal to Calvin in his works, and Swan look to the French Calvinist du Bartas, and would thereby by some be disbarred from the 'Laudian' camp, Andrewes and Laud both likewise appeal to Calvin, Andrewes going so far as to say 'the best Writers both old and new (I name of the new, Mr. Calvin; and of the old, Saint *Augustine*'.[14] That Laud was familiar with the *Commentaries* of Calvin is instanced by, for example, his reference to Calvin on Psalm 118 in the Dedication to the *Relation of the Conference*.[15]

Not only this, but there is a distinct parallel between the concepts of Calvin concerning the 'Civil Magistrate', and those of these Anglican Divines. There are significant parallels not only in general concepts, but also in development of argument and, indeed, in some instances, in phraseology itself, between Andrewes's sermons on State affairs, and John Calvin's concise thesis 'Of Civil Government' as set out in the *Institutes of the Christian Religion*.[16] That the civil authority is 'in the sight of God not only sacred and lawful, but the most sacred, and by far most honourable, of all stations in mortal life' is a concept shared by Calvin, Andrewes and Laud, standing as the common root of their observations on the nature of the powers that be.

Any charge of a doctrine of 'Divine Right', as it is mistakenly understood, is never laid at Calvin's door. Yet he shares common thought and language with the Laudian Divines in describing the chief powers in society. These civil powers have been appointed ministers of the divine justice . . . Their tribunal . . . that it is the throne of the living God . . . Their mouth . . . is an ordained organ of divine Truth . . . Their hand has been appointed to write the acts of God. . . . In a word they are the vice-regents of God.[17]

Such language might be suspected by some historians of being that of the most sycophantic of English divines. Yet it is John Calvin's. His doctrine of 'Divine Right', too, is tempered with its corollary of 'Divine Responsibility'.

The term 'Laudian', and the divines here included in it, is determined, therefore, not by anything but a common desire for the upholding of this concept of Order, which first concerns the doctrine of God, then the doctrine of Creation, the doctrine of Re-creation, and all that is subsequent on these – the Church, the Sacraments, Worship, Natural Law, the Authority of Kings and Governors, the Ordering of Society and the Individual's Place, as these were biblically and patristically understood. That such a concept of Order was not confined to theologians ordained, but was in the minds of other thinkers, has meant the inclusion of Francis Bacon to stand in company with the Laudian Divines. His theological observations, and his use of theology extended into other subjects and concerns, is of great value in assessing the influence of the Laudian emphasis on Order and its wide application. It is this emphasis which lies behind Bacon's deliberate application of the method used in interpreting 'the Books of God' to 'the Books of Nature', and providing, through this Order expressed in Christ, a unitary way of looking at God, Creation and mankind. This unitary way of thinking, as opposed to a dualistic way, where time and eternity, creation and Creator, mankind and God, were torn apart, mechanistic theologies (which tended to typify the Puritan mind) erected to bridge the gap, and an artificial framework imposed on society and the individual, was the genius and legacy of the Laudian divines and their similarly thinking contemporaries in other disciplines. It was Laud himself who stands as the martyr exponent of Order as expressed in Scripture, Tradition and Reason in their relation. It is the realization of the determinative role played by this theme of Order which, theologically, permits the title 'Laudian' to be applied to others.

The Laudians never speak of God in abstraction. They do not speculate about the being of God in eternity solely. For them, God is the God who not only *is*, but the God who *acts*. The action and work of God is manifested as order, or economy, and as such is the created corresponding expression of the order, or economy, which God eternally is in Himself as Father and Son bound in the bond of eternal love who is the Holy Spirit.

The order of the Triune God is revealed in the Incarnation. This is the prime economy of God towards and in His creation. All things have their meaning and place and function in the light of the Incarnation. All things depend for their season and their office in order, on the fact that the Word became flesh in the fullness of time, and, entering time gathered up all things in Himself. Time and space find meaning and destiny in the Triune Being of God through the Incarnation by the dispensation of the Spirit.

In the relation between the Incarnation and the Eternal economy or order of God as Father, Son and Holy Spirit in their unity and dispensation of office, the Laudians speak of the work of Father, Son and Holy Spirit towards creation, and penetrate back through the order of all time and things focused on the Incarnation, to the eternal relationships of the Trinity. In Christ, Natural Law is expressed and is seen to correspond, in its created dimension, to the uncreated nature of God and His will.

Every work of ordering is a work in which the whole Trinity, in apportioned balance, participates. The emphasis given to particular Persons of the Trinity in various aspects of the whole work of this ordering – the fullness of God's economy for creation – reveals the office, nature and mode of union of the Trinity. As God is, so He acts.

The work of ordering is a personal work. God is personally involved in revelation and redemption, and, through that, seen to be so in creation. In His Word all things consist by His Wisdom. This threefold, personal involvement is stamped on all things in the universal order of the economy of God. On this the concept of Natural Law rests.

The pattern is sustained from the consideration of this universal economy of all things and all time by decree of the Father, through the Word and in the Spirit, to a consideration of each nation in its time ruled by the monarch through the law administered in wisdom, farther down to each community ordered in this way by those set in authority and office, and yet farther down to each family with its parental government, pupils with their mentors, the needy with their benefactors. Every level and facet of creation is covered. Natural law, which runs through all this, has the same pattern as the law of Grace – the expression of God's love for His creation. Recognition of and obedience to this ordering makes for the good of all things.

Here we have to take account of the appreciation of the relation between the order which God is in Himself as He exists in His triune relations, the order which God decrees for His creation which order is above all encapsulated in the relation between Creator and creature personally and recapitulatively stated in the Incarnation, the order of the God-ordained creation which expresses itself in natural law, and the attempt to express the integrity of natural law in common law and statute law. The works of the Laudian Divines reveal, I would suggest, and hope to demonstrate in the chapters following, an intuitive or instinctive feel for the sense of an order expressing itself through various levels of created existence which in turn has to be formulated, in so far as is possible, in the ordering of the individual, the community, society as the nation in common and statute law.

This created order in all its manifestations, forms, expressions and applications, is related to that which gives it existence, identity, purpose and continuance, namely the Creator Himself in His triune and incarnate existence. It is the creaturely correspondent, within its own dimension, its temporal and spatial limitations, to the uncreated Order which God is. In view of this, the expression of the natural, created order, in common law and statute law, was regarded as being necessarily grounded on this relation between humanity and creation and Creator.

Natural law does not imply what is commonly perceived to be 'the law of nature', that is, 'nature left to itself'. It does imply that there is a rationality embedded in the created entities both as they are in themselves and in their relation with each other, and that that rationality can only be uncovered in the light of God's creative intent. In other words, natural law is that which is found in the relation between Creator and creation. That relation is one whereby the created order has an identity and a quality and a character and a dimension of its own. It is not the

Creator, nor an emanation direction from the being of the Creator. There is no confusion between Creator and creation. Inextricably linked with this perception is the recognition that creation can only be and have this in its dependency on the Creator for its beginning, that identity, quality, character and dimension, and its continuance. There is no separation between Creator and creation in this sense of contingent existence. This contingent existence is expressed implicitly but forcibly throughout the thought of these divines in what I call 'double contingency', that is, that the quality and identity of creation as its own is its contingency *from* God, yet it only has this in its contingency *to* God.

The perception of natural law in the writings of the Laudian Divines is to be appreciated, I propose, within this context of the relation of creation to Creator. Their subsequent view of common law and statute law, as the laws ordering and guiding the life of the realm of England, are therefore grounded on the same relation.

This brings into sharp focus the observed relation between statute law and common law. Lancelot Andrewes complained of 'Westminster Hall' laws,[18] which bear no relation to the laws of God, but which allow the corruption of the rich to slip through unchallenged like cobwebs which hold fast the small insects but allow the mighty hornets to fly through. Such cobweb laws are statute laws so designed, and are the direct result of 'cobweb divinitie'. Francis Bacon, too, warns of a danger of a surfeit of laws wrongly based:

> For this continual heaping up of laws without digesting them, maketh but a chaos and confusion, and turneth the laws many times to become but snares for the people.[19]

and of the statutory penal laws:

> So it is most certain, that your people are so ensnared in a multitude of penal laws, that the execution of them cannot be borne.[20]

> There is a learned civilian that expoundeth the curse of the prophet, *Pluet super eos laqueos*, of a multitude of penal laws; which are worse than showers of hail or tempest upon cattle, for they fall upon men. . . . There is a further inconvenience of penal laws, obsolete, and out of use; for that it brings a gangerene, neglect, and habit of disobedience upon other wholesome laws, that are fit to be continued in practice and execution; so that our laws endure the torment of Mezentius:
>
> > The living die in the arms of the dead . . .
>
> there is such an accumulation of statutes concerning one matter, and they so cross and intricate, as the certainty of law is lost in the heap.[21]

Bacon's *A Proposition to His Majesty touching the Compiling and Amendment of the Laws of England* contains a plea for the better understanding and interpretation of the 'Common Lawe', and a simplification and reduction of Statute Laws, the role of which is to clarify Common Law. He complains of the confusion over many Statute Laws and lists the abuses which arise from such a plethora of laws:

> But certain it is, that our laws, as they now stand are subject to great uncertainties, and variety of opinion, delays, and evasions: whereof ensueth:

That the multiplicity and length of suits is great.

That the contentious person is armed, and the honest subject wearied and oppressed . . .

That the chancery courts are more filled, the remedy of law being often obscure and doubtful.

That the ignorant lawyer shroudeth his ignorance of the law, in that doubts are so frequent and many.[22]

Behind this there lies two anxieties. The first is that expressed by Tacitus, and to which reference in legal circles was made from time to time – '*Corruptissima republica plurimae leges*' – that the multiplication of laws is directly related to the decay of the nation (and indeed vice versa). And second that Statute Law was being divorced from its proper reason and function of clarifying Common Law adding to its value, and becoming a substitute as an alternative to Common Law. The danger, therefore, was that Statute Law was uprooted from its proper matrix and estate and became groundless as a mere expression of political expediency and partisan convenience. There was nothing against which to test and prove it, save its application to the need of the moment. It was in danger of losing not only its context, but its authority. As Bacon pointed out, a multiplicity of Statute Laws could only lead not only to the difficulty of administering the law, but a debasement of it.

Law, in this misuse and proliferation of Statute Law, was removed from all stability of the inherent rationality of the creation and the creature, grounded in its double contingency beyond itself in Rationality itself, the Rationality of the Creator who gives all things genuine identity, right meaning and true purpose.

It is not to be without remark that hand in hand with the perception of the need for the right grounding of law in order, came the advance in natural science in that age, with its emphasis on what has been described as *kata phusin*, according to nature, thinking. The necessity of looking at objective realities as they are in themselves and as they are in relation to other realities was realized by those engaged in natural science. And, indeed, Bacon himself advocates the transference of the theological way of humble learning from scripture the Self-revelation of God as He is attested to in the biblical witness to the incarnation of the Word by whom all things were created, to the discipline of discovering the realities of creation in their integrities.

The disciplines of theology, science and law, are seen by the Laudian Divines, to engage in their respective ways in parallel modes of thought, by which the objective realities inform the mind of their integrities, the truth of what they are in themselves, and not in ways in which the objective realities are subjected to the authority of the supposed autonomy of the mind – what the mind thinks of itself as the natural adjudicator of what is truth. The mind, as it exercises and expresses itself in these respective disciplines, is, in the ways appropriate to the particular objects or area of its study, the servant of order as it reveals itself in the verities of a creation contingent to and from God.

With regard to law, thinkers such as Bacon and Coke saw that in so far as legislation is the sole source of law, that is, the corpus of common law interpreted and furthered by statute law, it can be regarded as a self-contained and self-sufficient system. Herein is the danger, for it can be used out of itself to justify itself, and there is no check against which it can be tested, save for that which it provided out of itself. Some of the legal thinkers of the period, and certainly Bacon stands foremost among them, realized that law had to be grounded in that which was constant in its constancy imparted meaning and purpose and direction. This is where the relation of common law to natural law is important, for it is there that the legislative integrity is guaranteed in that laws should be tested against the authority of that which is intrinsically and objectively true. Equally, a danger lay in grounding law in the status of the monarch. That in itself would be merely a self-perpetuating and self-justifying, closed system, without necessary reference to the fact that laws are true and right and good only in so far as they have reference to objective realities of existence beyond themselves. The systemization of law hangs not on a coherence dictated by itself, but in the coherence of how things are – that is, natural order – and it is to this that law was seen to be ontologically and dynamically related. Clearly there was here a parallel between the laws of science and the open nature of legislation grounded beyond itself as expressed in the making and administering of laws by which society and the nation were governed and ordered.

The dangers of a misinterpretation of the divine right of kings with regard to the potential autocracy of the law were evident. That is one reason, as hopefully will be shown, why the divines of the time, for the large part, are insistent that the divine right, that is the appointment of monarchy and government in the ordering of creation by the Creator, has as its inseparable corollary the divine responsibility of kings and those in authority, that is, their answerability to God for the exercise of their office. The dangers of transferring the divine right to the commons was also recognized.

To ground the justification of law on either an absolute monarch or an absolute elected body can only ground law on the inescapable subjectivism of either, for, in the last resort, if the body wielding power is absolute, its own perceived will is the final authority. Again, the danger of any such ground of law lay in the fact that the inheritance of common law would gradually become discarded on the grounds of mere subjective perception on the part of the legislator, and statute law lose its status of the interpreter and clarifier of common law and the developer of it in strict accordance with its direction, and become instead the substitute for common law and ultimately only utilitarian. Such a circumstance could only lead to the proliferation of laws not necessarily cohesive because grounded only on the reaction of the legislator to the pressing needs of the moment. Hence, Tacitus's dictum '*corruptissima republica plurimae leges*' was not far off in the awareness of those who thought more deeply about the nature of law.

The awareness and suspicion of much puritan subjectivity and fragmentation into factions (though subjective ways of thinking were by no means confined to the puritans) had grounds other than that of mere partisanship for the Anglican divines of the Elizabethan, Jacobean and Caroline periods. In general, their assessment of puritanism in all its forms and faces was that of various attempts to codify and encapsulate truth within a rigid system. The emphasis of the Anglican divines commonly was on unity in diversity, uniformity being conformity to the fundamentals of the faith and truth. Even in his comments on the nature of the law, Bacon appeals from time to time to this – in each case to Cyprian's observation:

It sufficeth that there be uniformity in the principal and fundamental laws, both ecclesiastical and civil: for in this point the rule holdeth which was pronounced by an ancient father, touching the diversity of rights in the church; for finding the vesture of the queen in the psalm, which did prefigure the church, which was of diverse colours; and finding again that Christ's coat was without a seam, he concluded well, in veste varietas sit, scissura non sit.[23]

This emphasis rested on the appreciation that truth was constant in itself. It maintained its integrity. Attempts to express the truth were unified in that it was to the truth that they were directed and from the truth they derived statements variously in an attempt, not to encapsulate it within the expression of it, but point to it in its integrity. In other words, statements about the truth were subservient to the truth itself and had to be tested constantly against it, by referring them again and again to its intrinsic rightness. This was not the seeking of a satisfactory, rounded-off and sufficient system, but a method of unfolding the truth in all its wealth while admitting its priority over all thoughts about it. Such is the majesty of truth that statements made about it were construed as always being under the judgment of the truth. The inability of the mind to encapsulate truth totally within its compass, led to the realization that while certain statements can be made with certainty, for they clearly agree with that which is self-evident about the truth, other statements had to be made on the basis of approximate possibilities. The theological method of these divines, which will be examined later, illustrates this, but as a *method* it was not confined to divine truth but also applied to the truths of the created entities.

Hence the distinction (and again Bacon on law makes the same discrimination) was between essentials and inessentials, between things fundamental and things 'indifferent'. In these latter, diversity was legitimate. The deterministic, factious and sectarian face of puritanism as a whole, however, did nothing to persuade the Laudian Divines that the puritan mind, of whatever hue, appreciated the concept of order and all that that entailed in the necessary truths of Creator and creation in their relation. For as there was an order of truth, so there was an order of knowing, which was of knowing what was subservient to the integrity of the truth itself and determined by it, it always holding the priority.

Hence Lancelot Andrewes can complain of the attitude of so many puritans regarding the counsels of God and the knowledge of God:

[God's] secret Decrees? May not they, for their *height* and *depth*, claim this Noli (touch not), too? Yes, sure: and I pray God, Hee be well pleased with this licentious touching, may tossing His Decrees of late; this sounding the depths of His Judgements with our line, and lead; too much presumed upon by some, in these days of ours . . . (Saith the Psalmist) *His judgements are the great deepe.* Saint Paul, looking downe into it, ranne backe, and cried *O the depth!* the profound depth! not to be searched, past our fadoming or finding out. Yet there are in the world that make but a *shallow* of this great deepe: they have sounded it to the bottome. God's Decrees, they have them at their finger ends, can tell the number and the order of them just, with 1, 2, 3, 4, 5. Men that (sure) must have been in God's *Cabbinet*, above the third heaven, where Saint Paul never came. *Mary Magdalens* touch was nothing to these.[24]

We are dealing here with a warning against confusing truth itself with the human reason dealing with that truth. In such a confusion, namely the identification of truth with human reason, truth becomes depersonalized and demeaned because it is eventually perceived as the system which the human reason produces. There is no idea of the ontological and dynamic relation between the truth and the thinker about truth. This is so particularly of the relation between God and humanity thinking about God, but it is also applicable to the relation between the thinker in all branches of discipline and the integrity and dignity of the objects of their respective studies, where respect for the integrity of what an object is in itself has to be held foremost in the process.

The personal way in which order is administered – be it by God, king, parent, or anyone with their particular gifts in their specific spheres – is to be noted. The Laudians were never concerned with systems or manifestos or impersonal institutions. They were concerned with the living relationships of persons; overall with the personal relationship of God with humanity in every time and place, and from humanity as the crown of God's creation, to all creation. This personal relationship is the gathering up out of its constrictions in its Adamic dimension of humanity and of humanity's sphere, in the Word made flesh.

Nor were the Laudians concerned with any idea of bare, sterile equality among people. All have their place in the dispensation of God, variously gifted, individually endowed. That is their equality. Nothing is too insignificant that it has no role, none is superfluous, nothing is so evil that it cannot be used despite itself by God for good, in this universal order. Everything works and moves together in this dispensation. Each person has his or her contribution to make in relation to others, and for this, each is personally and uniquely endowed in his or her time, place and office. Each has a personal sphere of order to administer, be it in matters ecclesiastical, affairs of state, the arts and sciences, the workings of the community, the circle of the family, the craftsman's art, the plebeian's toil, the creatures in nature's balance.

Nothing is mundane, nothing merely secular. Everything has significance within the Divine purpose and destiny. Every sphere of individual economy is a universe in microcosm. Every day in every sphere has eternal significance. And in every sphere in its time, the relationships within its economy, and in the relation of that economy to other spheres of order, are the stamp of the eternal order of the Triune God. All this hinges on the order revealed and worked out in the Incarnation, the economic way of the condescension of God's Grace, and the exaltation of this man Jesus to be the Head of all things, in whom all things consist, and by whom all things are gathered up into that triune Being of the eternal God. For the Laudians, this was the way in which Natural Law was construed. This is the ground of their existence and the declaration of that order by which alone they can live, move and have their being. This panorama of order, so set out, is the legacy of Laudian thought.

Notes

1   Cf. R.H. Tawney: *The Rise of the Gentry*, 1941; C. Hill: *Puritanism and Revolution*,
    Secker and Warburg, 1958; L. Stone: *The Causes of the English Revolution, 1529–
    1642*, Routledge, Keegan and Paul, 1972; Clarendon: *History of the Rebellion and
    Civil Wars in England*, 1704 edn. One quotation from Christopher Hill: *A Society
    Divided*, Open University, Block 3, A203 Course Text, highlights the disparity in
    historical judgement to which he himself contributes:

>   H.R. Trevor-Roper thinks there were no problems in 1641 which could not have
>   been solved by sensible men sitting round a table. Lawrence Stone regards the
>   English Revolution as one of the greatest revolutions of history, comparable with
>   the American, French and Russian Revolutions. F.S. Fisher, on the contrary, sees
>   the Civil War as 'the result of the breakdown of a clumsy political machine in the
>   hands of a remarkably ineffecient operator'. On this point I agree with Stone and
>   disagree with Trevor-Roper and Fisher.

    This opinion may be placed alongside that of A.L. Rowse: Reflections on the Puritan
    Revolution, Methuen, 1986, pp.1–4 and 226ff, for an example of diametrically opposed
    points of view.
2   A. Duke: 'The Face of Popular Religious Dissent in the Low Countries, 1520–1530',
    Journal of Ecclesiastical History, Vol.XXVI, no. 1.
3   H.R. McAdoo: *The Spirit of Anglicanism*, A. & C. Black, 1965, pp.24ff.
4   Ibid., p.25.
5   Romans IX:20.
6   Heylyn: *Historia Quinquarticularis* Pt.III, V.XVI, VI.
7   Ibid., C.V, V.
8   e.g. John Calvin: *Institutio* II:II:6.
9   Ibid., II:I:10.
10 McAdoo: *The Spirit of Anglicanism*, p.26.
11 Calvin: *Institutio* III:XIV:19.
12 Heylyn: *Historio Quinquarticularis* Pt.III, C.XIX.I.
13 Ibid. C.XXII,VII.
14 Lancelot Andrewes: *Ninety-six Sermons*, 'A Sermon preached at St. Maries Hospital,
    on the Tenth of Aprill, being Wednesday in Easter-weeke, 1588', 1635 edn, p.B8.
15 William Laud: *Relation of the Conference*, Dedication, 1639 edn, 14th page (pages not
    numbered).
16 John Calvin: 'Of Civil Government', Book 4, Ch. 20, *Institutes of the Christian
    Religion*, trans. H. Beveridge, Eerdmans, Chicago, 1979 edn, pp.650ff.
17 Ibid., cf. Lancelot Andrews: *Ninety-six Sermons*, 'A Sermon preached at the opening of
    the Parliament', 1635 edn, p. B149.
18 Lancelot Andrewes: *Ninety-six Sermons*, 'Sermons of the Gowries, sermon preached
    before the King's Magestie at Burleigh neere Okeham on the 5th August, 1616', 1635
    edn. p.847. Cf. Sermon preached at St. Maries Hospital, 1588, 1635 edn, p.B1.
19 Francis Bacon: 'A Speech on by Occasion of a Motion concerning the Union of Laws
    (that is between England and Scotland under King James VI and I)', *Collected Works*,
    1778 edn, Vol.II, p.185.
20 Francis Bacon: 'A Certificate to His Majesty . . . relating to the Penal Laws', *Collected
    Works*, 1778 edn, Vol.II, p.207.
21 Francis Bacon: 'A Proposition to His Majesty touching the Compiling and Amendment
    of the Laws of England', *Collected Works*, 1778 edn, pp.540–7.

22   Ibid., p.542.
23   Francis Bacon: e.g. 'A Brief Discourse of the Happy Union of the Kingdoms of England and Scotland', *Collected Works*, 1778 edn, p.157. He quotes Cyprian: De Catholical Ecclesiae Unitate, 7.
24   Lancelot Andrewes: *Ninety-six Sermons*, 1635 edn, Sermon 15 of the Resurrection, p.548.

Chapter 1

The Concept of Order Generally Accepted

The concept of the order of creation and that order which God is in Himself eternally, and the relation between them, was by no means confined to the awareness and works of the theologians of the sixteenth and seventeenth centuries. The whole appreciation of order coloured the thoughts and expectations of Elizabethan, Jacobean and Caroline society as a whole.

The subtleties of speaking about that order which God is eternally in Himself, as Father and Son, bound with the bond of eternal love, the Holy Spirit, may have been in their more sublime form restricted to theological works and sermons. Nevertheless, the idea of God as a God of order, and the contingent order of the universe, nature, society and individual identity, vocation and estate, subsequent on God's creative and sustaining activity, was commonplace. It formed attitudes to every aspect of human thought, endeavour and activity.

E.M.W. Tillyard, writing from the literary standpoint, in his *The Elizabethan World Picture*,[1] emphasizes in his analysis of the works of men of letters of the period, how much of their outlook rested on this idea of order. It is both explicit and implicit in their writings – and the implicitness shows how much it was taken for granted as an accepted fact in that period. (Tillyard uses the term 'Elizabethan' to cover also the Henrican, Jacobean and Caroline times: 'anything between the ages of Henry VIII and Charles I akin to the main trends of Elizabethan thought'.[2]) He points out that the pictures of civil war and disorder in the Histories of Shakespeare had no meaning apart from a background of order by which to judge them. When he looked into that background, he found that:

> it applied to Shakespeare's Histories no more than to the rest of Shakespeare or indeed than to Elizabethan literature generally. I also found that the order I am describing was much more than political order, or, if political, was always a part of a larger cosmic order. . . . Now this idea of cosmic order was one of the genuine ruling ideas of the age, and perhaps the most characteristic. [3]

'To look on this age as mainly secular is wrong',[4] says Tillyard and criticizes those historians and literary critics who overlook the fact that theological belief was such an automatic and accepted part of life then. He chides them for ignoring that 'Queen Elizabeth translated Boethius, that Raleigh was a theologian as well as a discoverer, and that sermons were as much a part of the ordinary Elizabethan's life as bear-baiting'.[5] The concept of order was not only a basic assumption behind literature – it was commonplace in the general attitudes of the educated populace. If there were no popular awareness of the concept of order, most of the drama of the day would have been totally meaningless to its audience.

As it is, so much of the drama surrounding the question of order takes over theological language and imagery to make its point. The theological language of order and its attendant symbolism is constantly employed by dramatists. It is resorted to particularly in looking at the body politic macroscopically in its relation to the body of the whole fabric of the universe with its interacting elements and spheres, or microscopically in its relation to the human body with its constituent and coherently working members. This employment in the business of the dramatist is without elaboration or explanation, thereby letting us assume that there was a general theological understanding of such devices in the minds of the general populace, which could be taken for granted by those whose business was to attract appreciative audiences.

Without this assumption there could not have been any comprehension on the part of an audience. A few examples may be noted: Ulysses's speech on 'degree' (which equals 'order') in Shakespeare's *Troilus and Cressida* ('Take but degree away, untune that string, / And hark, what discord follows') or Menenius Agrippa's 'Fable of the Belly' in *Coriolanus* ('There was a time when all the body's members / Rebell'd against the belly') or Canterbury's words in *Henry V* ('Therefore doth Heaven divide / The state of man in divers functions / Setting endeavour in continual motion; / To which is fixed as an aim or butt / Obedience; / For so worked the honey bees;').

This same notion of order is found in many works from different fields. It is the common factor which binds all disciplines of that age. It is as well to remember that many figures, pre-eminent in fields other than theology – Elyot, Tallis, Lawes, Harvey, Raleigh, Francis Bacon, Sir Thomas Browne, Clarendon, and King James VI and I himself, for example – were held in high regard for their theological erudition, as well as for their other pursuits and skills. The names outstanding in astronomy, mathematics, music, law, medicine, architecture, and all the other disciplines, cloaked the same persons as also appreciators of theology.

Tillyard cites by way of example of this, Raleigh's *History of the World*:

> For that infinite wisdom of God, which hath distinguished his angels by degrees, which hath given greater or less light and beauty to heavenly bodies, which hath made differences between beasts and birds, created the eagle and the fly, the cedar and the shrub, and among the stones given the fairest tincture to the ruby and the quickest light to the diamond, hath also ordained kings, dukes or leaders of the people, magistrates, judges, and other degrees among men.[6]

Sir Thomas Browne's *Religio Medici*, in the field of medicine, may be instanced here as well:

> Because the glory of one state depends upon the ruin of another, there is a revolution and vicissitude of their greatness, and must obey the swing of that wheel, not by intelligences [that is, the supposed souls of planets which were regarded as their motive force] but by the hand of God, whereby all estates arise to their zenith and vertical parts according to their predestined periods. For the lives, not only of men, but of commonwealths, and of the whole world, run not upon a helix that still enlargeth, but on a circle, where, according to the meridian, they decline on obscurity, and fall under the horizon again. [7]

Tillyard again remarks on an exposition of order which is close to that found in Shakespeare's works, though earlier. This is by Elyot, Ambassador to Charles V, concerning the office of magistrate and the exercise of judicial authority. In the first chapter of the *Governor*, prime place is given to the notion of order contingent upon God. The prominence accorded to order here is because all that follows is conditional on it – Tillyard asking 'for of what use to educate the magistrate without the assurance of a coherent universe in which he can do his proper work?'[8]

Elyot looks at order in this way:

Take away order from all things, what should then remain? Certes nothing finally, except some man would imagine eftsoons chaos. Also where there is any lack of order needs must be perpetual conflict. And in things subject to nature nothing of himself only may be nourished; but, when he hath destroyed that wherewith he doth participate by the order of his creation, he himself of necessity must then perish; whereof ensueth universal dissolution.

Hath not God set degrees and estates in all his glorious works? First in his heavenly ministers, whom he hath constituted in divers degrees called hierarchies. Behold the four elements, whereof the body of man is compact, how they be set in their places called spheres, higher or lower according to the sovereignty of their natures. Behold also the order that God hath put generally in all his creatures, beginning at the most inferior or base and ascending upward. He made not only herbs to garnish the earth but also trees of a more eminent stature than herbs. Semblably in birds beasts and fishes some be good for the sustenance of man, some bear things profitable to sundry uses, other be apt to occupation and labour. Every kind of trees herbs birds beasts and fishes have a peculiar disposition appropered unto them by God their creator; so that in everything is order, and without order may be nothing stable or permanent. And it may not be called order except it do contain in it degrees, high and base, according to the merit or estimation of the thing that is ordered.[9]

Tillyard writes that: 'The conception of order described above (he also notes Spencer's *Hymn of Love* as a poetic description of creation, emphasizing as it does the relations within creation and the relation of all to God) must have been common to all Elizabethans of even modest intelligence.[10] He also claims that Hooker's work 'assures us that he speaks for the educated nucleus that dictated the current beliefs of the Elizabethan Age'. Hooker, it may be said, is insistent on the concept of order, seen in terms of categories of Law – Law which is divine, cosmic, earthly and domestic.

Tillyard reminds us that the men of that age were merely repeating in their respective disciplines what the theologians had long stated. When Shakespeare places man 'in the traditional cosmic setting between the angels and the beasts', this was 'what the theologians had been saying for centuries'. He then quotes:

Nemesius, a Syrian Bishop of the fourth century . . . 'No eloquence may worthily publish forth the manifold pre-eminences and advantages which are bestowed on this creature. He passeth over the vast seas; he rangeth about the wide heavens by his contemplation and conceives the motions and magnitudes of the stars . . . He is learned in every science and skilful in artificial workings . . . He talketh with angels yea with God Himself. He hath all the creatures within his dominion.'[11]

The concept of order pervaded, captivated and moved the minds of the age. And this was a general phenomenon throughout all fields of learning, which worked its way down to the awareness of the populace at large. 'Order' was indeed one of *the genuine ruling ideas of the age, and perhaps the most characteristic*. It was the harmony of the interaction of the minds of men of the period employed in many disciplines in the whole orchestration of knowledge. A unitary way of thinking, whereby the relation of all created things to each other, and the relation of the whole to the Creator, is the hallmark of the way of thinking in that period.

There is no area of human vocation and activity which is not scrutinized from the vantage point of this concept of order by the divines of the late sixteenth and early seventeenth centuries. Explicit or implicit, order is the standard by which all things are judged. It is the *cantus firmus* which dictates the shape and harmony of every line of theological thought concerning every aspect of existence and circumstance. Because of this, the two great broad themes of the order which God is eternally in Himself and which He has revealed in the incarnation, and the resultant idea of order applied to created existence which is practically expressed in the tenets of Common or Natural Law, echo throughout every area of theological concern.

It is necessary to realize that in this the unitary way of thinking, creation and Creator, time and eternity, are profoundly bracketed together in an unconfused but inseparable relation. This means, first, that all created rationalities are contingent to and from God. That is to say, they depend totally upon God for their beginning, their sustenance and their fulfilment, yet, in this dependence they have their identity as things of a dimension qualitively different from God. They cannot be understood apart from a consideration of this relation. It means, secondly, that any study of the order of that created dimension will take into consideration that relationship to God's eternal Order and the fact that in the light of that relationship, Natural or Common Law is seen to be expressed in a broad sweep covering all aspects of human activity and endeavour and created entities. The two interrelated themes of the Order which God eternally is in Himself, and the Order of created realities which, contingent on the Divine Order, is expressed in Common or Natural Law, cannot be considered narrowly, as if they existed in neat compartments in the mentality of the age. Their proper significance can only be understood when it is realized how all-pervading these concepts were. It is therefore necessary to look at the way in which that mentality was formed under the compulsion of the concept of order, uncreate and created. Human rationality, theological method, the endeavours of the natural scientist, the estate and office of monarchy, social structure, the Church with its worship – all these are but differing themes on that relationship, and as such, come under the broad heading of Natural Law.

To take but one introductory example of this: Laud's concern for uniformity is based, not as some historians like Christopher Hill and Lawrence Stone would have it, on narrow piety and shallow politics. It is the declaration at the heart of religious observances that the profound truth of the relation between creature and Creator is at stake. When Laud observed that 'Ceremonies are the Hedge that fence the Substance of Religion',[12] he was voicing the claim that sound doctrine, whereby this relation is set out and safeguarded, has to be expressed visibly in the worship of the Church, so that that substance is clearly seen in that liturgical activity of man whereby all his existence is brought to, and sanctified by, that God. Dignity and rationality in worship serves only to the proper dignity and rationality of man's estate and vocation. The rationality of the truth of the God who has revealed Himself in Christ is acknowledged in the rationality of worship, liturgy being the handmaid of that truth, and in the exercise of that, the proper rights and dignity of each individual is witnessed to and realized. That Natural Law which speaks of man's estate and vocation under God is thereby brought out in liturgical concern. It is that relation between God and man which is the *substance* of religion.

It has been necessary, therefore, to look not just at the narrow use of references to Common or Natural Law in the works of the Caroline Divines, but at their implicit application of all its comprehensive bearing. To do otherwise would be to constrict the panorama of their vision that all things serve to the glory of God and find their true meaning and identity in that service. The harmony and interdependence of society and of all creation under God was that vision, and their insistence on God's Order and the Ordering of His household of creation, their attempt to realize it.

The method which the theologians, whose works are considered in what follows, employed, is the entrance into their insistence that Christ is Himself Order. This theological method was itself orderly, and regarded as part of the order which the Church must observe. It is necessary, first of all, to lay out the rationale behind this theological method, which is the characteristic of these divines.

Notes

1 E.M.W. Tillyard: *The Elizabethan World Picture*, Chatto and Windus, 1960.
2 Ibid., Preface, p.vii.
3 Ibid., Preface, p.v.
4 Ibid., p.3.
5 Ibid., Introduction, p.1.
6 Ibid., p.9.
7 Sir Thomas Browne: *Religio Medici*, 1642 edn.
8 Tillyard: *The Elizabethan World Picture*, p.9.
9 Elyot: *Governor*, quoted in Tillyard, *The Elizabethan World Picture*, p.9.
10 Tillyard: *The Elizabethan World Picture*, p.10.
11 Ibid., pp.1, 2.
12 William Laud: *Relation of the Conference*, 1639 edn, 20th page of Preface (pages not numbered).

Chapter 2

Order and Theological Method

The divines of the period operated with a theological method, which involved the three essential categories, as they saw them, of Scripture, Tradition and Reason. This method was the hallmark of Anglican thought at that time. Not only are there explicit statements regarding this procedure in the works of the Laudian Divines, but their whole approach both in sermons and in apologetic writings reveals an implicit, almost subconscious use of it. It may be permissible to say that they were imbued with this frame of mind. Behind this, too, there seems to be an ever-present awareness that these express the very centre, source, goal and horizon of order. They did not construct a theological system, for they were hesitant in describing truth as that which could be embraced and enclosed in statements about truth. Their theological method of the use of scripture, tradition and reason, was concerned to let truth speak on its own terms, and therefore for order to become apparent through this. Truth and order are seen as Christ Himself. This is why the works of these divines, while not systematic, were nevertheless orderly, and it may be the best approach to read their works with their aim in mind, which was to let order be apparent as Christ expresses Himself.

Richard Hooker was the foremost apologist for the Elizabethan Settlement, and, without doubt, the divines of the later Jacobean and Caroline periods with which we are dealing, are indebted to him for the decisive direction which he set out in his five books – *A Treatise on the Laws of Ecclesiatical Polity*. But the later divines developed his work and produced a more flexible theological attitude.

The prime example of this is the question of the theological method based on scripture, tradition and reason. In his *Ecclesiastical Polity*, Hooker tends to severely categorize these three – keeping them in neat compartments by themselves. The later attitude saw that the importance for theological method lay not just in the fact that there were the three categories – scripture, tradition and reason – but there was an essential relation between them. It is in this, the fruit of Jacobean and Caroline theological thought, that there lies the basis of both the comprehensiveness and the definiteness of what is known as the Anglican Theological Method.

Lancelot Andrewes (1555–1626), Bishop of Winchester, took up Hooker's three categories and restated them thus – and the three are to be taken together without as it were, to adapt one of Andrewes's own phrases from a sermon preached on another subject: 'without a breath, a pause, a full stop or a comma between them' –

One Canon reduced to writing by God Himself, two testaments, three creeds, four general councils, five centuries, and the series of Fathers in that period – the centuries, that is, before Constantine, and two after, determine the boundary of our faith.[1]

25

Implicit in all Andrewes's observations about scripture and tradition, is the insistence that these two are to be applied in their relation one with another, by reason, disciplined to the nature of scripture and tradition and under the enlightenment and guidance of the Holy Spirit. Here there must be amplified what Andrewes meant by this quotation.

Richard Hooker had already warned in his *Ecclesiastical Polity* that two opposing opinions regarding the Scriptures had to be rejected, both being 'repugnant unto truth'. The first is that view which states that scripture is insufficient, unless traditions are added to it, for of itself it did not contain all the necessary revealed and supernatural truth necessary for salvation. The second is stated by those who

> justly condemning this opinion grow likewise unto a dangerous extremity, as if Scripture did not only contain in that kind all things necessary, but all things simply. . . . We must . . . take great heed, lest in attributing to Scripture more than it can have, the incredibility of that do cause even those things which indeed it hath most abundantly to be less reverently esteemed. I therefore leave it to themselves to consider, whether they have . . . or not overshot themselves; which God doth know is quickly done, even when our meaning is most sincere, as I am verily persuaded their's in this case was.[2]

Hooker dismisses first the position of the Church of Rome on the matter of scripture, claiming that it is insufficient in things necessary and essential for salvation, the lack being supplied by the authoritative tradition of the Church from the beginning until now. He dismisses second, the reaction to this expressed by the growing Puritan faction, the attitude of which, to Holy Scripture, was that of that 'fundamentalism' which regarded the absolute truth of God and of all things as capable of being automatically, mechanically and immediately read from the written words of scripture – this is what Hooker means by 'Simply'.

In his view, Rome held the wrong relation between scripture and tradition – indeed had a wrong view of what tradition was – in that tradition was a necessary addition to scripture, while the opposite extreme held that there was no place whatsoever for tradition, and therefore that there was no relation to be acknowledged. Before coming on to the attitude of the Anglican Fathers as to the nature of tradition and the nature of its relation to scripture, two factors of fundamental importance regarding the nature of scripture must be noted.

Scripture is regarded as containing all things *essential* or *necessary* for salvation. There are other things which are *inessential*, though they may be edifying. This distinction between things essential and inessential is another mark of sixteenth- and seventeenth-century Anglican thought. *The* essential of scripture generally is regarded as its witness to the Incarnation – the fact that the Eternal Son or Word of God took to Himself our human flesh and nature and was born a son of man. The assent of the mind is required here, without dispute or question. This brings in the second factor of fundamental import with regard to the thought of these divines regarding scripture. And that is that the Word made flesh is the *scope* of scripture.

Operating implicitly with this concept of *scope*, the Laudian Divines saw clearly that scripture was a witness, pointing beyond its actual words to its inner content, nature and goal. It is the unique record which God is pleased to use through the inspiration of many and varied people whose work it is, to witness to that Word made flesh, Jesus Christ Himself. He is the inner content, nature and goal of scripture. Before the Laudian treatment of the matter, Richard Hooker again had written on the subject:

> The main drift of the whole New Testament is that which St. John setteth down as the purpose of his own history, *These things are written, that ye might believe that Jesus is Christ the Son of God, and that in believing ye might have life through His name*. The drift of the Old that which the Apostle mentioneth to Timothy, *The Holy Scriptures are able to make thee wise unto salvation*. So that the general end both of Old and New is one; the difference between them consisting of this, that the Old did make wise by teaching salvation through Christ that should come, the New by teaching that Christ the Saviour is come, and that Jesus Whom the Jews did crucify, and Whom God did raise again from the dead, is He. [3]

The argument runs: scripture is that which witnesses to Christ. He is its content and its goal. This is the unique nature of scripture. Hence, because of this nature, and only because of this, it does contain all things necessary for salvation.

But because Christ is the scope of scripture, the words of the Bible are not themselves coterminous with Him. Jesus Christ is Himself, He is not a collection of words. They witness to Him, and as witnesses, they come under the scrutiny of what we now call Biblical criticism. They must be understood within the context of their times, in as far as they are human words, and therefore they require scholarly interpretation. But that interpretation must have due regard to the nature of scripture and approach scripture accordingly, not doing violence to it on the basis of any authority other than its own, and forcing alien interpretations on it. Yet because of its scope, it has a peculiar nature which demands recognition and reverence.

John Hales (1584–1656), chaplain to Archbishop Laud, gathers this twofold observation about Scripture together. He warned both fundamentalists and liberal critics thus: 'The sense is Scripture, rather than the words', and that scripture must not be approached on the same level 'as chemists deal with natural bodies, torturing them to extract out of them that which God and nature never put in them', for 'Scripture interprets the interpreter'.[4] In this view, there cannot be a literalism of the words of scripture – that would be to confuse sign and thing signified, and that may be regarded as the essence of idolatry. These divines saw that there was such a thing as an idolatry of the Bible. Yet because of the paradigmatic nature of the words of scripture, in being the unique witnesses chosen to point to a unique essence, Jesus Himself, scripture itself is to be regarded with reverence as the lively oracles of God.

The Jacobean and Caroline Divines, following on from Hooker's work, were using exactly the same method as the Fathers of the fourth-century Church with regard to the interpretation of Scripture in accordance with its nature. St Athanasius had then spoken of Christ as the *skopos* of scripture, meaning by the Greek word, Christ as the essence, the content, the goal, of the Bible. It is in this sense that the word 'scope' may be used to describe the Biblical understanding of the divines of our period. St Athanasius wrote:

> Now the scope [skopos] and character of Holy Scripture, as we have often said, is this; it contains a double account of the Saviour; that He was ever God, and is the Son, being

the Father's Word and Radiance and Wisdom; and that afterwards for us He took flesh of a Virgin, Mary, Bearer of God, and was made man. And this scope is to be found throughout inspired Scripture, as the Lord Himself has said, *Search the Scriptures, for they are they which testify of Me*.[5]

Lancelot Andrewes (1555–1626) in his sermon preached on Friday, 25 December 1612, before the King's Majesty at Whitehall, on the text of Hebrews 1:1–3 notes that God spoke of old time by many persons and in different ways – that is, the old time of the Old Testament. But in these last times, that is, the time of the New Testament and since, He has spoken to us once and for all and sufficiently in His Son. These times of ours begin with the birth of Christ: 'the first day of *these last dayes*; the very *Kalends* of Christianitie, from whence, we begin our *AEra*, or Christian computation'.[6] There is a comparison in the text between this Christian era and the times of Israel of Old.

> betweene the times past, and these now. ... The point, wherein, is God's *speaking, speaking,* to both: but in a more excellent manner, and by a farre more excellent person, to us, than to them. The end, that so we might know, know and acknowledge ... what God hath done for us, and done for us, this day ... God is the same in both; He that *speaketh* to both: *of old,* to them: *of late,* to *Us*. Thus farr, even; they and we. One GOD, one *speaker*, to *both*. The oddes: Both spoken to; but not both *spoken to,* alike: Not alike in three Points ... Not in the Matter, *or Parts,* of which: Not in the Forme, or *Manner,* after which: Not in the Persons, by whom. To the Father(s?), He spake ... by *many peeces*; not entirely: To them ... *after sundry fashions*; not uniformely: To them, by His Servants, *the Prophets*; not by *His Sonne*. ... As the time grew, so grew their knowledge (peece and peece) of the great mystery, this day manifested ... it was *by peeces*, and *by many peeces*, they had it. Well said the Apostle that, *prophecying is in part*: One may now, in a few houres come to as much, as came to them in many hundred years. [That is, by reading the Old Testament.][7]

All the persons, institutions and history of the Old Testament point to Christ. Their full and final significance is found in Him alone, as their fulfilment. So Andrewes continues:

> the *Law* [of Moses] brings nothing to perfection: but, *Finis legis, CHRISTUS* [the end of the law is Christ]. And, all *prophecie* hangs in suspence (as imperfect,) till the fulfilling of it; which was done by *Christ*, to whom they all gave witnesse. Now, *when that, is perfect, is come; that, that is unperfect, must away*. Not to rest, in them, then: But, to CHRIST; and never rest, till we come to Him.
>
> And, as never to rest, till we come to him: So, there to rest, when we are come to Him: *As soone as His voice hath sounded in our eares,* that they *itch* no more after any new revelations. For, in, *Him,* are *all the treasures of wisdome and knowledge.*
>
> God spake *once and twice*: a third time, *He will not speake*. This, is His last time: He will speak no more. Looke fore no more *peeces*, nor phancie *no more fashions: Consumatus est,* there are no more to looke for. He is the *truth*: and, he that hath found the *truth*, and seeks further, no remedie, he must needs find a ly; he can find nothing else. To get us therefore to *Christ*; and never be got from Him; but, there, hold us.[8]

That was the problem as these divines saw it – how to treat of the scriptures that all might get to and be holden by, Christ. They understood the danger of the scriptures lying open and vulnerable to every man's gaze. Hooker, in his Preface to the *Laws of Ecclesiatical Polity*, points to the dangerous deficiency of using scripture as the sole source of ascertaining truth about polity and liturgy – and in so doing implies a wider concern. For the individual merely to seize, untutored, upon the Bible, means that authority has been transferred to the individual interpretation, and therefore to the subjective insight of the individual so engaged. In other words, the danger lies in the fact that every man's opinion is as good as the next man's – and in that, as Lancelot Andrewes saw so clearly, there is dormant and ready to awake the proliferation of sects.

These Divines recognized that the scriptures must have a rule of interpretation which was in keeping with the nature of scripture as that unique witness, the scope and horizon of which was Christ. So Andrewes again, in his 'Sermon of the Worshipping of Imaginations' preached in the Parish Church of St Giles, Cripplegate, 9 January 1592 – and this is a significant passage which deserves quite full quotation – remarks that there are two sorts of persons and two different

> meanes, whereby (as it were in two moulds) all *imaginations* have been cast, and the truth of God's word ever perverted. 1. From the Pharisee . . . adding to and eeking out God's truth, with men's phancies; with the *Phylacteries* and fringes of the *Pharisees*, who tooke upon them to observe *many things besideit*. 2. From the *Philosopher*, that wresting and tentering of the *Scriptures* (which *S. Peter* complaineth of) with expositions and glosses newly coined, to make them speake, that they never meant. Giving such *new* and *strange* senses to places of *Scripture*, as the Church of Christ never heard of. And what words are there, or can there bee, that (being helped out with the *Pharisee's* addition of a *truth unwritten*, or tuned with the Philosopher's wrest of a devised sense) may not bee made to give colour to a new imagination? Therefore, the ancient Fathers thought it meet, that they would take upon them to interpret the Apostles' Doctrine, should put in *sureties*, that their senses they gave, were no other, than the *Church* in former times hath acknowledged. It is true, the *Apostles* indeed spake from the *Spirit*, and every affection of theirs was an oracle: but, that (I take it) was their peculiar privilege. But, all that are after them, speake not by *revelation*, but by *labouring in the word* and learning: are not to utter their own phancies, and to desire to be beleeved upon their bare word . . . but onely on condition, that the sense, they now give, be not a *feigned* sense (as *S. Peter* termeth it) but such a one, as hath been before given by our fathers and fore-runners in the Christian faith. . . . Give I this sense of mine owne head, hath not *Christ's* Church heretofore given the like? Which one course if it were straightly holden, would rid our Church of many fond *imaginations* which now are stamped daily, because every man upon his owne single bond, is trusted to deliver the meaning of any Scripture, which is many times naught else, but his owne *imagination*. This is the disease of our Age.[9]

Here is the relation between scripture and tradition as seen by Andrewes. Tradition is that which interprets scripture in accordance with the nature of scripture – not adding anything to scripture, but distilling out of it the truth of its content, the doctrine of Christ Himself. Therefore scripture and tradition share a common scope – this same Christ. It would appear that for the Laudians, as exampled here by Andrewes, that the unveiling of this scope is the nature, business and goal of theology in dealing with Scripture and Tradition.

Andrewes is speaking in exactly the same tone as the early Fathers: for example St Irenaeus – 'The Church with one mouth traditions [catholic doctrine]'[10] – and also St Athanasius: 'The actual original tradition, teaching and faith of the Catholic Church, which the Lord conferred, the Apostles proclaimed and the Fathers guarded.'[11] And again, St. Athanasius – having spoken of Christ as the Scope of Scripture – writes of Christ as the 'Ecclesiastical scope',[12] that is, the true nature and content and horizon of the theological endeavour of the Church's life and works.

These divines were steeped in the study of the early Fathers of the Church, and everywhere in their works, there is an obvious familiarity, not necessarily through quotations from the Fathers (though these abound in profusion), but in the same thought forms and disciplined ways of theological thinking. Tradition for them meant three Creeds, four General Councils, and the works of the Fathers of the first five centuries of the history of the Church. Within this compass, the guidelines of how the scriptures were to be interpreted truly according to their essential nature were laid down. The reason for this was that they regarded these Councils – and the Creeds which were produced by them – as truly ecumenical, for they were representative of the whole, undivided, Church. In them, the Church with one mouth traditions Scripture. After this period, no Council can claim to be ecumenical, for the Church is divided and does not speak with one mind and voice.

Archbishop William Laud (1573–1645) is quite clear that the period of the Fathers was 'when the church was at the best'.[13] For Laud, the appeal of the Church of England was that of continuity with the early Church. The Apostolic Succession, for example, according to Laud, is a matter certainly of laying on of hands in succession, but not a 'bare' laying on of hands – there must be 'verity of doctrine' inseparable to the sign. Noting that the Fathers 'relied upon the Scriptures', making 'the creed the rule of faith'.[14] Laud points out that this is the state and position of the Church of England; the appeal to the Fathers demonstrates agreement with the early undivided Church.

These divines did not use the early Church and the writings of the Fathers as a quarry for material to justify and reinforce their own position. Rather, they were concerned to demonstrate that the Church of England was nearest to the early church, and therefore the most purely primitive. The primitive church was the yardstick against which their church was critically measured. This they did to counteract the vociferous claims of the Puritans on the one hand, and the militancy of the Jesuit apologists on the other.

The appeal to the Fathers shows that while the Anglican Divines of the period held firmly to the primacy of scripture, they did not regard the Bible as existing – or, indeed, as capable of being properly interpreted – apart from the continuous life of the church under the control of 'verity of doctrine'. The proper place and dignity of scripture, its enthronement as supreme, is in the seat of the 'rule of faith'. But that seat has been carved, and that rule measured, in strict accord with the nature of scripture. The scope of scripture determines exactly the nature of tradition, which thereby serves and exhibits the same scope, Christ Himself.

Hence, William Laud again, is at great pains to point out this. In this instance, he is dealing with Fisher's claims concerning the ecumenical status of the Council of Trent. He asks the same question and applies the same principle of judgment concerning the status of all councils apart from the four of the first five centuries:

Againe, is that Councell *Generall*, that hath none of the *Easterne Churches* Consent, nor presence there? Are all the *Greekes* so become *Non Ecclesia*, no Church, that they have no interest in *Generall Councels*?[15]

That is why there is this delineation of the first five centuries in the matter of describing and defining what is meant by tradition for the Jacobean and Caroline Divines. Andrewes writes of Scripture and Tradition and their relation as concerning the boundaries of the faith in his sermon 'preached before the King's Majestie at Halyrud (Holyrood) House, in Edenburgh on the 8th of June, 1617, being Whitsunday':

This *Booke* [that is, the Bible] chiefly; but, in a good part also, the *bookes* of the *Ancient Fathers*, and Lights of the *Church*, in whom the *scent of this ointment* [that is, the ointment of the nature, and therefore the proper interpretation, of scripture] is fresh, and the temper true; on whose *writings* it lyeth thick, and we thence strike it off, and gather it safely.[16]

Francis White (1564?–1638), Rector of St Peter, Cornhill, and then successively Bishop of Carlisle, of Norwich and of Ely, sets out the position of the Church of England with regard to her theological method and the related use of scripture and tradition:

The Church of England in her public and authorised Doctrine and Religion proceedeth in manner following.

It buildeth her faith and religion upon the Sacred and Canonical Scriptures of the Holy Prophets and Apostles, as upon her main and prime foundation.

Next unto Holy Scripture, it relieth upon the contentient testimony and authority of the Bishops and pastors of the true and ancient Catholic Church; and it preferreth the sentence thereof before all other curious or profane novelties.

The Holy Scripture is the fountain and lively spring, containing in all sufficiency and abundance the pure Water of Life, and whatsoever is, necessary to make God's people wise unto salvation.

The consentient and unanimous testimony of the true Church of Christ, in the Primitive Ages thereof, is *CANALIS*, a conduit pipe, to derive and convey to succeeding generations the celestial water contained in Holy Scripture.

The first of these, namely the Scripture, is the sovereign authority and for itself worthy of all acceptation. The latter, namely the voice and testimony of the Primitive Church, is a ministerial and subordinate rule and guide, to preserve and direct us in the right understanding of the Scriptures.[17]

Tradition, for these Jacobean and Caroline Divines, meant that scripture was best understood and properly interpreted in the first centuries of the Church. They claimed that then, there was laid down the method and pattern, to be followed in all ages, of regarding, reverencing, expounding and unfolding the scriptures. The Fathers of the first five centuries, and therefore tradition in this sense and description, were but the guardians of scripture, the stewards of the mysteries of God. They neither annexed something else in addition to scripture, nor did they seek to explain away scripture.

In this Laudian attitude, it may be seen that Christ, the scope of scripture and tradition, is the controlling and determinative self-giving, lively object, of all effort regarding scripture interpreted properly in the rule of faith of tradition. And here that third factor, *reason*, is to be seen in that context. Andrewes, preaching against 'imaginations', warned well of mental fancies giving rise to supposed new truths and grotesque interpretations. Implicit in this is the demand that the mind and reason should be disciplined to the nature of the object who so confronts us out of scripture and tradition. The mind is to be held by Christ, and objectively ordered according to who and what He is – the Word made flesh, God in all His Godness giving Himself in self-revelation to mankind, the very mouth of God speaking in human terms. The mind is not to force its own presuppositions on Christ, but to learn in obedience to Him, as He discloses Himself in scripture and through tradition.

But what these Caroline Divines were emphatic about is that the Christ who so gives Himself to be known by man, does not thereby give Himself up to be conquered by the mind of man, and explained away. The true nature of the Christ who reveals Himself, is that what He discloses Himself to be, that is, Lord – Lord over the mind and therefore Lord over theology. His true nature is that He reveals Himself to us the God who must always remain as Lord and therefore as Mystery to man. The genius and legacy of these divines was not that they erected a theological system, whereby God was determined by logic and held fast by philosophy, and all things explained to the satisfaction of the human mind. The human mind is not the judge and lord of God; rather, God is Lord and Judge of the human mind. Reason must bow in obedience to, and acknowledgement of what God is in Himself as He has revealed Himself in Christ. John Hales's phrase 'Scripture interprets the interpreter' is most pertinent here, for by it he rules out all arrogant assumptions of the mind of the interpreter in daring to deal with God, and reminds the interpreter that it is he who comes under the scrutiny of God who, in the insistence of these divines, searches the deep things of the heart and mind.

This third factor, reason, falls into a different category from scripture and tradition. Yet it is bound to them in a particular way. In Caroline thought, scripture and tradition are the trysting places of Truth, to which the mind must go if it is to meet with Truth. The mind, and therefore reason, is subservient to scripture and tradition. These inform the mind, and the mind must follow the pattern which Truth takes to reveal itself through them. In other words, reason must be obedient to the nature and way of Truth as declared in scripture and through the tradition of the Church. Reason operates by letting the Truth declare itself, and not by imposing irrational presuppositions, culled from other sources and authorities, and through natural prejudices, upon it. As such, the mind is the servant of scripture and tradition, not the master, and is bound to them by the scope common to each of them – Christ as the self-giving Truth and Light.

The fault of ascribing autonomy to the mind, and therefore of ascribing to reason a power of undisciplined subjective mastery, is avoided by these Carolines. It is a misrepresentation of the 'classical' Anglican position to regard scripture, tradition and reason as equal categories. The relation between them, emphasized so strongly in their works – namely, the common Scope of Christ Himself – and the status of these three categories in their respective relation to that scope, has been overlooked largely. It is reason's role, according to them, to take the unchanging Truth, objectively disclosing itself in scripture and through tradition, and let the Truth unfold itself in and for time and place. It is therefore the obedient and disciplined servant of the other two.

Andrewes exhibits a dread, characteristic of all his own and his contemporaries' works, of reason as an autonomous factor intruding into the mystery of God. His 'Sermon III of the Nativity, preached before the King's Majestie, at White-Hall, on Thursday, the 25th December, 1607', may be instanced here. Again, it is instructive to quote at some length, in order to let Andrewes's argument be seen to develop characteristically.

> *The manifestation of God in the flesh*, the *Evangelists* set downe by way of an *Historie*: the *Apostle* goeth further, and findeth a deep *Mysterie* in it; and for a *Mysterie* commends it unto us . . . this plaine *Mysterie* here . . . [the Apostle] esteemed himselfe not to know anything at all, but this.
>
> And as he esteemed it himselfe, so would he have us. It is his expresse charge, we see (in the Verse next before) where he tels his Bishop Timothie, how he would have him, his Priests and Deacons occupie themselves, in his absence: This he commends to them; wils them to be doing with this Mysterie. . . . God is manifested in the flesh . . . marke first, that it is not . . . any thing divine, or of God, but God Himselfe . . . God is manifested. . . .
>
> Manifested: wherein? . . . what say you to flesh? is it meet God be manifested therein? Without controversie it is not. Why, what is flesh? It is no Mysterie to tell you what it is: It is dust (saith the Patriarch Abraham.) It is grasse (saith the Prophet Esay;) . . . grasse . . . cut downe, and withering: It is corruption, not corruptible, but even corruption it selfe, (saith the Apostle Paul.) There being then (as Abraham said . . . Luke 16.) . . . so great a gulfe, so huge a space, so infinite a distance betweene those two, betweene God, and dust; God, and Hay; God, and Corruption; as no coming of one at the other . . . talke not of flesh. . . .
>
> We cannot choose, but holde this Mysterie for Great, and say (with S. Augustine,) . . . God, what more glorious? flesh, what more base? Then, God in the flesh: what more marvellous? . . . In clouts, in a stable, in a manger. The God, whom the heavens, and the heaven of heavens cannot contain, in a little Childs flesh not a spanne long: and that flesh of a Childe not very well conditioned, as you may reade in the 16. of Ezekiel.
>
> So, to day: but after, much worse. To day, in the flesh of a poore Babe crying in the Cratch, *in medio animalium* [in the midst of the animals]: After, in the rent and torne flesh of a condemned person, hanging on the Crosse, *in medio latronum* [in the midst of the thieves], in the midst of other manner persons, than Moses and Elias; That, men even hid their faces at Him; not, for the brightnesse of His glorie, but for sorrow and shame. Call you this manifesting? Nay, well doth the Apostle call it, the Veile of His flesh; as whereby He was rather obscured, than in any way set forth; yea, eclipsed, in all the darkest points of it.
>
> Verily, the condition of the flesh was more than the flesh it selfe: and the manner of the manifestation, farre more, than the manifestation it selfe was. Both still make the Mysterie greater and greater. [18]

And of those who sought to reduce this mystery standing central to the knowledge of God and to the propriety of all theological undertakings, Andrewes says this in an Easter 'Sermon preached before the King's Majestie at White-Hall, the 1. April, 1621' (the text was John 20:17: Jesus saith unto her, Touch Me not)

> [God's] *secret Decrees?* May not they, for their *height* and *depth*, claime to this *Noli* (touch not), too? Yes, sure: and I pray God, Hee be well pleased with this licentious

touching, nay, tossing His *Decrees* of late; this sounding the depths of His *Judgements* with our line, and lead; too much presumed upon by some, in these days of ours . . . (Saith the Psalmist) *His judgements are the great deepe*. Saint Paul, looking downe into it, ranne backe, and cried, *O the depth!* the profound depth! not to be searched, past our fadoming or finding out. Yet there are in the world that make but a *shallow* of this great deepe: they have sounded it to the bottome. God's *Decrees*, they have them at their fingers ends, can tell you the number and the order of them just, with 1, 2, 3, 4, 5. Men that (sure) must have beene in God's *Cabbinet*, above the *third heaven*, where Saint *Paul* never came. *Mary Magdalens touch* was nothing to these. . . [19]

The genius and legacy of the Caroline Divines was that they introduced – or rather rediscovered from the early Fathers – a theological method, flexible and unenclosed, whereby they endeavoured to let the truth of God ever be appreciated anew, and the conclusions of Reason, using Scripture and Tradition, be constantly reconstructed in accordance with the nature of the living Truth who confronted the mind out of scripture and tradition. Theirs was no inquisitive temper, bent on rounding off a self-satisfactory system, complete and finished. To them, this would have been a denial of the true nature of the God who reveals Himself in Christ. They shunned any presumptuous dealing with God, and this is how they proceeded in all their theological undertakings.

They neither sought to define completely the knowledge of God within a confession of faith, a documentary declaration of the fullness of belief in every article, nor did they recognize any authority vested in any institution which likewise defined and determined the faith within the compass of power and influence. Rather, the only authority they recognized was that of the Truth Himself, Who comes in His own Majesty, and demands not only the assent of the mind, but the adoration of the totality of the individual's existence. 'In Thy light, we see light', was their watchword. In the light of that God who revealed Himself in Jesus Christ, they sought to give all adoration and praise to that One who has not only created all things in grace, but has re-created them by visiting His creation and taking its temporal and spatial realities into union with Himself. Their theological method, therefore, expressed itself in their attitude towards the good order of creation, the harmony of society and the peace of the Church.

Scripture, tradition and reason, in their relation to each other, all being centred on the Incarnational revelation and reconciliation of God, were the conceptual tools with which they viewed all areas of existence. These areas they saw in terms of the order and truth of God as that order and truth is unfolded in scripture, through tradition and by reason all centred on Christ. It is these areas as they were dealt with in the thought of the Laudian divines we now examine.

Notes

1 Lancelot Andrewes: Oposcula (*Collected Works*), L.A.C.T. edn, p.91.
2 Richard Hooker: *The Laws of Ecclesiastical Polity*, II:VIII:7.
3 Ibid., I:XIV:4.
4 John Pearson: *The Golden Remains of the Ever Memorable John Hales*, 1659 edn, p.31
5 Athanasius: 'Four Discourses against the Arians', *Discourse* III:29.

6   Lancelot Andrewes: 'Sermon 7 of the Nativity', *Ninety-six Sermons* 1635 edn, p.53.
7   Ibid., p.53.
8   Ibid., p.55.
9   Ibid., p.B27.
10 Irenaeus: 'Contra Haereses', I:X:2.
11 Athanasius: 'Ad Serapionem', I:28.
12 Athanasius: 'Contra Arianos', III:58.
13 William Laud: *Relation of the Conference*, 1639 edn, p.34.
14 Ibid., pp.383ff.
15 Ibid., p.214.
16 Lancelot Andrewes: *Ninety-six Sermons*, 'Sermon 10 of the Sending of the Holy Ghost', 1635 edn, p.702.
17 Frances White: *A Treatise of the Sabbath Day, Containing a Defence of the Orthodoxal Doctrine of the Church of England against Sabbatarian Novelty*, 1635 edn, pp.11ff.
18 Lancelot Andrewes: *Ninety-six Sermons*, 'Sermon 3 of the Nativity', 1635 edn, pp.17–20.
19 Lancelot Andrewes: *Ninety-six Sermons*, 'Sermon 15 of the Resurrection', 1635 edn, p.548.

Chapter 3

Order, Creator and Creation

The concept of 'order' undergirds the theology of the Elizabethan, Jacobean and Caroline Divines. It is not therefore surprising that this emphasis in theology gained general recognition in an age when the sermon was commonplace to most of the population, and when theology made its impact on every other discipline of learning.

In the works of these Divines, order is seen in terms of God's *oikonomia* – the economy of God. While they refer to this generally in Patristic terms as 'the ordering of God's household of creation', it is seen primarily, again in Patristic terms, as that 'order' which God is eternally in Himself. Francis Mason (1566–1621) expresses this so: 'Order proceedeth from the throne of the Almightie, it is the beautie of nature, the ornament of Arte, the harmonie of the world.'[1]

John Swan in his *work Speculum Mundi, or a Glasse Representing the face of the World,* begins that section entitled the *Hexameron,* by setting out the relation of creation to the Creator.

Time, by whose revolutions we measure houres, dayes, weeks, moneths and years, is nothing else but (as it were) a certain space borrowed or set apart from *eternitie;* which shall at the last return to eternitie again ... for before *Time* began, there was *Eternitie,* namely GOD; which was, which is, and which shall be for ever: without beginning or end, and yet the beginning and end of all things. ... *Eternitie is substantially onely in the nature of God.* When Moses therefore would have known GODS name, he tells him, *Thus shalt thou say unto the children of Israel, I AM hath sent me unto you: By which name,* saith Junius, *he would have himself known according to his eternal essence, whereby he is discerned from all other things which are either in heaven, on the earth, or elsewhere.* ...

Thus we see that before ever any thing was, God only was, who* [*in the margin: When we behold the admired fabrick of the world, &c, we can no more ascribe it to chance, then a Printers case of letters could by chance fall into the right composition of any such book as he printeth.] gave both a beginning and a being, unto everything that is: and he, in respect of his divine essence, is but one. Yet so, as in that single essence of his there be three divine subsistences, or persons all truly subsisting; whereof every one is distinct from other, and yet each hath the whole Godhead in it self: and these are, *the Father, Sonne,* and *holy Ghost,* I John, 5.7.

1. The Father is a person who from all eternitie hath begotten the Sonne.
2. The Sonne is a person from all eternitie begotten of the Father.
3. The holy Ghost is a person eternally proceeding from the Father and the Sonne,* [*in the margin: Psal. 2.7. John 15.26.] as the holy Scriptures witnesse.

*These thus distinct in person, not divinitie
All three in one make one eternall Trinitie
[*in the margin: Du Bart. I, day of the I. week.]

37

> From which eternall and undivided Trinitie, the whole world, consisting things visible and invisible, took beginning . . .[2]

What is of note here, first, is the precise way in which Swan follows the orthodox maxim of Athanasius, that God is beyond all *created* being. There is no thought of falling into the dualistic assumption of Origenistic thought that God is beyond all *being* – and therefore in the last resort unknowable. God is knowable in His Triune existence as He is pleased to reveal Himself in the Incarnate Son.

Secondly, and following from this, He is the source, the sustainer and the fulfiller of all created being. Creation is therefore contingent to and from God. It is contingent *to* God, for it utterly depends on Him for its existence and its upholding and its destiny. It is contingent *from* God, because it is created distinct from Him in His uncreate nature, and has the quality of its own identity. If it is to be that creation which God intends it to be, contingency *to* and contingency *from* have to be in exact balance.

Thirdly, the nature of eternity has to be noted. There is no eternity apart from God. It is because God is eternal that he has His 'time' and His 'space', namely eternity. It is not that there is existing by its own independent right an eternity which God happens to inhabit. The relation between time and eternity is therefore the relation of time to the eternal God, and the relation between things and eternity is therefore the relation of created entities to the measureless God. It is a relation of being. The time and space of creation is contingent on the 'time' and 'space' of the eternal God. Hence time is 'a certain space borrowed or set apart from eternitie; which shall at the last return to eternitie again. . . . Eternitie is substantially onely in the nature of God.'[3] Swan goes on to speak of the creation as a work of the Trinity: 'From which eternall and undivided Trinitie, the whole world, consisting of things visible and invisible, took beginning.'[4] He points out that the word 'Elohim' in the creation narrative is a plural word, signifying *Dii, Gods*. But the verb used 'Bara', which is Created, is singular. In the reasoning of the age, he deduces that the plural subject and the singular verb juxtaposed

> shew that there are three persons in the Deitie, and that the three persons are but one God, who did create. Or thus; Those two words, being the one of the singular, the other of the plurall number, do note unto us the singularitie of the Godhead, and pluralitie of the persons. And not onely so, but they also shew that the three persons being but one God, did all of them create: For such is found to be the proprietie of the Hebrew phrase, *Elohim bara, Creavit Dii, The Gods created.*[5]

Swan then sets out, by way of Biblical appeals, the nature of each of the Persons in the work of creation. This is carefully set out, for on it rests two important interdependent factors upon which he insists: that all the Persons of the Trinity are confederate in the work of God, and that God in Himself is all sufficiency and company. The conclusion to which these factors lead points to the nature of creation itself.

> 1.   Of the Father it is witnessed, that he created as the fountain of goodnesse. For saith S.James, *Every good and perfect gift is from above, & cometh down from the Father of lights*, Jam. 1.17. *Of whom and through whom*, saith S.Paul, *are all things*, Rom.11.36.

2.   Of the Sonne it is witnessed that he created as the wisdome of the Father. For, *when he created the heavens*, saith Wisdome, *I was there*, Prov. 8.27. And again, *By him were all things created that are*, Coloss.1.14,15. namely by him who did bear the image of the Father, and was the Redeemer of the world.

3.   And lastly of the holy Ghost it is witnessed, that he createth as the power of the Father and the Sonne. For *by his Spirit he garnished the heavens, and by his hand he hath formed the crooked serpent*, Job 26.13 and chap. 33.4. Or, as the Psalmist hath it, *By the word of the Lord were the heavens made and all the hosts of them [spiritu oris] by the spirit of his mouth*, Psal. 33.6.[6]

Having set all this out, Swan immediately remarks as consequent:

All which considered, and found to be done in the beginning, must needs be then when there was no pre-existent matter to work upon. For . . . the Hebrew word *Reshith*, which is Englished *the beginning*, doth not signifie any substance; neither doth the other word *Bara, to create*, signifie any way to create but of nothing: and thereby it is distinguished from the word *Jatzar, to form, & Gnasha, to make*. And therefore though now we behold a glorious something wherein appears in every part more than much matter of wonder; yet at the first, saith noble *Bartas*,
Nothing but nothing had the Lord Almightie,
Whereof, wherewith, whereby to build this citie.[7]

Creation owes nothing to anything but to God Himself. It owes it only to this God who exists as the God He eternally is in His interior relations. To this God, and to no other sort of God, it owes its beginning and its existence, its nature and its identity. Creation is the work of this God, and therefore it is a specific sort of creation. This is why Swan is so carefully detailed in outlining the creative work of the Trinity from the outset. Creation is contingent to and from God. Specifically it is contingent to and from the Triune God.

This further enhances the idea of contingency as a contingency of sheer grace. God, eternally existing as Father and Son bound in the bond of eternal love which is the Holy Spirit, is in no need of anything. He is, in Himself, all company, conversation, majesty and dominion – total sufficiency. There is no necessity or compulsion upon Him from within (as though there were a personal lack) to create. Nor is there any necessity or compulsion upon Him from without (as though there were a co-eternal other with which He had to deal) to create. Here Swan's emphasis is on the Nicene concept of creation *ex nihilo*, which he approaches through the doctrine of the sufficiency of the Triune God in His eternal, interior relations as Father, Son and Holy Spirit.

Heaven and earth had a beginning. They were not always. But at that beginning, they were not distinguished, the one from the other. All lay in a confused heap, 'like a disordered and deformed Chaos'. This is 'said to be void and without form, and not able to be kept together, had not the Spirit of God cherished it'.[8] What is of interest here is Swan's clear implication of the tendency of created matter towards annihilation, or reverting to nothingness, even in the most primeval and chaotic state, were it not for the action of God. This emphasis is his awareness that all things are upheld, not by their own natural force, but by the grace of God. This he maintains consistently throughout this work, and in so doing underlines continuously, the principle of the contingency of creation from and to God.

Appealing to the 'Nightingale of France' (the poet Du Bartas) he calls the chaotic mass an 'EMBRYON', likening it, and the process of bringing order out of chaos, to the foetus:

> *The shapelesse burden in the mothers wombe,*
> *Which doth in time into good fashion come.*[9]

The first degree of the sensible world is that matter is expressed *ex nihilo*. The second degree, or principle, is that in origin it was without form and void 'rather to be believed then [than] comprehended of us'. The second principle, says Swan, following the sixteenth-century work, *Purchas's Pilgrim* is this

> privation . . . acquired in regard of generation, not of constitution. . . . This was the internall Constitution. The externall was darknesse upon the face of the deep. Which deep compriseth both the earth before mentioned, and the visible heavens also, called a depth, as to our capacitie infinite, and pliant to the Almightie hand of the Creatour: called also waters, not because it was perfect waters, which was yet confused; but because of a certain resemblance, not onely in the uniformitie thereof, but also of that want of stability whereby it could not abide together, but as the Spirit of God moved upon the face of the waters to sustain them.[10]

So here we have the first principle – a creation out of nothing – and a second principle, that it is without form and void (or *without variety*) and receives sustained existence and stability only by the action of God.

The concept of contingency is firmly to the fore here in the stating of these two principles, as it is in the third following. What also is of note here is that Swan, following Purchas, notes the propriety of biblical imagery – 'water . . . the deep . . . darkness' all combine to convey the impossibility of our comprehension of the creative act of God. It also conveys the idea of the state of fluidity and flux which the creative action of God alone can contain and stabilize. For the imagery points to the fact that there is no natural ability or resource inherent in the primal matter, to be self-contained and to achieve its own stability. The subsequent containing, stabilizing and development of the primal matter into created order is a question of the sheer incomprehensible grace of God.

The third principle is the form which God decrees for creation:

> The Hebrews call the whole masse, as it is comprehended under the names of Heaven and Earth, *Tohu Vabohu: tohu, without order; bohu, without varietie*. But it was not long that it continued in this imperfect state: For in one week it was (as I may say) both begotten and born, and brought from a confused Chaos, to a well-ordered and variously adorned Universe.[11]

The question as to why God did not make everything perfect instantly, is then entered upon. Swan argues that, far from God disabling His omnipotence by not doing so, He demonstrates the quality of that power by ordering all things according to His counsel, which in this work of creation (prosecuted both by an order of time and degrees) is so farre from eclipsing his power, that it rather doth demonstrate both his power and wisdome to be infinite.

An entrance is made here into the qualitively different natures of Creator and creature. The parenthesized phrase in the above quotation – 'prosecuted both by an order of time and degrees' – is of note. For by it Swan emphasizes that God holds time and space in His counsel and in His creative work. He determines to bring that form of temporal and spatial realities (for 'degree' means 'things in their place') as the nature or quality of creation. These temporal and spatial realities, time and space, He takes seriously. These are the identity of His creation. Here, again, the notion of contingency is underlying. There is a contingency *to* God, in that time and things are totally dependent on Him for their origin, existence and form. There is a contingency *from* God, in that they have this, their peculiar identity bestowed upon them by Him. They can only be what they really are, that is, entities separate in their quality from Him, by virtue of their very relationship to Him.

Swan notes that the question as to why God did not create perfection instantly, is improper: 'God's will is a sufficient reason in all his actions; and therefore it is better left then [than] looked into.' But, he continues, if a humble probing of the question will help man to understand his status –

if they instruct man in any thing pertinent to his present condition, and inform him so as he may be somewhat reformed by them: then they may be urged without the brand of nicenesse or imputation of curiousitie.[13]

Had God created perfection instantly, he argues, and had He not taken His leisure in the matter, it might first be thought that things were increate, divine, and not made at all. There would be little distinguishing of order, and no sense of the essential identity of creation in its contingency, which we can perceive, seeing one thing is created before another and there is place and order for things.

Secondly, it demonstrates the great kindness of God towards mankind. For man who is 'the chief inhabitant' of creation has his dwelling place prepared for him by God 'thus perfected by degrees before man was ... methinks so orderly to raise such a sumptuous palace for mankind, whilest yet mankind was not.'[14] The careful and timely preparation of God for the making of man, holds out and demonstrates His continuous graciousness to mankind after its making, for which He had so much forethought.

Here we must question Swan's observations on the forethought of God. There seems to be a departure in this matter from the Patristic insistence – for example in Basil's *Hexaemeron*, where there is followed out the fourth-century Greek Fathers' insistence that as soon as God thinks or wills He acts. That is to say, Swan has no concept of an instantaneous creation, and indeed contradicts Basil's observation that

Thus then, if it is said *In the beginning God created*, it is to teach us that at the will of God the world rose in less than an instant, and it is to convey this meaning more clearly that other interpreters have said: *God made summarily* that is to say all at once and in a moment.

By 'other interpreters', Basil seems to be thinking of Origen, at least Aquila's version of Origen's *Hexopla*. But it would appear that there is a possible disparity here between Swan's observations and the Greek Patristic tradition, and, indeed, between Swan and the English tradition of the Hexaemeron as instanced by Bede and Grosseteste both following Basil. It may be that Swan has allowed the influence of Augustine of Hippo in the general matter of the division of thought and act by God to sway his opinions.

Swan continues:

> And thirdly, it is a lesson to man how to proceed in his works under God, not heedlessly or hastily, but soberly and by degrees with careful thought, holding God's likeness in so working in mind.[16]

Swan quotes Bishop Hall (lib.1.): 'How should we deliberate our actions which are so subject to imperfection; seeing it pleased Gods infinite perfections (not out of need) to take leisure.'[17]

In this first section of *Speculum Mundi*, Swan looks at the nature of creation under the grace of the Triune God, who in His total sufficiency in His eternal and internal relations, existing as He does as Father, Son and Holy Spirit, creates in His overflowing love and out of His grace, an entity separate from Him yet dependent on Him, with which to share His glory.

Swan's work shows the transition from mediaeval scholastic cosmology and, indeed, mythology, to the flowering of objective observation and interpretation. There are still more than traces of the former in this work, but it does represent the renewed face of properly grounded natural science. (Grosseteste was an exception to the Scholastic mind prevalent in his day, in his rejection of Aristotelian concepts of creation. To give one example of Grosseteste's rejection of Aristotelian concepts and the tenets of most of his contemporaries: 'With the hammer of these words [that is, In the beginning] Moses crushed the philosophers who assert with Aristotle that the world has no beginning.'[18] We may conjecture that had Grosseteste's works been available to him, Swan might have grounded his observations even more objectively.)

Nevertheless, there is surely an insistence in Swan's work that objective interpretation, as far as he saw it, holds prime and determinative place. This is seen in his emphasis on theological interpretation, on letting God and the works of God, speak out on their own terms. In other words, the attempt is being made, despite the clinging to the fantasies of a past age and outlook, to discipline the mind according to the nature of the object studied.

The nature of Truth, as that which comes in its own intrinsic authority, is what is at stake here. Swan is careful to distinguish, for the most part (again despite the lingering medieval attitude) between Truth itself and statements about Truth. He is well aware that God and the things of God cannot be comprehended and reduced to the boundaries of the limitations of human thought, however sublime. It is here that there can be appreciated a repetition of what happened in fourth-century Alexandria. There, the Nicene fathers in particular, made an impact on rational thought with their insistence that theological science dealt with the Truth on the Truth's own terms. They equally insisted on the obedient assent of the mind to the nature of that

Truth, that is the revelation of God in Christ. This mode of thought opened the way for natural science to look objectively at creation. For natural science, such as it was, had been constricted by the dictates of a dualistic way of thinking, which ignored things as they were in themselves, and sought the truth about them in their supposed eternal forms, clamping down on reality a framework of rigid idealism. This meant that the creation was regarded as but a temporal shadow of eternal verities, and it was in the light of the latter that creation was to be interpreted. It also meant that, in the last resort, all things material and corporeal were discardable and of little significance in themselves.

This way of thinking, dominated by then current trends in Greek philosophy, rested on the tearing apart of Creator and creation, eternity and time, the heavenly and the earthly. The doctrine of the Incarnation was the corrective to all this. Here, with the union of God and man, was the formation of a unitary way of thinking, where things were seen in their relation to the God who gave them existence, and who personally took the created realities into union with Himself in Jesus Christ, establishing them, as He had decreed at creation, with their own qualities and contingent natures. The idea of the contingency of creation to and from God, and what this meant for the nature of the created realities, has its foundation here. It was this, in fourth-century Alexandria, which gave impetus to the schools of natural science, letting them throw off the shackles of philosophical idealism and speculation, which in its dualistic attitude, had constricted a true understanding of the nature of God's handiwork.

This same unitary way of thinking, and the resulting observations of the contingency of creation in its relation to the God who created all things out of nothing by the Word and in the operation of His Spirit, colours Swan's thinking. His observations on the creation of light, as God's first creature, and the way in which he sets out the orders of creation to that created light and the relation of the whole to the uncreated Light on which all depends for existence and rationality, have already been underlined.

But all this is arrived at by obedient and objective treatment and interpretation, without imposing any idealistic framework constructed by mere surface and formal observations on creation for a supposed understanding of its nature. It is the same mode of thought which was formed by obedience to the nature of the revelation of the living God in Christ, which was transferred to the interpretation of creation, and therefore to the properly scientific mode of investigation.

It was Francis Bacon, *par excellence*, who delighted in transferring the same mode of interpretation of the 'Books of God' to the 'Books of nature'. He was insistent on the necessity of objective thinking, of letting whatever was the object of study reveal itself on its own terms. In two important passages (*Of the Proficience and Advancement of Learning*, and *In Praise of Knowledge*[19]), he repeats 'The truth of being, and the truth of knowing, is all one.' That is to say, as an object is in itself, so it is towards us in our obedient observation and interpretation of it. He introduces this statement about truth of being and truth of knowing in *In Praise of Knowledge* so: 'The mind itself is but an accident to knowledge; for knowledge is a double of that which is.' Here, of course, we are in the same parallel mode of thought as the Patristic observation that what God is eternally in Himself, He is towards us in Christ. That is, God reveals Himself as the God He is in His eternal existence, and we know Him in His revelation as the God He is in His eternal Being. This Patristic maxim directs the thinking of so many of the divines, and through them the general thinkers in fields other than theology (though these other disciplines were never far removed from theology) in this period.

Bacon, in the second instance of his statement about the truth of being and knowledge, in *Of the Proficience and Advancement of Learning*, says that

> the essential form of knowledge . . . is nothing but a representation of truth; for the truth of being and the truth of knowing are one, differing no more than the direct beam and the beam reflected.

'Light of Light' is the basis of such modes of thought here, and again, the image is a Patristic one, much used in wide application in such matters of the nature of knowledge by writers contemporary to Bacon – Lancelot Andrewes in his 'Sermons of the Nativity', for example.

Bacon sets knowledge – its nature and quality – on firm foundations in the same book:

> First, let us seek the dignity of knowledge in the archetype or first platform, which is in the attributes and acts of God, as far as they are revealed to man, and may be observed with sobriety; wherein we may not seek it by the name of learning: for all learning is knowledge acquired, and all knowledge in God is original; and therefore we must look for it by another name, that of wisdom or sapience, as the Scriptures call it.
>
> It is so then, that in the word of creation we see a double emanation of virtue from God; the one referring more properly to power, the other to wisdom; the one expressed in making the subsistence of the matter, and the other in disposing the beauty of the form. This being supposed, it is to be observed, that, for any thing which appeareth in the history of the creation, the confused matter and mass of heaven and earth was made in a moment, and the order and disposition of that chaos, or mass, was the work of six days; such a note of difference it pleased God to put upon the works of power, and the works of wisdom: wherewith concurreth, that in the former it is not set down that God said *Let there be heaven and earth*, as is set down of the works following; but actually, that God made heaven and earth: the one carrying a style of manufacture, and the other of a law, decree, or council. . . .
>
> To descend . . . to sensible and material forms; we read the first form that was created was light, which hath a relation and correspondence in nature and corporal things to knowledge in spirits and incorporal things. . . .
>
> After the creation was finished, it is set down unto us, that man was placed in the garden to work therein; which work, so appointed to him, could be no other than work of contemplation; that is, when the end of work is but for exercise and experiment, not for necessity; for there being then no reluctation of the creature, nor sweat of the brow, man's employment must of consequence have been matter of delight in the experiment, and not matter of labour for the use. Again, the first acts which man performed in paradise, consisted of the two summary parts of knowledge; the view of creatures, and the imposition of names. As for the knowledge which induced the fall, it was . . . not the natural knowledge of creatures, but the moral knowledge of good and evil; wherein the supposition was, that God's commandments or prohibitions were not the originals of good and evil, but that they had other beginnings which man aspired to know, to the end to make a total defection from God, and to depend wholly upon himself.[20]

Here we have, in the thought forms of the time, a survey of the quality and the nature of knowledge. The essential unitary way of thinking which Bacon employed is clear – the contingency of all creation to and from God, the proper interpretation of all created realities in the light of that relation of the whole to its Source lying qualitatively beyond it as uncreated Being, the refusal to separate form and content, and the necessary discipline of man's mind to the order which God has decreed. The fall, and false knowledge, are intertwined, for the fall, in essence, is the temptation to man to see himself as the orderer of all things and the decider of good and evil. In other words, man is turned in upon himself in his self-ascribed autonomy, and turns away from the true centre of his being and knowledge, which is God. We have here the juxtaposition of the good ordering of all things in their contingent nature, and the appreciation of true knowledge by minds disciplined to this order of God, and the malevolent technology of man's false knowledge, springing as it does from his own aversion to God and the ordering of God's decrees.

Bacon is laying the ground for the true direction and method of natural science, which is the obedient observation and experimentation and discovery of things according to what they really are in themselves, and not the violence done to them by disregarding their essential nature, by man's self-centred and self-seeking decree, manipulation and invention.

True knowledge, moreover, will be content with the fact that all things, which can be observed and interpreted within the bounds of their compass as created being – although related to that which lies beyond them as uncreated Being – rest on the mystery of that uncreated Being, which can never be encompassed within the bounds of minds limited by time and space. Theology and Natural Science share the same disciplined method with regard to the objects of their respective studies, the one, as it were, from Creator and His revelation to creation, the other from creation to the indescribable and indefinable Source of all things. This is expanded in Book II, but the gist of the matter is that the order of all things, and therefore the rationality of all things and the possibility of true knowledge of them, depends on that order which God is eternally in Himself.

> Faith containeth the doctrine of the nature of God, of the attributes of God, and of the works of God. The nature of God consisteth of three persons in the unity of Godhead. The attributes of God are either common to the Deity, or respective to the persons. The works of God summary are two, that of the creation, and that of redemption; and both these works, as in total they appertain to the unity of the Godhead, so in their parts they refer to the three persons: that of the creation, in the mass of the matter, to the Father; in the disposition of the form, to the Son; and in the continuance and conservation of the being, to the Holy Spirit.[21]

The order and rationality of creation, is in correspondence, though in its qualitatively different nature as created being, to the Order and Rationality which God is in Himself in His uncreate and eternal Being. It is this understanding which typifies the work of so many writers of the period in all disciplines of learning, and it is that which gave cohesion and comprehension to the relation between all such various and varying branches of study at that time. There was also a discernible order in the relation between these disciplines as they occupied the minds of the period. Bacon ends this work with the remark that 'Thus I have made, as it were, a small globe of the intellectual world.'[22]

Again, in *Valerius Terminus: Of the Interpretation of Nature*, Bacon, in the section 'Of the Limits and End of Knowledge' follows out this same course of thought:

> I thought it good and necessary in the first place, to make a strong and sound head or bank to rule and guide the course of the waters, by setting down this position or axiom, namely, *That all knowledge is to be limited by religion, and to be referred to use and action.*[23]

Bacon then removes the ground of false natural theology – attempting to read the Uncreated off the created, so that he can establish the ground of true knowledge with respect to the genuine nature of created realities:

> For if any man shall think, by view and inquiry into these sensible and material things, to attain to any light for the revealing of the nature or will of God; he shall dangerously abuse himself. It is true that a contemplation of the creatures of God hath an end, as to the natures of the creatures themselves, knowledge, – but as to the nature of God, not knowledge, but wonder: which is nothing else but contemplation broken off, or losing itself . . . God is only self-like, having nothing in common with any creature . . . Therefore attend his will as himself openeth it, and give to faith that which unto faith belongeth . . . To conclude; the injury hath been infinite, that both divine and human knowledge hath received by the intermingling and tempering of the one with the other: as that which hath filled the one full of heresies, and the other full of speculative fictions and fantasies.[24]

He is warning against that dualistic mode of thought which so separated the Divine and human, that it bridged the gap by reading the Divine off the idealization of the earthly and temporal, and so projected created concepts into the status of the eternal.

He is also stressing the fact that realities are to be treated as those which are in themselves what they are. The created realities are, by nature, of the dimension and status of the created order. They are not Divine or eternal, and are not to be treated in interpretation or application, as such. They are to be respected for what they are as they are in themselves. Therefore we are concerned here, according to Bacon, with a particular mode of thought. This way of thinking places the emphasis on the objective reality which is being studied. The subjective thinker and interpreter holds but a secondary, though connected place. The thinking subject disciplines his thoughts and interpretation of the objective reality to what that object is. That is, *truth of being and truth of knowing are one*. As the object is, so it will reveal itself in a mode entirely consistent with what it is. It is the thinking subject's role to let this happen, and to let his mind be filled and formed so.

Of the Interpretation of Nature is part of Bacon's *Novum Organon*, which has as its first part 'The Advancement of Learning'. In this first part there is stated a fundamental aphorism:

> Man, nature's servant and interpreter, effects and understands just so much as he may have observed of nature's order either in fact or thought; beyond this, he has neither knowledge nor power.[25]

This has several implications which Bacon follows through scrupulously in the second part of the work:

1   It is the vocation of man to come to an understanding of that order by which nature – the realm of created things – exists and moves.
2   An appreciation of that order can only be gained, not by imposing upon nature hypotheses by which it is supposed to work, but by diligent and objective observation and reasoning on the basis of what nature reveals itself to be.
3   Man's knowledge of, and power over, nature is limited by what nature so reveals, and all things must be done by man with respect to that and not contrary to it.

Thus, he says in the next aphorism: 'Neither the naked hand, neither the intellect left to itself, can achieve much' – by which he means that brute, uninformed dealing with the things of nature, or an undisciplined mind self-deludedly free to roam as it will, is useless, and no truth or proper action can result.[26]

It is noteworthy that the Latin word Bacon uses to describe futile speculations about nature is *idola*. By this he means not 'idols', but rather that which is indicated by the Greek *eidwla* – false projections of human ideas imposed on things to make them what they are not by nature. He concludes his *The Interpretation of Nature* with an observation on false methods in Theology and in Natural Science:

> The access also to this work hath been by that port or passage, which the Divine Majesty, who is unchangeable in his ways, doth infallibly continue and observe; that is, the felicity wherewith he hath blessed humility of mind, such as rather laboureth to spell, and so by degrees to read in the volumes of his creatures, than to solicit and urge, and, as it were, to invoke a man's own spirit to divine, and give oracles unto him. For as in the inquiry of divine truth, the pride of men hath ever inclined them to leave the oracles of God's word for the mixture of their own inventions; so in the self-same manner, in inquisition of nature, they have ever left the oracles of God's works, and adored the deceiving and deformed imagery, which the unequal mirrors of their own minds have represented unto them. Nay, it is a point fit and necessary in the front and beginning of this work, without hesitation or reservation to be professed, that it is no less true in this human kingdom of knowledge, than in God's kingdom of heaven, that no man shall enter in to it, except he become first as a little child.[27]

Humility of mind – taking a secondary place and giving pride of place to the objective realities confronting one, so that they inform the mind, and the mind does not impose its own images on them – is the necessary stance in matters theological and matters scientific. This presupposes that there is an inherent rationality in the things of the Creator and the things created by Him, and that the mind is to allow the order by which this rationality – uncreate rationality in the things of God's Being and acts, and created rationality in the things which God has created – is decreed and in which it is observable, in the respective qualitive difference of their fields, to unfold itself on its own authority, without the mind's subjective and unwarranted intrusions and impositions. The mind has to be open to that order which God is in Himself and as He is pleased in Christ to reveal it, and likewise to be open to that order, contingent to and from that same God, which is displayed to like humility of mind towards the created realities He has brought into being.

Herein lies the true estate and vocation of man. In this, man discovers his place *vis-à-vis* the things of creation and the God who has so ordained him:

> it is a restitution and reinvesting, in great part, of man to his sovereignty and power; for whensoever he shall be able to call the creatures by their true names, he shall again command them, which power he had in his first state of creation.[28]

Bacon is saying here that man is the king and priest and prophet of creation, so called and endowed by God, and only in humility of mind towards God and creation, in their respective truths of being and truths of knowing revealing themselves to be what they are in themselves, can he fulfil this role and find his true identity and proper dignity.

> God hath framed the mind of man as a mirror, capable of the image of the universal world, joying to receive the signature thereof, as the eye is of light: yea, not only satisfied in beholding the variety of things, and vicissitude of times, but raised also to find out and discern those ordinances and decrees, which throughout all these changes are infallibly observed. And although the highest generality of notion, or summary law of nature, God may still reserve within his own curtain, yet many and noble are the inferior and secondary operations which are within man's sounding.[29]

In this view there is a proper Natural Theology, which does not confuse the created dimension with the uncreated, but has respect to the created order as it is decreed by God, and which man properly engages on when he fulfils his God-given function to explore, care for and guard, God's handiwork, having respect to it as a created entity in relation to the One who brought it into being out of nothing. The theologian is the scientist of Divinity, the scientist the theologian of nature, both concerned with order, that order which God is in His eternal rationality, and that order by which created rationality exists as it is in itself from God, and by which it points to that eternal rationality beyond man's discovery and comprehension, but which is revealed in Christ.

Notes

1   Francis Mason: *The Authoritie of the Church in Making Canons and Constitutions Concerning Things Indifferent*, 1607 edn, p.11.
2   John Swan: *Speculum Mundi*, 1643 edn, pp.39, 40.
3   Ibid. p.41.
4   Ibid., p.42.
5   Ibid., pp.40, 41.
6   Ibid., p.41.
7   Ibid., p.41.
8   Ibid., p.43.
9   Ibid., p.44.
10 Ibid., p.44.
11 Ibid., p.44.

12   Ibid., p.43.

13   Ibid., p.46.

14   Ibid.

15   Basil: *Hexaemeron*, I:6.

16   John Swan: *Speculum Mundi*, 1643 edn, p.46.

17   Ibid., p.46.

18   Robert Grosseteste: *Hexaemeron*: I:VIII:4, Dales and Geiben text.

19   Francis Bacon: *Of the Proficience and Advancement of Learning* (Novum Organon, pt.1), 1778 edn, published by J.Rivington, London, Vol.I, and *In Praise of Knowledge*, Vol.I, p.370.

20   Francis Bacon: *Of the Proficience and Advancement of Learning*, 1778 edn, Vol.I, pp.22, 23

21   Ibid., p.129.

22   Ibid., p.130.

23   Francis Bacon: *Valerius Terminus, The Interpretation of Nature* (Novum Organon, pt.2), 1778 edn, Vol.I, p.373.

24   Ibid.

25   Ibid. This Quotation is the aphorism with which this work begins. It does not appear in the 1778 edn, other annotations also being omitted – see note on p.372 of the 1778 edn. It is found in the folio vol. of 1620, published as a separate work, p.1.

26   Francis Bacon: *The Interpretation of Nature*, 1620 edn, p.1.

27   Francis Bacon: *The Interpretation of Nature*, 1778 edn, vol.1, p.376.

28   Ibid., p.375.

29   Ibid., p.374.

Chapter 4

Order, Knowledge
and the Rationality of Man

Swan, in his second section of Chapter 3 in *Speculum Mundi*, deals with the creation of light:

> Thus having (as it were) considered the first part of the first dayes work, we may now come more nearly to that which is the beauty of it, I mean the Light, which some call Gods eldest daughter, or the first distinguished creature, wherewith the Lord* [*in margin: Psal.104.2] decked the world as with a garment.[1]

There is an immediate, and indeed fundamentally significant, relation between Word and Light:

> And now concerning this bright creature, no sooner did God say, Let it, but lo it was. He* [*in margin: 2. Cor. 4.6.] commanded that it should shine out of darknesse, as speaks the Apostle.[2]

Swan regards the biblical witness to the One who is the eternal Word of God, as that which indicates that He is eternal Wisdom and eternal Light. Word and Wisdom and Light coinhere in the existence of the Triune God. But just as the Word, or Son, is uncreate, and is one with the Father and the Spirit in His 'Godness', so too this Light is uncreate. Here, in the ending of the first day's work of creation, we are concerned with created Light. Yet, in its qualitatively different nature of a created thing, it corresponds, nevertheless, in that created status, to the One who brought it into existence out of nothing. By the uncreate Word of God, Who is Himself Light, and, being God of God and Light of Light – that is fully God and of one substance with the Father – there is a correspondence in the nature of the creature to His uncreate Being. God's Word is His Light and God's Light is His Word. He, the One by Whom all things were made, is the source of all intelligibility within His created universe. So too, created light, is the first factor and principle in all intelligibility for us to comprehend the nature of things.

It is significant that the creation of light is the first act of the Word of God. Swan discusses the nature of light, and notes the necessity of light for the intelligible discernment of all other levels of creation: 'But of this resplendent creature (without which the beauty of the rest could not be seen) there are no few opinions.'[3] He goes on to discuss these opinions – that first, some think that the creation of angels is meant. This Swan dismisses, deducing that the creation of angels came later, but more importantly, emphasizing this relation between this created light and created intelligibility.

1.   Some would have it a spirituall Light; and so under it they comprehend the creation
of Angels. But surely in my judgement their opinion is the sounder who make it a
naturall and materiall Light onely, such as now is in the Sunne, the Index of time, and the
worlds bright eye. For as the office of the Sunnes light is now to distinguish between the
Day and the Night; so was the office of this Light being commanded to shine out of*
[*in margin: Which was the locall, but not the materiall of it, as saith Pareus] the
darknesse before the Sunne was made: which being made, was the subject ever after to
retain it. If it were otherwise, or any other light, where is it now? shall we say it is either
extinguished or applied to some other use? surely I think not; because God (who made
all by the power of his word) needed no instrument to help in the work of his creation.
. . . And yet perhaps, as* [*in margin: Aquin. Sum.1.par.Quest.70.artic.1] *Aquinas* thinketh,
it was *but Lumen informe . . . An informed light*.[4]

As for the claim by some that the creation of Angels is meant by the reference to
the creation of light here, Swan dismisses this by pointing out that this is to forsake
objectivity and stoop into the realms of an allegorical interpretation of creation.
Here he certainly parts company with Scholastic thought.

Secondly he deals with the claim of others that think the element of fire is really
meant here, and thirdly dismisses the claim that the creation of the sun is indicated.
He then makes some positive assertions about light. It is made 'in motion'. And this
moving first creature is that on which all else in creation depends: 'This is the
beauty of all the beauties else: for even all the beauty of the world had been as
nothing if so be this bright shining creature had never been.'[5]

What Swan is doing here is to point to the unique status of light in the created
orders. Everything else is in relation to that created light, and therefore is to be
defined in terms of that relationship. Although he could not have known it, his
insistence on the mobility of light was an important observation, as future theories,
Einsteinian and post-Einsteinian were to appreciate. The Einsteinian claim that 'light
has a unique metaphysical status in the universe', revolves round the constancy of the
speed or motion of light, which is an ultimate principle, independent of anything else
in the created orders. This constancy of mobility is that which gives a reliable and
invariable point of reference for the understanding of all else, for even in natural
change, decay and seemingly confused fluctuation, in aspects of the universe, there is
a constancy and an intelligible pattern and course, which is discernible by reference
to the constancy and nature of light. So careful is Swan to be objective in the matter
of discussing the nature of light, that he sets out these self-same principles in embryo,
according to the limitations of the knowledge and concepts of his time.

Implicit also in this work, is the fact that created light depends on no higher
element within the whole created order. Its unique status is that it is not contingent
to or from any higher created order, but is directly contingent to and from uncreated
Light, which is God Himself, the source of all things. There is therefore, a hierarchy
of created orders, all interpenetrating and dependent on the level above them –
which he brings out in the rest of this *Hexameron*. But with regard to created light
itself, that is unique in the principal place which it, and it alone, occupies, and in
the correspondence it bears in its created nature to the qualitively different uncreated
Light of God.

In all this, Swan stands in that tradition of a theology of light which comes down
from John Philoponos of Alexandria in the east and St Augustine of Hippo in the

west, and in England through Bede and Robert Grosseteste. In the last named's
Hexaemeron and *De Luce*,[6] the same emphasis is found, that the universe is a
universe of light, for created light, the prime and fundamental substance of God's
creation, is unceasing throughout the universe in such a way that it constitutes all
form and causes all movement and development. This created light is in relation –
though qualitively different – from God, the Creator, whose eternal Light is that by
which the light of all things is illumined. However, it seems to be clear that Swan
knew nothing of Grosseteste, and was unwittingly following the same reasoning in
this matter at least, no doubt building on what Hexaeramic literature he knew.

The appropriateness of the nature of light to be the first of creatures ('God's
eldest daughter') and its unique quality, is also emphasized by Swan. He asks:

> *Quest*. But if God made the Light, was he not before in darknesse?
> *Answ*. No: for he needs not any created light, who is himself a Light uncreated; no
> corporall light, who is a spiritual one. *God is light and in him is no darknesse at all, I.*
> *John I.5*. He made this Light for our mortall journey on earth; himself is the Light of our
> immortall abode in heaven: neither did he more dwell in this Light that he made, then
> [than] the waters were the habitation of the Spirit, when it is said that the Spirit moved
> upon the waters.[7]

There is a created and temporal correspondence which points beyond itself to the
uncreated reality and eternal purpose of God. God is not to be interpreted by the
limitations of creation. The very fact that there was this light created and that there
was day and night, light and darkness before any sun was created 'sheweth that we
must allow God to be the Lord of his own works, and not limit his power to means'.
The very nature of light, as created, corresponding in its state to the nature of
uncreated Light, is appropriate to remind us that God is God on His own terms, and
not capable of being contained within the concepts of mere creaturely understanding
and expectation. Created light itself is the foremost creature and the corrective to
all such attempts.

There is also a correspondence between the status of light and the Person and act
of Christ, the Word and Wisdom and radiance of God's Light, and therefore Light
of Light. In this, the paradigmatic role of light, the basis of all created order, is
seen.

> God made light on the first day; so Christ rose from death on the same day, being the
> first day of the week: And *He is the true light which lighteth every one that cometh into*
> *the world*: Of which light if we have no portion, then of all creatures man is the most
> miserable.[8]

We have here a polarization of the concept of light, and therefore of intelligibility,
in Jesus Christ. This, in turn, stretches back to the creative work of God whose
Word and Wisdom and Light is Jesus Christ, the Word made flesh, and forward, to
the fulfilment of all things, when that Light will be all in all, and all things seen to
be the eternal dwelling-place of God's glory, enlightened by that uncreated Light.
The viewing of the orders of creation, their intelligibility, estate and function, then,
is only properly within the understanding of the relationship of created light to
uncreated Light – and that is a Christocentric exercise. Order is firmly seen in the

context of where uncreated Light Himself, comes into the realm of created light, where darkness would threaten to extinguish all things, and there to bring His creative presence to bear within the realities of His creation. Light, in all its forms, the physical, the light of reason, the light which is the life of men, coalesce and find their meaning in the One who is uncreated Light in their midst, and to and from whom they exist in their contingency. Herein alone is the true nature of order to be seen.

The place of man in this, is a matter of great comment in the cosmology and the theology of the time. Swan sees an especial relationship between the work of the first day in the creation narrative of Genesis, and the work of the sixth day – between the creation of light and the making of man. He deals, in *Speculum Mundi* with all the orders of creation set out in the 'days' of the work, but in the sixth day's work he sees the recapitulation of it all in a particular way.

In his analysis of the other days' works, Swan is somewhat fanciful in a great number of his observations concerning the nature and functions of the various levels of creation produced in their orders. There is, indeed, an impression of true empirical science, objectively grounded, struggling against a veritable web of medieval fancy, legend and mythology.

However, his main thesis is that:

> God made the world for Man, and Man for himself. It was therefore a daintie fancie of*
> [*in margin: Hug. in Didase. lib.I] one, who brought in the World speaking to Man after
> this manner . . . *Vide homo, dicit Mundus . . . See oh man, (saith the World) how he hath
> loved thee, who made me for thee. I serve thee, because I am made for thee, that thou
> maist serve him who made both me and thee; me for thee, and thee for himself.*[9]

Swan then goes on to sum up poetically all that he has so far observed regarding the other orders of creation and to introduce his commentary on the making of man.

> Herbs cure our flesh: for us the winds do blow,
> The earth doth rest, heav'n move, and fountains flow.
> United waters round the world about
> Ship us, new treasures, kingdomes to find out.
> The lower give us drink; the higher meat,
> By dropping on the ground nigh parcht with heat.
> Night curtains draws, the starres have us to bed
> When Phebus sets, and day doth hide his head.
> One world is Man, another doth attend him;
> He treads on that which ofttimes doth befriend him.
> Grant therefore (Lord) that as the world serves me,
> I may a servant to thy greatnesse be.[10]

The making of man is referred immediately to the eternal Being of the Triune God. Swan begins his observations on the making of man in section 2, chapter 9, of *Speculum Mundi*:

> Though mankind were the last, yet not the least. God onely spake his powerfull word, and
> then the other creatures were produced: but now he calls a counsell, and doth consult, not
> out of need, but rather to shew the excellencie of his work; or indeed, to shew himself: he

speaks not therefore to the Angels but the Trinitie, saying, *Let us make man*. Wherein the Father, as the first in order, speaketh to the Sonne and holy Spirit: and the Sonne and Spirit, speak and decree it with the Father: and the Father, Sonne, and holy Ghost, all Three in One, and One in Three, create a creature to be the other creatures lord. He was therefore the last, as the end of all the rest; the last in execution, but first in intention; the Map, Epitome, and Compendium of what was made before him.[11]

The importance of this statement is far reaching for an understanding of the concept of order and man's estate and vocation in creation in the minds of the time. It is to be first noted that this especial work of God is a matter in which the eternal rationality of God is emphasized in the counsel taken, the decree made, by the Persons of the Trinity in their unity and distinction. What rationality man has as a creature is therefore immediately in correspondence with that uncreated rationality which is God's. As with created light and uncreated Light, so here with created rational existence and the Uncreated Rationality of God.

It may be seen, secondly, that although man is the last of the works of God, in the Rationality of God – God's reasoning as to creation – he is the first. The reason for all other orders of creation in their relation one to another, and for the whole in its relation to God, is the making of man. The order of creation hangs on the decree of God to make man, a rational being in correspondence with His divine life. Creation, in other words, is typified by the presence of man as its *crown*.

Swan's view is that in man there is gathered up the whole meaning and rationale of creation. He therefore stands in a particular relation to God, as does no other creature. This gathering up and this unique status of man is described by him in a way typical of his age.

Three worlds there are, and Mankind is the fourth: The first is Elementarie; the second a Celestiall world; the third Angelicall; and the fourth is Man, the little world. In the first is *ignis urens, a burning fire*: and this in the heavens, is *ignis fovens, a nourishing* and *quickning fire*: but in those creatures above, seated in the supercelestiall world, it is *ignis ardens, & amor Seraphicus, an ardent, burning, and Seraphicall love*: and in the fourth are all these found at once. . . . Neither was [man] made like other creatures, with a groveling look, or downward countenance, but with an erect visage beholding the heavens, and with lordly looks well mixt with majestie.[12]

It is in this way that Swan describes man as standing on the horizon between heaven and earth, eternity and time, bearing a special relation to the Creator in the midst of creation. Man's gaze is directed heavenward. That is, he is turned to the source of knowledge. It is in this that his rationality consists. Specifically, his rationality is properly grounded on the fact that he is created in the image of God.

Swan notes that the image of God is not the shape of man. But

God breathed in his nostrils the breath of life, and man became a living soul: he then took his second part, when his first was finished, neither was that second made until then: for in the infusion it was created, and in the creation it was infused, to be the dweller in that house built out of clay, and reared from the dust.

And in this last piece, God stampt his image: for it consisted not in the figure of the bodie any otherwise then [than] as the organe of the soul, and in that regard being a weapon with it unto righteousness, it had some shadow thereof.[13]

He rejects several other ideas about the meaning of the phrase 'the image of God'. Its meaning does not reside in any supposed resemblance between the soul and the 'essence of God'. Nor yet in any supposed 'emblemes of the Trinitie' – the natural faculties of understanding, will and memory. Here, at least, Swan rejects Augustinianism. He appeals to St Paul:

> The Apostle sheweth how we are to understand the image of God in man; in one place speaking thus, *Which after God is created in righteousnesse and true holinesse, Ephes.4.24.* And in another place, *Put on the new man, which is renewed in knowledge, after the image of him who created him*, Coloss.3.10.[14]

The image of God, therefore, is a matter of the knowledge and light of God and their attendant virtues and qualities. Swan emphasizes that this is a matter of grace, not of natural possession because of the fall – man's turning away from God as the ground of his being. The image of God is a matter of:

> the knowledge and illumination, holinesse and justice [that is, in the usage of the time, the 'right ordering'] of the soul, which are now wrought in man by grace, and then were given by creation. For that image is now lost, and cannot be had till it be renewed: for the substance of the reasonable soul, with the naturall faculties and powers thereof are not lost, therefore is not expressed therein this image according to which mankind was made.[15]

The renewing and restoration of the image of God is again a Christocentric matter, for only in the re-creative work of the One by whom all things were made, and Who is Himself the Image of God, can this be achieved.

Man is the soul of his body and the body of his soul. In that unity he is created as a rational creature whose orientation is to God in whom alone he lives, moves and has his being. This is a matter of the grace of God in Christ, and this is the direction and the posture of true knowledge. This pervades all Swan's observations on man throughout this work. When, for example, in the midst of his anatomical analysis of the organs of the body, he considers the feet, he writes:

> The feet be the bases of the bodie, carrying man like a lordly creature, with his face from earth, and eyes to heaven; that he might thither strive to come at last, where he inhabiteth who gave him these, and all his other members else.[16]

Man is so ordered and placed at the crown of the other orders of creation, that he bears this stamp and status, his unique estate and vocation directed to and upheld by the light of the knowledge of God.

This awareness of the dignity accorded to man by God, man's place as the crown of God's creation, and his responsibility towards God in that estate and vocation, permeates the works of the divines of this period, and colours their thoughts on many subjects. Lancelot Andrewes, in his 'Sermon 7 of the Gun Powder treason, preached on the 5th November, 1615', even in the midst of a sermon on such a subject, reverts to it. His text was Psalm 145, verse 9 'The Lord is good to all: and His mercies are over all His workes'.

For, if the reason, why *mercy is over all His workes,* be, because they be, *His workes*: then, the more they be *His workes,* the more *workmanship* He bestowes upon them, the more is *His mercy over them.* Whereby it falls out, that as there is an unequalitie of *His workes,* and one worke *above another*; so there is a diverse graduation of *His mercy,* and one *mercy above* another; or rather, one and the *same mercy* as the same *Planet* in *Auge,* in the top of His *Epicycle,* higher than it selfe, at other times.

To shew this, we divide His *workes,* (as we have warrant) into His *workes* of *Fiat* (as the rest of His creatures:) and the Worke of *Faciamus,* as *Man,* the master-peece of *His workes*; upon whom He did more cost, shewed more workemanship, than on the rest: the very word [*Faciamus*] sets Him above all. 1. . . . that Hee did deliberate, enter into consultation (as it were) about his *making,* and about none else. 2. . . . that Himselfe framed *his body of the mould,* as the *potter,* the *clay.* 3. Then, that He *breathed* into him a two-lived soule, which made the *Psalmist* breake out, *Domine, quid est homo &c? Lord, what is man, thou shouldst so regard him,* as to passe by the heavens and all the glorious bodies there, and passing by them, breathe an imortall soule, put thine owne image, upon a peece of clay? 4. But last, *Gods* setting him *Super omnia opera manuum suarum, over all the workes of His hands.* Making him (as I may say) *Count Palatine* of the worlde; this shewes plainely, His setting by man more than all of them. As he then, *over them*; so, Gods mercy over him. *Over all His workes*; but, of *all His workes, over this worke. Over His* chiefe *worke,* chiefly: in a higher degree. And, not without great cause. Man is capable of eternall either felicitie or miserie; so are not the rest: Hee sinnes; so doe not they. So, his case requires a *Super* in this *Super,* requires *mercy* more than all theirs.

Upon men then, chiefly. They, the first *Super* in this *Super.* But, of *men* (though it be true in generall, *He hath shut up all under sin, that He might have mercy upon all,* yet) even among them a *Super* too, a second. Another *workemanship* He hath yet; *His workemanship in Christ Jesus*: the *Apostle* calls it *(Ephes.2.10.) His new creature (Gal.6.15.)* which His *Mercy* is more directly *upon* than *upon* the rest of mankind; *Servator omnium hominum,* the *Saviour* of *all men* (saith the *Apostle*;) marrie, *Autem,* most of all, *of the faithfull Christian men.* Of *all men, above all men* upon *them*: They are His *Worke* wrought on both sides; *Creation* on one side, *Redemption* on the other. For (now) we are at the worke of *Redemption.*[17]

Creation, and its analysis, is invariably and immediately followed by a consideration of re-creation in Christ. The writers of the period are aware that creation cannot be understood as a self-explanatory entity, existing in, by and for itself. Not only is creation a work of God's grace, there being no internal or external necessity upon God to create, but its necessary re-creation is likewise a matter of sheer grace. In both, creation and re-creation, the act and being of God are involved. There is no disjunction – God's being is expressed in His acts and His acts are the expression of His being. Creation and re-creation, therefore, are accomplished in relation to the being of God. The nature of creation as that which has been brought into being out of nothing by the Fiat of God, and its nature as that re-created by God in Jesus Christ, can only be understood in reference to this. It is light which is God's first creature, demonstrating the rational nature of His creation which is in correspondence to His uncreate and eternal Light and rationality. It is His eternal Light which enters the darkness of a fallen and darkened creation, to restore and re-create it in reference again to Himself.

Man stands at this relation between created light and uncreate Light, as the 'chiefest' of God's handiworks. His rational being, made as it is in the image of God and re-created as this in Jesus Christ, can only be such in reference to this.

Otherwise he stands as the Adamic iconoclast, and his true ground of reference by which he is truly man, and in which true knowledge is possible, is shattered, and the light of rationality darkened.

Only as man is properly orientated and made to 'look up' to God, is true knowledge possible. The ordering of all things in light is only seen in this Light, the contingent nature of all things to and from God realized, and his own existence as a life corresponding to God. True knowledge, therefore of the right ordering of all things – and of the estate and vocation of man himself – rests on Jesus Christ, uncreated Light and Wisdom and Word of God, re-creating the light of the true existence of all things. Only in Christ can man properly be God's vice-regent on earth, the *Count Palatine* of the world, and true knowledge be correctly and effectively exercised.

Notes

1   John Swan: *Speculum Mundi*, 1643 edn, p.46.
2   Ibid., p.47.
3   Ibid., p.47.
4   Ibid., p.47.
5   Ibid., p.51.
6   Robert Grosseteste: *Hexaemeron*, I:XVIII:2, II:VIII:2, II:X:4, De Luce, Iff, Dales and Geiben text.
7   John Swan: *Speculum Mundi*, 1643 edn, p.51.
8   Ibid., p.52.
9   Ibid., p.488.
10 Ibid., p.488.
11 Ibid., p.489.
12 Ibid., pp.489, 490.
13 Ibid., pp.492, 493.
14 Ibid., p.493.
15 Ibid., p.493.
16 Ibid., p.492.
17 Lancelot Andrewes: 'Sermon 7 of the Gun Powder Treason', 1635 edn, p.965.

Chapter 5

Order, Monarchy
and the One Body Politic

That work entitled *The Authoritie of the Church in Making Canons and Constitutions Concerning Things Indifferent*, was based on a sermon preached

> in the Greene yard at Norwich the third Sunday after Trinitie, 1605. By Fran. Mason, Bachelor of Divinitie, and sometime Fellow of Merton College, Oxford. And now in sundrie points by him enlarged.

Mason was Archdeacon of Norwich, and it was his desire to see all things settled in the Church (bearing in mind the troubled area of Puritan influence over which he had archidiaconal authority) which settlement he sought to ground in the rational realities of God's order for creation. This is the object of this work.

In common with so many of his contemporaries, Mason emphasizes the importance of order for the Church. This concerns the whole of the Church's life – its ministry, its worship, and here particularly, that which gives framework and authority to all church order, canon law itself. Closely attendant to the concept of order is the principle of uniformity. This, since the days of the Elizabethan Settlement of 1559, had been regarded as a matter of prime importance for the life and identity of the Church of England. Indeed, the whole nature and character of the Church revolved around this principle.

Uniformity, as understood by the divines of the Jacobean and Caroline eras, in their work of bringing the concepts of their Elizabethan forerunners to their fulfilment and fruition, has sometimes been dealt with superficially by historians as diverse as Christopher Hill, H.R. Trevor-Roper and A.L. Rowse.[1] This is because behind the ideal of uniformity, there lies the complex theological concept of order, and a grasp of the theology underlying the latter is necessary before any proper appreciation of the former can be stated in fairness to the intent of these divines.

The general attitude of these divines towards order may be summarized generally so: Order is primarily the revelation of God as Father and Son bound together in the bond of eternal love which is the Holy Spirit. Order therefore resides fundamentally and determinately in the fact that God is all order, and yet variety, in His eternal existence. But what God is in Himself in His intrinsic and internal relations, He is in His external acts. He is true to Himself in His works. Act and Being are consistent and harmonious. There is no disjunction or contradiction between what God is and what God does.

Creation, therefore, is a work of order. It is not an extension of the Divine being, but as a contingent entity brought into being out of nothing by God, it corresponds in its order, peace and harmony, its unity and its variety, to the nature of the One

Who so begun it and crafted it. Particularly is this so of humankind, standing at the heart of creation, as its 'crown', for man, if he is God's man, lives out a life in correspondence to God's life. This is the significance of Jesus Christ. It is in Him that true humanity and all good order is to be found.

All order is Christocentric. What God is eternally in Himself, He is towards us in Christ. And here is the Divine life taking a particular human identity and giving this existence in all the realities and the limitations of creaturely status, in union with itself. Here is the One by whom all things were created, standing in the midst of, and bearing the needs and limitations of, the creaturely dimension. So here, then, is the focal point of all order. Order must concern the Church fundamentally. Indeed, the Church is the servant of that order established in Christ. That is its business. And as its work is so its existence must be.

Mason treats of all this most beautifully. Having spoken of the necessity of observing Church order, he continues:

> And that no marvell, seeing the whole fabricke of the World, both the celestiall orbes and the globe of elements are framed and upholden by order. The fixed starres in their motions and revolutions, keepe a most firme and fixed order. The Planets, though compared with the fixed, they may seeme to wander, yet in trueth they observe a most certaine and never wandring order. The day in opening and closing, the Moone in waxing and waining, the sea in ebbing and flowing, have their interchangeable course, wherein they continue an unchangeable order. *The Storke, Swallow, Turtle, and Crane, knowe their appointed time,* & the Cranes doe also flie in order. The Grashoppers have no King, yet goe they foorth all by bands. The Bees are little creatures, yet are they great observers of order. Amongst men in peace nothing can flourish, in warres nothing can prosper without order. Order proceedeth from the throne of the Almightiie, it is the beautie of nature, the ornament of Arte, the harmonie of the world. Now shall all things be in order, and the Church of God onely without order? God forbid. The Church is a *Garden inclosed*, and a *garden* must be in order. The house of God, and Gods house should be in order; an *armie with banners*, and an armie should bee marshalled in order. Therefore in the Church of God, *Let all things be done honestly and by order*.[2]

It is Mason's purpose to divide this sermon into two parts. First, 'an explication', and second, 'an application; a briefe application of the text, and a more ample application of the text to the present estate of the Church of England'. Mason notes that St Paul is the speaker of these words of the text, the Church at Corinth those spoken to. As Paul himself said: 'What things soever were written before time, were written for our learning.' So this text concerns 'not the Church of Corinth onely, but the Church of England, the Church of Geneva, and all the Churches of the Saints'. Mason emphasizes that the gift of prophesying is extolled in this chapter (I Corinthians XIV, of which his text is the 40th verse) over all else. By prophesying, he says, is meant not 'foretelling things to come, but the word of edification, exhortation, and consolation, that is, the Preaching of the Gospell'.[3] With this, the chapter interlaces certain points of Church government – 'the publicke performance of Prayer, thanksgiving, and prophecying'[4] – the observing of proper and seemly order by those who perform these duties. St Paul's discourse is 'sprinkled. . . . with Ecclesiasticall orders* [*in the margin: Calvin is noted]'. Mason closely follows Calvin's Commentary on I Cor. for his argument.[5]

Mason, in passing, makes an observation which is of fundamental importance concerning the nature of the Church of England as he sees it, and its relation to other Churches. The Corinthians were so in love with themselves that they would not countenance any questioning of their own orders,

> but rather went about with singular arrogancy, to impose them upon others, as though other Churches were bound to follow their patterne. Finally, there followeth a generall direction concerning all Church orders. . . . Let all things be done honestly and by order.[6]

Lying behind this is that constitutional understanding of the English nation, which had evolved since the reign of William I. That is the 'Principle of Empire' – the construing of England as a free, independent and sovereign nation. This Principle, restated in the Magna Charta in 1215, reaffirmed by Henry VIII's seven Acts of Parliament accomplishing the English Reformation, and refined and strengthened in the Acts of Supremacy and Uniformity composing the Elizabethan Settlement in 1559, was by this time undergirded by the concept of each nation as a microcosm – a small instance on the same pattern, and governed by the same order, as the whole universe with its Divine governance. In this concept the office and rule of each monarch in his time and place, may be regarded as pointing to the universal rule and order of God over all things.

Lancelot Andrewes was, at this same time, stressing this concept in various sermons.

> Now then of this great Monarchie of mankind, of the whole world, the severall Monarchies of the world are eminent parts . . . Wherefore doth God give salvation unto Kings? Namely, because they are His viceregents upon earth; because they are in God's place, because they represent His person; because they are His 'ministers' (Romans 13:4&6).[7]

Monarchy is contingent from and to God – held by God's appointment, and answerable to God for the exercise of its high office. The nature of the Monarchy is also personal, for it is derived in this contingent manner from the God whose person is involved in His acts and decrees. God exists in all eternity in the personal order of His internal relations, as Father, Son and Holy Spirit, and the creative, re-creative and sustaining decrees and acts of the Triune God are Personal decrees and acts. Monarchy, by its personal nature is paradigmatic – pointing beyond itself to the nature of God's personal sovereignty and governance of all things. Bound closely to the institution of Monarchy is the concept of Natural Law and Common Law, man's Amen to the divinely ordered way in which creation, with mankind at its heart, had been decreed and disposed by God. Common Law stemming from Natural Law, and Natural Law itself, had a Christological foundation. Natural Law is not the Law of Nature, based on an observation of the way in which things are perceived to exist in and for themselves. All creation is fallen from its true course in its contingency to God, and truth cannot be read out of the surface appearance of things as they exist in this state. Natural Law was Christocentric, in that it takes stock of Creation as it is to be viewed in the light of God's Personal visitation and re-creation of it – the declaration of His intent and destiny for all creation – in the incarnation, death, resurrection and ascension of His Eternal Word (by whom all things were made, for whom all things were made, and in whom all things consist) made flesh, Jesus Christ Himself. It is the estate and vocation of monarchs to uphold and execute this Common Law resting on the Natural Law of what God has decreed creation should and will be, for the true welfare and dignity of the commonwealths over which they are severally set to rule.

The bounds of each nation were sacrosanct. Each boundary was the territory allotted to the particular body of which a monarch or governor, as the appointed *minister* of God, was the head. The Principle of Empire ruled out any external interference in the internal affairs of a kingdom. This was the axle round which the whole evolutionary process of the English Constitution had revolved. The constitutional history of this country is interspersed with various Acts reiterating and safeguarding from time to time as need arose, this self-same Principle. The medieval Acts of Praemunire and Provisors, for example, dealt with various aspects of this protection of England's sovereignty.

It is in this general constitutional context that Mason is laying down here, as an axiom, that no one Church has a right to interfere in the governance, structure and custom of another. He later makes this clear in writing about those who take their colour from Geneva, or outside England, and seek to impose what has been found right for these churches on the English Church.

Mason lays out clearly the constitutional position of the Church, *vis-à-vis* this national sovereignty:

> By the ancient lawes of this realme, this kingdome of ENGLAND *is an absolute Empire and** [**in the margin: *Sir Edw. Cooke de iure Reg. eccls. folio 8b*] *Monarchie*, consisting of one head, which is the *King* and of a *bodie politike*, which bodie politike the law divideth into two generall parts, the Cleargie and the *Laitie*.[8]

Here is a definitive statement of the unity of the nation in its two aspects, the ecclesiastical and the temporal. They are not separated in any way, yet are not confused. In each commonwealth, the monarch is the head, and the realm, in all its aspects, is the body. There is a unity of one organism. That is why it is entirely erroneous to speak of 'Church' and 'State' as though they were two separate entities. The English Constitution has historically defined that interwoven relationship within the one body under one head.

That head, the monarchy, with its duty of sovereignty, cannot be separated from a consideration of Common or Natural Law. It is this Law which is the binding factor of head and the whole body. It is the foundation which bears all the overlapping and interwoven strands of the nation's life as a totality. It is therefore, again, equally mistaken to speak of the 'Established Church', as though the State had taken on a particular partner. It is clear from general constitutional usage, particularly in the Jacobean and Caroline eras, that the correct term is 'the Church by Law Established'. Again, the principle by which the Church is so established is not, in the first instance, Statute Law (though this may be used to clarify and codify certain features of this relationship) but Common or Natural Law, which is concerned with the nature of the whole body of the single nation under its head and governor.

Mason sets out the particular place and role of the Church as part of the fabric of the whole nation under the rule of monarchy. It is to be noted how all these aforementioned concepts are brought to bear here:

Now the King of England being an absolute Soveraigne, and consequently by the law of God supreme governor over all persons and causes Ecclesiasticall and Temporall, within his owne dominions, may, by the ancient *prerogative and lawes* of England, make an Ecclesiasticall* [*in margin: Ibid (as above, Sir E. Coke)] commission by *advise whereof*, or of the* [*in margin: Act for Uniformity] *Metropolitane*, he may according to his Princely wisedome, *ordaine and publish such ceremonies, or rites, as shall be most for the advancement of Gods glorie, the edification of his Church, and the due reverence of Christs holy mysteries and Sacraments*. And it is further enacted by authoritie of* [*in margin: Anno 25. H.8] *Parliament*, that the *Convocation* shall bee assembled alwaies by vertue of the *Kings Writ*, and that their Canons shall not be put in execution, unlesse they be approoved by Royall assent.[9]

Here Mason appeals to past legislation, quoting as his authority Sir Edward Coke, and instancing the Act of Uniformity and the Statutes of King Henry VIII. He then notes the relationship between the sacred synod of Convocation (and how it was constituted) and the monarch, and the legal procedure involved, the consultations, the constitution of the synod, being:

presented to the King, ratified by his roiall assent, confirmed by his Highnesse letters Patents, under the great Seale of England, and by his soveraigne authoritie published, commanded and enjoined to be diligently observed, executed, and equally kept by all the subjects of this kingdome, have a binding force, and are in the nature of a law, and therefore may bee justly called the Kings Ecclesiasticall lawes, in making whereof the Church of England without all controversie proceedeth honestly and in order.[10]

'Order' refers in the first instance to that order which God Personally is in His eternal Being. It then extends into the concept of *oikonomia* – that order which God has ordained for creation, His great household. The other side of this *oikonomia* is Common and Natural Law, which is man's Amen to this dispensation of God for created existence, an existence which is contingent to and from God. The concept of order then proceeds, for the Jacobean and Caroline mind, to the ordering of the household of the nation, each nation being a microcosm of all creation. As God is the sovereign, universal ruler and orderer of all things, so He has appointed His vice-regents, answerable to Him, over each nation and people, for the true dignity and order and welfare of humanity.

Again, Lancelot Andrewes, in his sermon 'On the Right and Power of Calling Assemblies, preached at Hampton Court before the King, on Sunday, 28th September, 1606, sums up the relation of Creator to His vice-regents, via the concept of Common or Natural Law:

This is the Law of God; and that no judiciall Law, peculiar to that people alone, but agreeable to the Law of Nature and Nations; (Two Lawes of force thorow the whole world.) For even in the little Empire of the body naturall, Principium motus, the beginning of all motion, is in, and from the head. There, all the knots, or (as they call them) all the conjugations of sinewes have their head, by which all the body is moved. And as the Law of Nature, by secret instinct by the light of the Creation annexeth the organ to the chiefest part: even so doth the Law of Nations, by the light of Reason, to the chiefest Person.[11]

The Divine Right of Kings, their appointment in the dispensation of God, has its corollary in the Divine Responsibility of Kings. This responsibility lay in the upholding of Common or Natural Law. As God is order in Himself, so His acts express His being and He is seen to be the God of order in His creative and re-creative dispensation declared in, and accomplished by, His Word. And in the same qualitative way, His vice-regents, appointed in this natural dispensation to their estate, exercise their vocation in terms of this order. This 'rectitudio Regis, A power Regall', however, is concerned with the totality of Common or Natural Law. This has bearing on all aspects of the life of the one body politic, with its two aspects, the ecclesiastical and the temporal.

The relation between Order, Common Law and Natural Law, Monarch, and the One Body Politic, is comprehended in two sermons in particular by Lancelot Andrewes. The first of these was preached on the anniversary of the coronation, 24 March 1606 – 'Sermon On the Coronation Day, preached before the King's Majestie at Whitehall'. This was on the text Judges 17:6, 'In those dayes, there was no King in Israel: But every man did that, which was good in his owne eyes'. Having first disposed of the idea that human sight of itself is 'no competent judge', Andrewes elaborates on the chaos which resulted in Israel from the lack of order and monarchy to minister that order. That chaos is felt in religion, with Micah setting up an image to worship and instituting a priesthood to serve his god. It is felt in things civil and moral, with the anarchic behaviour of the citizens of Gibeah and the tribe of Dan:

> By this time wee see, what a masse of mischiefe there is in these few words. . . . See then now, what a wofull face of a Common-wealth is here? . . . Micah, a private man; Gibeah, a city, Dan, a whole tribe: Tribes, Cities, families, all out of course. . . . Out of course, in Religion; and not in religion alone, but in morall matters. . . . Last, this was now not in a corner, but all over the Land. Micah was at Mount Ephraim, in the midst; Gibeah, was at one end, and Dan at the other. So in the midst and both ends, all wrapped in the same confusion.[12]

The ordering of the household of Israel in all its aspects was at stake in Andrewes's view. This was for lack of a monarch – God's Vice-regent, charged with upholding the Divinely appointed order in his or her appointed territory. Andrewes was no sycophant. This view of the Divine Right of the King as God's Ambassador, is always tempered by the view of the grave responsibility of the office: there is a Divine Responsibility inherent in Kingship's Divine Right. The office of kingship is always regarded as an office of duty, for which Kings are answerable to God.

This is set out in a second sermon by Andrewes – 'Sermon on Giving Caesar His Due, preached at Whitehall on the 15th of November, 1601' on the text St. Matthew, 22:21, 'Give therefore to Caesar, the things which are Caesar's: and to God, those things which are God's.' His argument runs:

> If we aske then, what is Caesar's? Our answer must be; what God hath set over to him. For though Quae Dei stand last in place; yet sure it is, the former quae cometh out of the latter, and Quae Caesaris is derived out of quae Dei.[13]

This is a statement of the dependence of earthly power on the power of God. It is seen in terms of *contingent*, not *derived*, authority, not a personal possession by mere right alone.

> Originally, in the person of all *Kings*, doth *King David* acknowledge [the idea of Scripture by way of recapitulation speaking out to every generation] that, *All things are of Him*, and *all things are His*. But the sovereigne bounty of God was such, as He would not keepe it all, in His owne hands; but as He hath vouchsafed to take unto Himselfe a secondary meanes in the governmente of mankinde; so hath He set over unto them a part of His own duty, that so one man might be one anothers debtor, and (after a sort) *Homo hominis Deus*. To the conveiance then, of diverse benefits, He hath called to Himselfe diverse persons: as our *Parents*, to the worke of our bringing forth; our *Teachers*, in the worke of our training up; and many other, in their kindes, with Him, and under Him, His meanes and *Ministers*, all for *our good*. And in the high and heavenly worke of the preservation of all our lives, persons, estates and goods, in safety, peace and quietnesse, in this His so great and divine benefit, He hath associated *Caesar* to Himself: and in regard of his care and travell therein, hath entitled him to part of His owne right; hath made over this *Quae*, hath made it due to *Caesar*, and so commeth he to claime it.
>
> In which point we learne, if we pay *tribute*, what we have for it back in exchange: if we *give*, what *Caesar* giveth us for it againe; our *penny* and our *penny-worthes*; even this, *Ut fit pax et veritas in diebus nostris*.[14]

In this view, the monarch occupies a special office and duty in the *oikonomia* of God to all creation, within the sphere allotted to him, his realm and people. In Caroline thought, the monarch is a type of Adam, that is to say, he is to exercise the estate and vocation given to Adam at creation, to be God's vice-regent upon earth, and hold dominion, answerable to God. The Carolines viewed the Israelite Kingship in these terms. An unwarranted criticism of them is sometimes made, that they went straight to the Old Testament, and quarried there for an interpretation of Kingship, which they then directly applied to their own circumstances under James VI and I and Charles I. But they only used the Old Testament in the light of its fulfilment in Christ, to whom all power in heaven and earth is given, and who reminds Pontius Pilate, Caesar's representative, that he would have no power unless it were given to him from above. This process of Christ/Old Testament/Christ/ contemporary Kingship, as a progress of thought in interpreting Kingship is followed out scrupulously in all Andrewes's sermons – particularly those preached on the anniversaries of the Gowries Conspiracy and the Gunpowder Plot. It is to the understanding of Kingship and universal order as revealed in Christ, and as accomplished by Him, the true and good ordering of all creation in the creative intent of God, and to the Old Testament as a pointer to that and a foreshadowing of it, to which the Caroline Divines appeal. In the same way, they look back from what they say of contemporary Kingship to Christ and His universal rule.

Andrewes interprets disorder in the estate and vocation of persons who should be fulfilling their God-ordained duties and responsibilities, with primeval chaos and disorder. The Hebrew *tohu/bohu* of the creation narrative in Genesis, is employed by Andrewes to link the disorder of society in all its aspects with the manifestation of the threat of chaotic nothingness and darkness. In 'A Sermon Prepared to be Preached on Whitsunday, 1622, being Sermon 15 Of the Sending of the Holy

Ghost', he does this, but begins first with that order which God is eternally in Himself.

> Order is a thing so highly pleasing to God, as the three *Persons* in *Trinitie* (we see) have put themselves in order, to show how well they love it. And *order* is a thing so neerely concerning us, as breake *order* once, and breake both your *staves* (saith God in *Zecharie*) both of *Beauty*, and that of *Bonds*. The *Staffe of Beauty*: For . . . no manner of *decencie* or *comlinesse* without it; but all out of fashion. The *Staffe of Bonds*; For . . . no kind of *steddinesse* or constancie, but all loose without it. All falls back to the first *Tohu*, and *Bohu*. For all is Tohu (*empty*, and *voyd*) if *the Spirit* fill not with His *gifts*: And all is *Bohu* (a disordered rude *Chaos* of confusion) if CHRIST ordereth it not by His *Places* and *callings*. Every body falls to be doing with every thing, and so nothing done: nothing done well, I am sure. Every man, therefore, whatever his gift be, to stay till he have his place and standing by CHRIST assigned him.[15]

In the Laudian view, the place and standing of the monarch, in the ordering of Christ, through the enabling of the Spirit, in the decree of the Father, is to uphold and order that *oikonomia* of God, the only sure foundation of man and states. That is to say, these divines saw monarchy as bound inseparably to Common Law and Natural Law, as their advocate and defender, for, as a human institution, it is the echo, in human affairs and in the natural sphere, of the ordered will of God for all things. But this institution is of Divine appointment and by such, the monarch is concerned with the welfare of the totality of his particular nation, his microcosm, the life of the one body politic over which he has been appointed, and for which he is answerable to God for his stewardship of the office.

Notes

1   Cf. C. Hill: *Change and Continuity in Seventeenth Century England*, Weidenfeld and Nicolson, 1979; *Puritanism and Revolution*, Secker and Warburg, 1958; *Economic Problems of the Church from Archbishop Whitgift to the Long Parliament*, Oxford University Press, 1956. H.R. Trevor-Roper (Lord Dacre): *Archbishop Laud*, 1962. A.L. Rowse: *Reflections on the Puritan Revolution*, Methuen, 1986. C.V. Wedgewood: *The Trial of Charles I*, Reprint Society, 1966.
2   Francis Mason: *Authoritie of the Church in Making Canons and Constitutions Concerning Things Indifferent*, 1605 edn, p.11
3   Ibid., p.2.
4   Ibid., p.3.
5   Cf. John Calvin: 'Commentary on I Corinthians', *Commentaries*, Oliver and Boyd, 1960.
6   Francis Mason: *Authoritie of the Church in Making Canons and Constitutions, etc.*, 1605 edn, p.3.
7   E.g. Lancelot Andrewes: 'Sermons of the Gowries – Sermon Preached before the Kings Majestie at Ramsay on the 5th August, 1607', 1635 edn, p.779.
8   Francis Mason: *Authoritie of the Church in Making Canons and Constitutions, etc.*, 1605 edn, p.15.
9   Ibid.
10 Ibid., p.16.

11 Lancelot Andrewes: *Ninety-six Sermons*, 'Sermon on the Right and Power of Calling Assemblies', 1635 edn, p.B106.
12 Lancelot Andrewes: *Ninety-six Sermons*, 'Sermon on the Coronation Day', 1635 edn, p.B120.
13 Lancelot Andrewes: *Ninety-six Sermons*, 'Sermon of Giving Caesar His Due', 1635 edn, p.B94.
14 Ibid., pp.B94–B95.
15 Lancelot Andrewes: *Ninety-six Sermons*, 'Sermon 15 Of the Sending of the Holy Ghost', 1635 edn, p.761.

Chapter 6

Order, the Rule and Law of Man and the Rule and Law of God

The sermons preached by Lancelot Andrewes on the anniversaries of the Gunpowder Plot and of the Gowries Conspiracy (the attempt on the life of King James VI on 5 August 1600, by the Earl of Gowry and his brother), might seem by way of only superficial scrutiny to be narrow in intent and application and contrived in text and exposition. While their content was necessarily dictated by the two events commemorated on their respective days, nevertheless, the way in which Andrewes handled his texts and brought out from them a breadth of theological insight bestows greater value upon these sermons than the occasion of their preaching would seem to dictate.

In this chapter I cite several sermons by Andrewes preached on the Gunpowder Plot anniversary to illustrate how he uses a specific incident centred on the person of the monarch and of national significance, to derive from such seemingly constricted circumstances what he saw as theological truths regarding the Christocentric foundation of order, law and rule, and Christian responsibility within these. The attitude revealed in these and such other sermons preached on these occasions are symptomatic of the common approach by the Laudian Divines in general to such issues, and lay bare the way of thinking behind the approach to them. They emphasize above all, the way in which order, law and rule was perceived to be grounded dynamically in the verities of creation in its contingent relation to God, and, beyond the created dimension, in the very existence of God himself. They deal with the interaction of human and divine rule and order.

We may begin with two such sermons – the first, 'Sermon 7 of the Gunpowder Treason', preached before the King at Whitehall on 5 November 1615 on the text of Psalm 145:9, 'The Lord is good to all, and His mercies are over all His works'[1]; the second, 'Sermon 8 of the Gunpowder Treason', preached on 5 November the following year on the text of Isaiah 38:3 (wrongly printed Psalm, Chapter 37:3 in the 1635 edition), 'The children are come to the birth, and there is not strength to bring them forth.'[2]

In the first sermon, the rule of God is interpreted as 'mercies'. It is in mercy that the power of God consists, and Andrewes cites the collect for the ninth Sunday after Trinity – 'God, which sheweth Thy almighty power most chiefly in shewing mercy'[3] – as a correct insight into this. This is done in the context of a long and exhaustive interpretation of the use and significance of the word 'mercy'. He indicated the Hebrew word for 'mercy'

> which . . . is properly the *bowels* . . . And what *bowels*? Not the *bowels* of the common man . . . but . . . the *bowels* of a *parent*. . . . And this ads much: ads to *mercie* . . . *naturall love*. To one strong affection, another as strong, or stronger than it.[4]

69

Andrewes asks 'what parent?' and answers that it indicates the mother, for it is holden that the mother is the one more inclined to show pity and to be more passionate and compassionate. Moreover, the singular of the Hebrew word for 'mercy' can also mean 'womb' (he could have added 'maiden' as well).

> You may adde this: that one mother hath but one wombe, for all her children; but, he speakes (here) of God in the *plurall*; as if He had the compassion of more wombes than one, the *pity* of many *mothers* put together.[5]

In 'Sermon 8 of the Gunpowder Treason', Andrewes employs the same figure of the womb. This time he refers it not to the mercies of God but to the conception, development and attempted accomplishment of the evil of treason, the Plot itself. Of the text 'The children are come to the birth, and there is not strength to bring forth', he notes that the Hebrews quoted it as a proverb on the occasion of any abortive plot,

> as a By-word, upon the defeating of any plot. Not, every defeating; but then, when a plot is cunningly contrived, and closely followed, and is neere brought to the very point to be done, yet not done though; but defeated, even then.[6]

The occasion upon which this particular text was spoken by King Hezekiah, was the treacherous blasphemy of Rabshakah hand in hand with the invasion of Sennacherib so near to Jerusalem. The words of the text then are by way of allegory:

> All is spoken by *Allegorie*; and no *woman*, but the *State* of the *Kingdome*, here meant. And it is no new thing to set forth *States by women*. The *Prophets doe it oft: Esays Hephsiba; Ezekiels Ahola, and Aholiba; Hosee's Loruhamah*, all shew it. Nothing more common with them, than *Daughter of Babel* for the *State* of the *Chaldeans*; the *Daughter of Sion* for the *State of the Jewes*.[7]

Here Andrewes applies the text to the kingdom at the time of the Gunpowder Plot. There had been, historically, other such plots. The Trojan horse was a womb

> full of armed men: and so many armed men as there were, so many children, after a sort, might be said to be in it. And, if that: may we not affirme as much of the *vault*, or *cellar*, as with as good reason?[8]

He cites (not named) Virgil *Aneid* 2:20 regarding the Trojan horse in order to parallel it with the Gunpowder Plot:

> *Uterumque armato milite complent*, the belly or *wombe*, when it was full of armed men ... the verse will hold of it too – *Uterumque nitrato pulvere complent*. The *uterus* or *wombe* of it, crammed as full with *barrels of powder*, as was the *Trojan Horse*, with men of armes. This ods onely. Every one of these *children*, every *barrell of powder*, as much, nay more force in it to doe mischiefe, than twenty of those in the *Trojan horses belly*.[9]

Then follows a detailed analogy of the process of conception and birth with the beginning and progress of the Plot. The vessels containing the powder as so many embryos; the vault as the womb in which they lay so long; the mothers were they who devised and conceived the plot; the fathers were 'the fathers' (that is, the Jesuits) who animated and gave soul, as it were, to the treason; the conception was the time when the powder, as seed, was conveyed in; the articulation was the couching of them in order, just as they should stand; the covering of them with wood and faggots was the development of the embryos with the drawing of the skin over them, the midwife was that conspirator found ready with the match, the instrument to assist the birth; and if the fire had come near the powder, 'the children had come to the birth'.

What is to be noted here, says Andrewes, is that the mind of man conceives as well as the womb.

[T]he word (*conceiving*) is like proper, to both. Men have their *wombe*, but it lieth higher, in them; as high as their *hearts*; and that which is there *conceived*, and *bred*, is a *birth*. So, I finde, the *Holy Ghost* in the *Psalme* calleth it; *Behold, he travaileth with mischiefe, he hath conceived sorrow and brought forth ungodlinesse*. And that is, when an *evill man*, in the *evill wombe* of his *heart*, shall hatch or *conceive* some *devillish device*, and goe with it as *big* as any *woman goes* with her *childe*, and be even in paine, till he have brought it. This is the *birth* here meant: and there, in the *heart*, is the *matrix* or *conceptory* place, off all *mischiefe*. Then (saith our *Saviour*) *de corde exeunt, From the heart* they come all. Usually they say in Schooles, *Conceptus, conceptio; partus, opus*: the *conceipt* is a kinde of *conception*; and the work, a kinde of *birth*: the *imagination* of the heart is an *embrio*, conceived within.[10]

The conspirators lacked nothing but the final strength and opportunity to bring the Plot to its hideous birth. They had strength enough except in the final issue, but

the *strength to issue is Gods* ever, and He tooke it from them.
Domini sunt exitus: The *Issues* of all attempts are in the *hands* of God, them He reserved to Himselfe[11]

God is not in the beginning of the conception of evil, but his mercy has the last word in such ventures. Andrewes cites two previous occasions when the design of man was overruled – the failure of Queen Mary to produce a child, an heir for the Roman Catholic throne, and on the event of the Armada –

How farre was the *invincible Navie* suffered to come sailing in LXXXVIII, to cast *anchor* even before the *Thames mouth*, every houre ready to deliver her *children ashore*. In an instant, a fatall fell upon them; their *strength* and courage taken from them; about they turned, like a wheele; fled and had not the power to looke behind them. But, *non erant vires pariendi*, we all know. *God* loves thus to doe: and then to doe it.[12]

Over and above all that the human mind or the desire of nations may conceive, there is a higher conception – and that is the eternal mercy of God. In all positive works of the mind so conceiving, God is at both the beginning and the fulfilment of them. This mercy of God as the rule of God, his dispensation, is set out in 'Sermon 7 of the Gunpowder Treason'.

In Sermon 7, Andrewes applies female analogies to God. The mercy of God is as the pity which the mother takes upon the child of her womb, the child that lies therein. He notes that the text speaks of the 'mercies' of God, 'as if He had the compassion of more wombes than one, the *pity* of many *mothers* put together'.[13] Here the work of creation is portrayed in terms of conception, gestation and birth. God has conceived all his works of and for creation, greatest and least, nothing excluded, and that conception, ordering and genesis is a matter of the divine mercy alone. There is no other cause. The register of all God's works in Psalm 136 is underlined in these orders of creation with the refrain 'For His mercy endureth for ever':

> It was *Mercy*, and nothing but *mercie*, set the *creation* in hand. For, it is well knowne, *in non ente*, there could be no moving cause at all. Nothing we were; We and all His *workes*: In nothing, there can be nothing to induce, why it should bee brought out of the state of being nothing. So that, His *mercy* it was, that removed that universall defect, of *non entitie* at the first.[14]

'That universall defect of non entitie', Andrewes's statement of creation *ex nihilo*, emphasizes the total unqualified and free mercy of God in the conception and genesis of creation. There is no other cause of creation; God suffers no compulsion to create; there is no coercion from without for God to so act, no constraint from within his own being. This work of God is conceiving and bringing forth creation is different qualitatively from any other conceiving and birth, and therefore the mercy which causes it is qualitatively different from all other mercy. It brings out of nothing that which now is, but this mercy of God is not only the cause but the sustenance of all being as well. This merciful sustaining means that all things in their order and the order of all things kept from reverting back to the primeval chaos of nothingness.

> And having then made them, it is kindly, that *Viscera misericordiae* should be *over* those *opera* that came *de visceribus*; whom it brought from nothing, to be *over* them and not see them case away, and brought to nothing againe. The *Eagle* (saith *Moses*) the poor *Hen* (saith our Saviour) will doe it for their young ones: stretch *their wings over them* to preserve them, what they can.[15]

This essence of parental care of creation runs throughout this sermon, as an extended analogy of God's mercies over all things. Mercy, then, is the quality of the power and rule of God, the measuring rod of his ordering of all creation. Andrewes carefully analyses this elevation of mercy, implied in the text with its observation that the mercies of God are *over* all his works. The *over* of the text is *super* which means *above*. *Above* certainly implies height – but it is not a one-dimensional, vertical measurement which is meant by the use of the word in the text. It is not to be construed in the sense of the measurement of created dimension, for such quantitative measurement is a mark of material bodies, of which mercy is not one:

> The meaning is, that it is the *chiefest*. So, heaven in the greater World [that is the macrocosm]; so, the Head, in the lesse [that is humanity as the microcosm]: both of them the highest, both of them the chiefest; chiefest of all, and rule all. As (indeed) of whom is *Super* said, so rightly, as of the *Soveraigne*?[16]

Yet the text holds more, however, in its *above*. It also has an *over*:

> All that are *above*, are not over. It is not *above* onely, as an *Obelisk* or *Maypole*, higher than all about them, but have neither shadow nor shelter; no good they doe. *Mercy* hath a broad top, spreading it selfe *over* all. It is so *above all*, that it is *over* them, too. As the vault of this Chappell is *over* us, and the great vault of the Firmament *over that*. The *super* of *latitude* and *expansion*, no lesse than of *altitude*, and *elevation*.
>
> And this, to the end that all may retire to it, and take covert: It, *over* them; and they, *under* it. Under it, under the *shadow* of it as of *Esay's great rock in the wildernesse*, from the *heat*. Under it, under the *shelter* of it, as of *Daniel's great Tree*, from the *Tempest*.[17]

The scope of God's mercy is enlarged upon by a consideration of the works over which it is exercised. Mercy is over all his works, and Andrewes appeals to Psalm 104: 'How manifold are Thy works', noting that we could never enumerate even half of the created verities and entities of God's handiwork. He divides them into 'opera' and 'opuscula', the great works and the minute ones, and thus, in the extremes, taking all between.

God's mercy is at once both immensely grand and intensely personal. Here there is much parallelism in thought with one of John Calvin's emphases, that the divine rule over all things comprehends not only the vast and majestic tracts of the cosmos, but is particular and scrupulous in its personal attention to the small and seemingly insignificant. Their thesis was over against that of Democritus and Epicurus and Aristotle (and, indeed, that tendency stemming from the latent Aristotelianism in Lutheranism) that some things and events are too insignificant and trivial to warrant divine attention.

> Now, as none so high; none of His *opera*, His *Folio-workes*: So, none so meane, none of His *oposcula*, but *over* them too. As His art no lesse wonderfull, in making the Ant, than the Elephant: So, His care no lesse *over* the one, than *over* the other. *Naturas rerum minimarum non destituit Deus*: The very *minims* of the world, His *Mercie* leaves them not destitute.[18]

There is nothing too high or too low in the creation for it to be covered with God's mercy. Even the highest of creatures, the most splendid and sublime, require that covering. Heaven itself and the brightest part of heaven, the stars, are 'not clean in His sight'. Not only they, but the angels themselves are found wanting by God – he finds 'somewhat amiss' even in them.

> So, over them too; they need it. The very *Seraphin* have something to *cover*. As for the *Cherubin*, they will set *Mercie a seat upon the top of their wings*: So glad and faine are they to have it over them. All the tongues of Saints and Angels must say this verse with us, *Misericordiae Domini super omnia opera eius*. Both say it, for both need it: And if both they, I would faine know, who needs it not.[19]

Here is the cosmic aspect – physical and spiritual in its sphere – of God's merciful rule and care. The course of the worlds and the courts of heaven are ordered by mercy and upheld by mercy. From the immensities, Andrewes descends to the intensities of creation. Absolutely nothing is destitute of that mercy which is not '*Pallium breve*; the *Mantle* is wide enough, it leaves none out'.[20]

The ubiquitous yet particular mercy of God, is shown in comparison with that other virtue of God which would seem to be its contradiction or opposite, namely, his judgment. Here is the same theme, the relation between mercy and judgment, which is set out in Andrewes's 'Sermon XI Of the Nativitie' on the text of Psalm 85:10–11. Andrewes continues his descent from the incomparable mercy of God as He exists in Himself, as a quality of His divine nature, through the highest qualities of creation which need that mercy for their being and their sustaining, to where He is to speak of the divine mercy in terms of the incarnate Word, the creator of all bringing to bear that mercy in His Person in to the midst of the needs of His creatures in the depths of the need for mercy.

In 'Sermon XI Of the Nativitie', Andrewes notes that the text from Psalm 85 personifies the apparently opposing qualities of Mercy and Truth, Righteousness and Peace. The very juxtaposition is contrary. The sequence is not Mercy and Peace, two compatible virtues congenial to us, or Truth and Righteousness, equally conformable in their severity towards us, but a mixture whereby Mercy and Truth meet together and Righteousness and Peace kiss each other. This concourse and embrace of such diverse qualities comes about at the incarnation of the Word. At the first and recapitulative rebellion of humanity against God, Truth, or Justice, had fled the earth, become a stranger to it, and Righteousness could scarce look down from heaven. Only Mercy remained to plead for God's handiwork. And now, in Christ, Mercy is seen to prevail without ignoring the demands of divine justice and righteousness. Herein lies genuine peace, in the harmony of Truth and Justice and Righteousness. Mercy is the patient and all-embracing virtue of God which comprehends and covers all that God has made.

In his 'Sermon 7 Of the Gunpowder Treason', Andrewes cites St James, that

> *Misericordia Super-Exaltat judicium, Mercie is exalted (more than exalted, Super-exalted) above judgement, nominatim.* That *worke* of *His* [justice and judgment]), we most stand in awe of, *ever that work* by name, *Mercy triumpeth.* And, in the very *Decalogue*, there may you see the *Super* of a *thousand* to *foure*, in *Mercy over justice.* Even there, even in the rolle of His *Injustice* (the Law;) there, *God* would have it extant upon record, that *Mercie is above* it. And if *mercy be above* it, thither (to *mercy*) wee may remove our cause, as to the Higher Court. There lieth an Appeale thither, *A Solio Iustitiae ad Thronum Gratiae*, from the Bench of Justice, to the Throne of *Grace* and *Mercy*. There, we may be relieved.[21]

Andrewes scrupulously avoids any lurking dualistic thought on the matter of the expanse and corrective operation of God's mercy. It reached everywhere; it is over our most wicked disposition and action, and indeed over whence such stem, even the dimension of the satanic depths. The 'Devill' is one of God's works, and, since mercy is over all God's works, it is over him as well. That is not to say that God is the prime cause of evil, for the devil is one of God's works:

> He [the devil] also, is one of them: Of *God's* making, as an *Angell*; Of his own marring, as a *devill.* *Above his workes* (I say) and *above the workes* and practices of his limmes, and they can doe or devise against them, *over* whom His *mercy* is. The Sonne of *God* (saith *Saint John*) in *mercy* therefore appeared, *Ut solveret opera Diaboli,* that *He might loose, undoe, quite dissolve the workes of the Devill.* No worke shall he contrive, never

so deepe under ground, never so neere the borders of his owne region, but God's *mercy* will bring it to light; it and the workers of it. His *mercy* will have a *Super*, for their *Subter*. There shall be more in *Mercy*, to save; than in *Satan* to destroy: More, *dicat nunc Israel*; more, *may this Realme now say*.[22]

Andrewes here plays on the 'below' of the works of evil and the 'below' of the vaults housing the gunpowder barrels. The general lesson of the supremacy of God's mercy has been particularly expressed in the recent event of the thwarting of the Plot, and the Israel of this realm of England is to be grateful. The superiority of mercy to wickedness is a matter of recognizing that 'Great is the *whirlpoole* of my wicked *workes*, but greater is the *Bethesda*, the wide and deepe gulfe of the *mercy of God* that hath no bottome'.[23]

Even if our sins are over and above us as an accusing cloud which we cannot dispel, yet in Christ mercy and justice meet, and Christ has done for us what we cannot do of ourselves, incapable as we are of dealing with our sins. This is the essence of the gospel and the fact that God's mercy is God's grace. There are no sins of the world which the Lamb of God does not take away. Here we see that behind Andrewes's thought regarding the heinousness of sin, even that of the Gunpowder Plot with its destructive aim, there is nevertheless a universality of God's mercy. This is not to dismiss sin as of little import. Mercy and justice are together. Nevertheless, there is evident throughout Andrewes's sermons a generosity of mind which does not outline the fate of evil men only in terms of the justice of God. That he leaves to God. He preaches only what he has received and will not go beyond the scriptural witness to whatever subject with which he is dealing in any sermon. That alone governs his thought and preaching and he does not add to it what might be regarded as suitably vengeful. Thus, he declares, with regard to the wickedness of humanity,

Our *sinnes, over* us; judgements over them; but *mercy over all, Super omnia*. Alwaies, where there is *Super*, there is *Satis*; *Satis superque* shows, *Super* is more than *Satis*. Enough then there is, and to spare, for them all.[24]

He draws no line at the *all*, but allows it its implications, but, again, without compromising the role of justice in all this. Mercy is freely offered, if it is rejected the cause is not from God but from those who refuse it.

Andrewes gathers this together in his observations on the place of humanity in creation. Mankind as an especial work of God, stands central to all the works of God. Humanity stands in an essential relation to the whole cosmos, in its macroscopic and microscopic dimensions as the work and works of God. Therefore mercy, in its universal operation, astonishingly centres on humanity as the particular work of God with a unique nature and estate bestowed upon it. This centring and this operation characterizes the whole universe, all that exists, as the dwelling place of mankind under the especial mercy of God. And all mankind, upon whom God wishes to have mercy and upon whom to bestow it, and therefore humanity's great cosmic dwelling place, centres in turn upon that unique and personal expression of God's mercy for humanity, the fact and event of the Word made flesh, God born man, the Householder become a servant, the creator a creature. Andrewes set this out. Apart from man, all God's other works are of 'fiat, let there be'. But man is the work of 'faciamus, let us make'. This centrality of humanity in creation as expressed in this sermon has been dealt with in Chapter Four, so it is sufficient to note here that the rule of God's mercy in strict accord with his justice, centres on man but because of the man which the Word became. The rule of God is Christocentric, and it is only in Christ that man can perceive and exercise that necessary balance, whereby just rule is merciful rule above all. It is in Christ that mercy, and therefore rightly ordered rule, is seen to mean a right relation with God. That due order may prevail means first that the necessary order of man's relation to God in Christ must avail. It is there, and there only, that the perception of, and ability to exercise, the balance of order, both just and merciful, is gained.

This theme of the necessary response to the mercy of God shown to us is carried forward in 'Sermon 9 Of the Gunpowder Treason'. This sermon was preached on the text Luke 1: 74–5, the seventh and eighth verses of the canticle *Benedictus*. Andrewes notes that the text begins with an 'Ut – That, In order that – we are being delivered . . . might truly serve God'. Throughout this sermon, Andrewes has an underlying criticism of the fashionable and prevailing attitude of his courtly hearers towards the observance of God's deliverance, a particular manifestation of which should have been in the remembrance of the national deliverance from the Gunpowder Plot. The lapse of 12 years from the actual plot had evidently dulled their sense of awe and gratitude for the acts of God worked on the nation's behalf. By this time, it would appear, the annual remembrance of the Plot's foiling and the nation's deliverance had become an excuse for secular jollification and tended away from a national and solemn sanctification. Andrewes was not slow to remind the courtiers of their prime duty in this matter. '*We* are', he says, 'delivered':

> Were we *liberati*, to become Libertines, to set us downe, and to eat, and to drink healths, and rise up, and see a play? Was there no *Ut* in it? Yes: what was that? *Ut serviamus illi*.[25]

Delivered from the hands of enemies requires the human service of God in recognition of, and thanksgiving for, that deliverance. Andrewes resorts to legal analogies to explain the relation between the act of deliverance done and the response of those on whose behalf it was accomplished. It is a 'contract, in the nature of a Bond, or Covenant'. The deliverance was from 'the hands of our enemies'. Those hands were of the self-same sort, he notes, which had carried knives taken from the Spanish Armada in 1588 and which were 'thus engraven, *To cut the throats of the English heretikes* . . . divers so engraven, in Spanish, were brought from the Fleet, and shewed'.[26] Such hands also held the match for the gunpowder's igniting. Out of these hands of these our enemies were we delivered. This is an illustration pointing to the 'great delivery of the world' by the incarnate Word: 'what time the world little thought, either of their owne perill, or of His pains and passion, that *delivered it*'.[27]

This is what makes us 'lieges' of the 'King of Kings', and beholden to him. This sets the pattern for all other deliverances. In other words, the true interpretation of events is Christocentric. The fact and event of Jesus Christ is the determinative for the Christian assessment of all other facts and events, for they happen, and are, under this prime deliverance. The *Benedictus* was itself occasioned by:

the *deliverance of deliverances*, our finall *deliverance*, from our *ghostly enemies*, and from their fire (the fire of hell) by our Blessed Saviour; which was so great, as was able to open the mouth, and loose the tongue of a dumbe man, and make him break forth into a *Benedictus*. But, inasmuch as in every kind, the chiefe giveth the rule (or, as we may say here) the *Ut*, to all that are from, and under it: And that, ours and all other *deliverances*, that have beene, or shall be, are from or under that of His . . . as comming, all from the same *principium a quo*: and tending all, to the same *finis ad quem*.[28]

Such a deliverance puts us under obligation. It is a covenant between God and us, and the equity of the covenant on God's part is that he freely and without our first serving him, delivers us, for he would have our service of him, which is itself freedom. Our responsive duty to God in this deliverance is not servitude, a bondage, thraldom, slavery or tyranny. If it is bondage, it is our binding to the bond of love; if it is service, we discover it as freedom – our freedom for God, and therefore our freedom to be free humanity, God's humanity – grow out of love and thankfulness. Indeed, had there not been this particular deliverance from the conspirators, then the nation would have itself under servitude, bondage and thraldom. This response of service from that which is beholden to that which bestows is a law of nature. Here Andrewes appeals both to natural law and to the law of nations.

This *Ut* is naturall: there groweth a naturall obligation betweene him that doth, and them that receive a good turne: (And a deliverance, specially such an one is a good turne.) The fields we till, the trees we plant, shew it. They returne their fruit to them, that bestow labour, or cost upon them. That (I know not how) but so it falls out, in matter of benefits, we be not so soone loosed, but we be tied againe: Nor eased, but loaden afresh: not freed, but bound anew. It is the Law, the bond of nature, this, *Liberati Ut*.

And that *Ut*, is *Ut serviamus*. And this particular, *Ut*, groweth out of the Law of Nations. There the Law is, *ut victus sit in potestate victoris*, the conquered, ever, in the power of the Conquerour, to take his life, or to save it, at his pleasure. But if he will save it, then comes the voluntary Ut, or Covenant . . . This being the Law of Nature, and Nations, why should not the God of Nature, the King of Nations, be allowed it? that if our lives have beene by Him saved; we should, from thenceforth, come to this *Ut, ut serviamus Illi*.[29]

The service that such love and thankfulness ought to call forth – and the law of nature and of nations stands in judgment upon human carelessness in this – is, according to the text, that humanity is in 'holiness and righteousness'. Andrewes again, with more than implicit criticism of his congregation of courtiers, analyses the meaning of holiness and righteousness in terms of the ordering of the totality of human existence and conduct. His hearers had grown sadly slack in this respect. There is a deliciously almost subtle passage in this sermon which excuses none, not even the highest in the land, from such service.

What are we to the glorious Saints in heaven? Doe not they worship thus? Off goe their crownes, *downe before the Throne they cast them*, and fall downe themselves after, when they worship. Are we better than they? Nay, are we better than His Saints on earth, that have ever seemed to goe too farre, rather than come too short, in this point? There was one of them, and he was a King (no less person) when it was thought, he had done too much. What? uncovered? yea, *uncovered* (saith he) and if that be too vile, *vilior adhuc fiam plusquam*, I will yet be more vile; Why, it is before the Lord, before whom we cannot be too low. ... No more then, is sought from us, than Kings on earth, than crowned Saints in heaven, in their *holy service*, doe before *Him*.[30]

Lest there by any misapprehension as to the full implications of the terms 'holiness' and 'righteousness', he says that these are neither an

unrighteous holinesse; nor ... an *unholy* kinde of *unrighteousnesse*. Neither with the *Pharisee*, to have all our *holinesse* in *our Phylacteries* and *fringes*, and frequenting the Lectures of the Law (no matter how we live:) Nor with the *Saducee*, live indifferently honestly, but neither beleeve *spirit*, nor looke for *resurrection*: be *Christians*, like *Aggrippa*, *in modico*, a little Religion, upon a knives-point, will serve us. Neither in *holinesse* then onely, nor in *righteousnesse* onely, but in both.[31]

In the meaning of righteousness and holiness the totality of human existence is involved. Religious observance and care, civil carriage and conduct, lie together in this thankful service evoked from us by God's deliverance. Yet, though both are necessary, they are distinct, and a priority determines that distinction.

That priority lies with holiness, that is, service to God alone. It must come first, for it is the well-spring from which all rightness of existence and conduct, the natural law of created rationality, flows. However good we may be to our fellows, that is of little avail if its quality is not determined by the fundamental rightness of our existence in relation to God. This holiness, Andrewes divides into private devotion – about which he will say little, for this is a matter between God and the individual – and public observation of the service of God. This is undertaken too lightly, he complains.

He laments that the highest service we can render God, the sacrament of Christ's body and blood, is attended in such a way that there is 'denied any reverence at all. ... No *service* then: No servants there: but bidden guests, haile-fellowes, homely and familiar, as one neighbour with another.'[32] He further complains that some think that the service of God only consists of attending lectures and sermons, but these are a matter of 'eare-hearing', comparable to that 'eye-service', that observation only of externals which God despises. The body is neither an eye nor an ear alone, and in the matter of hearing sermons there is no sense of the necessity of hearing and saying '*Speak on, Lord for thy servant heareth* ... but, *speake on Lord*, whether thy servant heare or no.'[33] Thus there arises the scandal that such persons

thinke *holinesse* a discharge from *righteousnesse quite*. So they serve God, and heare Lectures (as the terme is) they take themselves the liberty to pay no debts, to put their money out to usury, to grind their tenants; yea, and so they misse not such a Lecture, in such a place, they may doe any thing then.[34]

A second misuse of surface hearing is that men may indeed deal honestly, pay their debts, but are so imperious and high-minded in the distribution of their piety 'so like great Lords', as if righteousness were divorced from service.

Yet again, there are others who confine their righteousness to the dictates of the law of the land only, who make the law a scantling of their *righteousnesse*: and farther than that will compell them, they will not goe, not an inch: not so farre neither, *sine timore*, but for feare. Yea, not only our *righteousnesse* to men: but even our *feare to God, is taught us by man's precepts*: and in both, so that *Statutes of Omri* be observed, all is well. But, whatsoever a man else may make sure, he cannot make sure his soule, by the Law of the Land. This *righteousnesse* here, goes up to God and His Law: and pierces deeper beyond the outward act, even to the inward man: whence, if ours come not, or whither, if it reach not; Man wee may (perhaps) but *God in righteousnesse, serve* we not.

But even according to mans Law, our *righteousnesse* goes not well so, neither. The Philosopher gives a rule, when a people is just or righteous, according to mans Law: (God's he knew not) and that is, when Justice wants worke, hath little to doe. By which rule, ours is in no very goode case: Men are so full of suits, so many causes depending before every seat of justice, so much to doe: and all, to repaire the wrongs of our unrighteous courses, while each one seeks rather, to over-rule men by wrong, than to *serve* God by right.[35]

Moreover, Andrewes continues his complaint, each department of justice is intent in enlarging its sphere of influence and power. If the evil were contained only to the misuse of the law, then that, while of itself wicked, would only be one evil, but there are other evils. If the seats of justice themselves were right, that would be of some hope. But, 'as the Prophet *Hosee* saith, *The Princes of Israel are as they that remove the land-marke*'.[36]

Andrewes is not hesitant in condemning the corruption of the administration of the law. Neither the use of the law by suitors, nor the governance of the law itself in its self-seeking, have anything to do with that righteousness which is necessary as the foundation of all good order and orderly conduct. Here there is a perception of how and where the law ought to be grounded. Of itself it cannot uphold that which it is meant to safeguard. It assumes an independence which is the very covering and excuse for the wickedness of people. It itself becomes sin and the occasion of sin. The relation between the law of the land and the Law of God has to be maintained. The hearing of the Word of God in truth is the perception of that, which corrects both the substance and administration of the law and the use of the law by those who have recourse to it.

Here we have the idea of a double contingency of the law. It is the law of the land, but if it is to be truly that and serve its purpose, it has to be seen to be dependent upon the Law of God expressed in the Word made flesh. It has its own sphere and reason, yet it can only have this rightly in its grounding in the higher Law. It is to be noted how Andrewes gathers together in a unitary way of thinking, the self-revelation of God in the incarnate Word, the Law of God, the hearing rightly of that Word and therefore the appreciation of that Law, the law of nature and of nations, and right and righteous existence and conduct. It is to be appreciated, however, that this is not mere moral relation, but one of actuality concerning existence itself. The implicit but clear concept of the double contingency of creation, with humanity at its heart – its contingency to and from the Creator, with his personal relation to creation as the Word made flesh – is what underlies Andrewes's observations here.

Andrewes brings out again the relation between theology and jurisprudence, the Law of God and the law of man, the divine decrees and the civil legislation, in

'Sermon 6 of the Conspiracy of the Gowries', preached on the text of Esther, 2:21–3, 'In those dayes, when Mardochai sate in the Kings gate'. The particular issue with which Andrewes deals here is the crime of 'laying hands' on the king. In the course of his argument he lays out his concept of the relation of human and divine law in the context not only of the relation of the monarch to God but of the relation of monarch to subject and the relation of that bond to God. In former sermons on this anniversary, he notes, 'we have beene all in *Divinitie*; that a heynous sinne it is there (this attempting on *Princes*:) But now shall we goe to the *Common Law*, what it is there.'[37] The two offenders against the king, mentioned in the text, Bigthan and Teresh, and their execution for the attempt on the king's life, thwarted by Mordecai and the queen Esther, were subject to, and dealt with under, not the law of Jewry, but the law of Persia. That that law was just, argues Andrewes, is an indictment on Christians, should such an offence be found among them. Such is the context of Andrewes text that, concerning the two would be regicides, 'We will empanell no *Christian*, a *quest* [that is, a duly appointed jury] of heathen men shall serve to attaint them.'[38]

This law was an ancient law among the Persians, written down in the Chronicles of that nation, and here written out of them into scripture. This book of Esther is properly

> not called *a booke*, as others are (not the *booke*) but the *Roll of Esther*. Originally, it was but *Persian law* (this:) and it had not been much, if that had beene all; but, by virtue of this *enrollment*, it is made the law of God.
>   . . . For, of this (whether *Divinity* or *Law*) this we may safely say; it is no new *Portugall Divinitie*, this almost three yeare old, taken up *in diebus hiis*. Nor no new *Law* of *heri* and *nudiustertius*: nay, not of *Edward the third*, then, *Et a principio non fuit sic*. No: it is old this, *in diebus illis*; in those dayes. And, those *dayes* are as old, as the *Second Monarchie*, the famous *Monarchie of Persia*: the reports of which Nation are more ancient, than any save those of the *Jewes*: no booke but the *Bible*, so ancient as they.[39]

Andrewes does not mean here that because of the antiquity of the Persian monarchy and its laws, this law is thereby a law of God. It is taken out of the law of Persia in the dispensation of God and seen to be a divine law by the 'direction of God' in that he enrols it and enshrines it in scripture.

What Andrewes is seeking to do here is to show that the law (here of treason, but the law in general) must be grounded on the law of God:

> Well may we talke of *Law*, the *Law of the Land*; but when all is done, never doe men rest, with that quiet and full contentment, as when they see, it is warrantable by the *Word of God*; hath the ground there, as this hath the ground there.[40]

This relation of the law, that it is grounded for its validity and efficacy on the Law of God, is the only guarantee of the rightness of law. There is a mutual support here of jurisprudence and divinity, law and theology, *facultas juris and facultas theologiae*. Common law and statute law can never be treated in isolation from the divine precepts as a political, social or fiscal expediency. Nor, of course, can the theological dimension of the divine law be treated in isolation from the law of the land. The divine decrees must be expressed tangibly in the created realities of human existence, and they should be so formulated in the common law and in the statute laws interpreting that corpus. Sin is a matter of humanity under God's judgment, and this dimension must be held to with regard to humanity under the law, otherwise that which is deemed wrong has no ground to be perceived as wrong, no standard against which it can be deemed to be so. It is the ultimate standard of how we stand before God, and how wrong is seen in that light which gives the fundamental standard of right and wrong.

> What care men for *sinne*, if there by no action at the Common Law for it? None but *Westminster-hall sins* do men care for. God saw it would come to this; Men learne no more duty, than *penall Statutes* did teach them; He tooke order therefore, to bring it within them too.[41]

Wrong can become relativized if it is not grounded in ultimate judgment. The law itself can become a matter of mere convenience or expediency if it is not related to the natural law of the integrity of the created realities in their relation to God.

Andrewes had the gift of preaching at certain occasions which called for the noting of a particular subject and the choice of a text relevant to that occasion, yet introducing the broad issues underlying these concerns. In all his sermons preached on state occasions and anniversaries, his concern for a unitary presentation of the order of created existence in its relation to God, is shown to be paramount, and his fearless criticism (which must have made his congregations of courtiers and those in positions of authority within the national and civic governments uncomfortable to say the least) of accepted practices and contemporary standards, reveal that his concern for law was more importantly with the larger issues, of which the particular occasion was but an instance. The good ordering of all things, as expressed by right laws and the fitting administering of the law, seen in the double contingent relation of creation to Creator, is the *cantus firmus* which runs throughout the counterpoint of his sermons.

Notes

1 Lancelot Andrewes: *Ninety-six Sermons*, 'Sermon 7 of the Gunpowder Treason', 1635 edn, pp.958ff.
2 Lancelot Andrewes: *Ninety-six Sermons*, 'Sermon 8 of the Gunpowder Treason', 1635 edn, pp.971ff.
3 Lancelot Andrewes: *Ninety-six Sermons*, 'Sermon 7 of the Gunpowder Treason', 1635 edn, p.961.
4 Ibid., pp.960–1.
5 Ibid., p.961.
6 Lancelot Andrewes: *Ninety-six Sermons*, 'Sermon 8 of the Gunpowder Treason', 1635 edn, p.972.
7 Ibid., p.972.
8 Ibid., p.974.
9 Ibid., pp.974–5.
10 Ibid., p.974.
11 Ibid., p.976.

12   Ibid., p.980.
13   Lancelot Andrewes: *Ninety-six Sermons*, 'Sermon 7 of the Gunpowder Treason', 1635
     edn, p.961.
14   Ibid., p.963.
15   Ibid., p.963.
16   Ibid., p.961.
17   Ibid., p.962.
18   Ibid., pp.962–3.
19   Ibid., p.962.
20   Ibid., p.963.
21   Ibid., p.964.
22   Ibid., p.964.
23   Ibid., p.964.
24   Ibid., p.964.
25   Lancelot Andrewes: *Ninety-six Sermons*, 'Sermon 9 of the Gunpowder Treason', 1635
     edn, p.984.
26   Ibid., p.987.
27   Ibid., p.988.
28   Ibid., p.984.
29   Ibid., pp.988–9.
30   Ibid., p.991.
31   Ibid., pp.989–990.
32   Ibid., p.991.
33   Ibid., p.992.
34   Ibid., p.993.
35   Ibid., p.993.
36   Ibid., p.993.
37   Lancelot Andrewes: *Ninety-six Sermons*, 'Sermon 6 of the Conspiracy of the Gowries',
     1635 edn, p.845.
38   Ibid., p.845.
39   Ibid., p.845.
40   Ibid., p.845.
41   Ibid., p.847.

Chapter 7

Order, Monarchy, Parliament and Church

The relation between Common and Natural Law and Church or Canon Law is of supreme importance. It is a fundamental principle for an understanding of the Jacobean and Caroline position *vis-à-vis* the Church by Law Established. The estate of the monarchy and its vocation regarding the upholding of Common Law and Natural Law figure largely in this. However, the context of this is a sequence of thought moving from the order which God is eternally in His eternal relations, through the *oikonomia* which God, in consistency with the nature of His Being as a God of order, decrees for creation in His creative and re-creative acts in His eternal Word. The sequence continues through a consideration of Common Law resting on Natural Law as man's attempt at obedient understanding of the nature of creation in the light of God's revelation. It then moves through the concept of the ordering of each kingdom with its appointed Vice-regent 'in God's place', for the true dignity and welfare of humanity within its bounds, to the ordering of the Church as an aspect of that ordered one body politic. The dictum of King James VI and I – 'No Bishop, no King'[1] – was not a mere clever statement of political expediency. It comes from a far deeper understanding of the issues involved concerning the concept of *order.*

The responsiblity of monarchy was the upholding of God's order within each kingdom over which a king rules, and that order is by the upholding of common and natural law, for the true welfare of all things and their proper establishment and existence, and for the holding back of chaos and lawlessness. The responsibility of monarchy, therefore, is the safeguarding of the rights and dignities and estates of all things within the *oikonomia* of God. The realization of this was never far from King James VI and I – an able theologian, underestimated by the greater part of historians. In his *True Law of Free Monarchies*, published anonymously in 1598, he claimed regarding common law:

> a good King will not only delight to rule his subjects by the law, but will even conform himself in his own actions thereunto; always keeping that ground, that the health of his commonwealth be his chief law.[2]

In 1607, Dr Cowell, Professor of Civil Law in the University of Cambridge, published *The Interpreter*, in which he made exaggerated claims for the estate and function of monarchy. The King, he wrote, 'is above the law by his absolute power'.[3] This James repudiated, asserting that he was the upholder of Common Law. In his 'Speech to the Parliament, 1610', he declared

> anent the Common Law, which some had a conceit I disliked, and (in respect that I was born where another form of law was established) that I would have wished the Civil Law

to have been put in place of the Common Law for government of this people. And the complaint made amongst you of a book written by Dr. Cowell was a part of the occasion of this incident; but as touching my censure of that book, I made it already to be delivered unto you by the Treasurer here sitting.[4]

The distinction is here introduced between civil and common law. Strictly speaking, in the constitutional evolution of England, civil (or statute) law, was the codifying of certain aspects stemming from common law which dealt with particular issues for the clearer (and, if need be, temporary – for statute law can always be repealed when occasion arises) ordering and governing of the people. Again, strictly speaking, all statute law was to be tested against common law, of which it was but the secondary, but immediately practical, expression. Statute law could not be contrary to common law; it was merely the codification and clarification of particular aspects of it. The essential nature of all things, and therefore their order and function, was firmly embedded in common law, and beyond common law in the *oikonomia* of God of which that law was but the human expression. Hence Mason's observation already cited from his *Authoritie of the Church*: 'Order proceedeth from the throne of the Almightie, it is the beauty of nature, the ornament of Arte, the harmonie of the world.'[5] It is here that common law and natural law are rooted, and, dependent on that, statute law. It is necessary to examine the function ascribed to Monarch and Parliament as the authorities responsible for law, common or statute, and then to examine the relation between common and canon law in that light, if the Caroline Divines' attitude towards canon law and the ordering of the Church, is to be grasped.

The King, as head of the whole body, is regarded as the source and seat of such law, and it is his duty to maintain and exercise it. We turn here to Lancelot Andrewes's sermon, 'On the Right and Power of Calling Assemblies, preached before the Kings Majestie at Hampton Court, on Sunday the 28. September, 1606, on the text of Numbers, chapter 10, verses 1&2':

> Then God spake to Moses, saying, Make thee two Trumpets of silver, of one whole peece shalt thou make them, and thou shalt have them . . . to assemble the Congregation, and to remove the Campe.[6]

This sermon is particularly important as an exposition of Andrewes's attitude towards the question of the right of the monarchy to order the Church, and it requires careful scrutiny.

His argument is that the trumpets, the use of which was to be the calling of lawful assemblies, were made of one piece, and given to only one person for lawful use, Moses. Only one was permitted their use, by God's command:

> every body must not be allowed to be a maker of *Trumpets*: nor when they be made, that they hang, where who that lift may blow them: (that is) that every man, hand over head, is not to be in case, to draw multitudes together: There will be (saith *St. Luke*: [Acts 19:13] *Turbatio non minima*, no small adoe, if that may be suffered. If *Demetrius* getting together his *fellow crafts-men*, they may of their owne heads, *rush into the common Hall*, and there keepe a shouting and *crying two houres* together; *not knowing* most of them, *why they came thither*, and yet thither they came. There is not so much good, in *publike meetings*,

but there is thrice as much hurt, in such as this: No Common-wealth, no not Popular Estates could ever endure them. Nay . . . (say both Scripture [Acts 19:36] – and Nature) *Let all be done in order*: Let us have . . . *Lawfull* orderly *Assemblies*, or else none at all. Away then with this confusion, (to begin with:) away with *Demetrius* Assemblies.[7]

Moses had the power of the use of these trumpets, and only Moses. The two trumpets made from the single piece of metal symbolize, for Andrewes, the two sides of the one body politic, the secular and the ecclesiastical. The fact that only one person (here Moses) may blow them, is the pointer to one person being authoritative over both sides of that one body. Here Andrewes is laying the ground for an exposition of where authority lies and how the instruments of authority are to be severely guarded for proper use by the one person so qualified and called to use them.

God had first summoned the people of Israel Himself

as at the first He took this *Power* into His owne hands, and called them still together Himselfe: so here, He deriveth this *Power* immediately from Himselfe, unto *one*: without first settling it, in any *bodie collective* at all.[8]

God Himself was the authority and the power. He alone can summon the people for His purposes. All authority and power therefore reside in God alone, and they are His alone to give. This He does as a matter of grace. But it is to an individual that God so gives, not to the whole body of the nation. Andrewes sets out the reasons why:

It is from our purpose to enter the question, Whether the *Power* were in the *whole body* originally? Seeing though it were, it is now by the positive ordinance of God otherwise disposed. . . . The two *Trumpets* may be blowen, two diverse wayes, if they be in two hands; and so shall the *Trumpet give an uncertaine sound* (I Cor.14:8) and how shall the *Congregation* know whither to *assemble*? Nay (a worse matter yet than all that) so may we have an *Assembly* against *Assembly*: and rather than so, better no *Assembly* at all.

Therefore, as *God* would have them, both made of *one peece*: so will He have them both made over to *one Person*. . . . Who is that *one*? It is to *Moses* God speaketh. . . . Him doth God nominate . . . No man to *make*, no man to have the hammering of any *trumpet*, but he.[9]

Andrewes makes it clear that it is not to Aaron, 'the High Priest anointed and fully vested in the rights of it', and his Levites, that the right is given to blow the trumpet and summon the Assembly. It is to Moses alone, and he is given the power of summoning the Assembly as Chief Magistrate – the trumpets are given to him with a Ceremony investing him, and him alone, with the right of them. And this was '*rectitudo Regis*, A power Regall'.

There is a double use for the trumpets, for the Congregation, that is for times of peace, and for moving the camp, that is for times of war. But peace and war both concern the civil side of things and the ecclesiastical. Affairs of state have to be seen to by Assemblies in war and peace, but the Church has its peace and its wars, too – in building up the faith, and in attacking, and defending against, heresy. The two trumpets – one is for peace and the other for war – are both for things civil and things ecclesiastical. It is not that one trumpet is for Church concerns, and the other for affairs of state. They are both of one piece, the civil and the ecclesiastical are not separate, and one is for peaceful concerns in either things ecclesiastical or things civil, the other for alarums in both. The use of the trumpets is the Chief Magistrate's alone, even if he delegate that. They are his property.

> This is the Law of God; and that no *judiciall Law*, peculiar to that people alone, but agreeable to the *Law of Nature* and *Nations*; (Two *Lawes* of force thorow the whole world.) For even in the little Empire of the body naturall, *Principium motus*, the *beginning of all motion*, is in, and from the *head*. There, all the knots, or (as they call them) all the *conjugations* of sinewes have their head, by which all the body is moved. And as the *Law of Nature*, by secret instinct by the light of the *Creation* annexeth the organ to the chiefest part: even so doth the *Law of Nations*, by the light of *Reason*, to the chiefest *Person*.[10]

We may note Andrewes's appeal to the natural law whereby the head moves all the other members of the body, and the familiar description of the human body as a microcosm. As God rules the creation, so the little world of the body is ruled by the head, and so too, a nation is ruled by its governor, the chief person placed there for the purpose by God.

Then follows a comprehensive and scholarly list, beginning with the time of Moses, through all the generations and into the Christian era of the General Councils of the early Church and beyond, of Assemblies called and authorized by Kings and Emperors. The monarch, it is to be noted here, is supreme Governor in matters Civil and Ecclesiastical. The body, over which the head rules is one. There is no concept of two separate bodies existing together, the body of the state and the body of the Church. There are things civil and things ecclesiastical, but they are conjoined, inseparably, though unconfusedly, in the one 'body politike' under one head.

This had always been the generally accepted and practised constitutional position in England. In the dispensation of its office, the monarchy is assisted by Parliament. Andrewes's 'Sermon Preached at the Opening of the Parliament, 1621', is pertinent here. Again, careful scrutiny is required here, for this sets out best Andrewes's ideas concerning the monarch as the one for the many, and how the monarch's exercise of office may lawfully be assisted by others without encroaching upon its substance and dignity. It is on the text of Psalm 82, verse 1:

> God standeth in the Congregation of Princes (in the Psalter), or, in the Assembly of the Gods (in the Geneva Bible) or, of the Mighty (in the New Translation) [that is, the 1611 version, of which Andrewes was one of the principal translators].[11]

This sermon was preached before the King and the Three Estates – the Lords Spiritual, the Lords Temporal and the Commons. In it, Andrewes reminds them of their status and duty under God. They are termed 'Gods' – the title applied to all in authority in scripture. But they are 'not all Gods alike'. In this collective body which is as a

> *God-head, Some are before or after other, Some are greater or lesser than another. There are some higher than other* (saith *Salomon, Ecclesiastes*. 5.12) *And there are*

others yet higher than they. For the Powers that are, are by God, both *ordained,* and *set in order* (saith *St. Paul.* Romans [13.2]) So *in order,* (saith *St Peter* [I Peter. 2.13]) as there is one . . . (he saith) . . . the King by name, *Supereminent above the rest,* and the rest *ab eo missi,* have their *mission,* and *commission* from *him.* Many *Superiors,* but one *Soveraigne.*[12]

The word 'Gods' as applied to them, is but a title, and the ways in which they are variously called Gods are not to be construed as 'swelling words of vanity'. They are called such because of God's appointment, the duty they owe Him, and the answer they must make to Him for the exercise of their office.

There would seem to be a principle of derivation at work here in Andrewes's thought. God is the Source of power, indeed Power and Authority Himself; the monarch derives his power and authority from God, those set in office in the nation's affairs derive their power and authority from the king. However, there seems to be a deeper understanding than this at work in Andrewes's mind. A careful reading of the general context and of particular phrases, suggests that the principle of contingency rather than that of derivation underlies the reasoning. It is not a question of the king exercising the power of God in a straight line from God, as it were, but exercising that which God permits him to hold as befits, and as is required for, his office as monarch. The monarchy is part of the *oikonomia* of God, and, being so placed and ordered by God, holds its own peculiar power by God's grace. Likewise, those set to assist the monarch have their own positions and authority which they hold by virtue of the fact that they, too, are placed and ordered by God in their offices and positions, and are called to use these to assist the monarch in the exercise of his duties. In this way they all participate in furthering the *oikonomia* of God by God's good pleasure. As such, those under the monarch are little monarchs in their own fields. This is dealt with at greater detail below, and in order to clarify this, some full quotes from this sermon are given. But here it must be noted that it is the principle of contingency which is the controlling factor in the question of the monarch's estate and vocation, that is, his power is contingent to and from God, and that it is not some simplistic principle of derived Divine power which colours Andrewes's thought. We may perhaps say that he regards the king as God's representative and not God's representation.

Andrewes then appeals to the early Fathers, to Gregory Nazianzen in the fourth century, speaking of Magistrates (that is, those in authority) as

of the *Images of God,* and sorting them, compareth the *highest* to a *picture drawne cleane through downe to the feet;* the *middle sort, to halfe pictures drawne but to the girdle;* The *lowest,* to those same *Idyllia,* no further but to the *neck* and *shoulders.* But all in some degree, carry the *image of God,* as all have the honour to be called by *His Name.*
. . .
What infer we of this? Nothing, but that, what they are, they would be: *having obtained so excellent a Name,* they would be even what their name bodeth. They that weare *Gods* name, hold *Gods place,* represent *His Person, what manner persons ought they to bee:* Choice persons they would bee.[13]

Now it may be objected that to 'hold God's place' may be construed as meaning 'in place of God', but the other phrases and descriptions Andrewes employs put a somewhat different interpretation on this statement. It is straining too far, perhaps, to interpret it as 'to hold God's placing', for he is insistent on the high dignity of the holder by virtue of the office. It is possibly better to treat it as 'to be in God's place insofar as our mortality and frailty allow'. For the subsequent emphasis is on the limitations of the holders, and such limitations are far from divine in any way.

Andrewes goes on to list the reasons for the high dignity and sacredness of this assembly, a Congregation of Gods. But their dignity and estate consists of the proper exercise of their duty, bearing in mind God who has so appointed them. In the midst of these reasons, he points out that they are, as a Congregation, called in the Hebrew of the text a 'Synagogue, which is a Holy Place, a Sanctuary, a High Place, or Court of Refuge'. He notes that God, to further the high end to which He has called them, and to heighten an awareness of the sacredness of their duty 'hath . . . spared them a peece of His owne Temple, to have their eetings in . . . that so their feet might stand on holy ground'. This for those present then, as it was for those called Gods in authority in ancient Israel. Andrewes is referring to the fact that the affairs of Israel were conducted in part of the south side of the Temple in Jerusalem, and here, in Parliament, were dealt with by the Congregation of those in authority, meeting in St Stephen's Chapel, which they had done since 1550, having previously gathered in the Chapter House of Westminster Abbey.

Contrary to what could be a much mistaken impression, the title God is not applied only to the monarch. It is given to all in any sphere of authority whatsoever. It is a title, not, as Andrewes had already said, 'of swelling words of vanity', but a reminder of the *oikonomia* of God who has so appointed to positions of responsibility. This is ignored in so much historical comment on the seventeenth century's view of the Divine Right of Kings. There was, in fact, a Divine Right in every estate and vocation of man throughout all levels of society.

Robert Sanderson (1587–1663), Regius Professor of Divinity in Oxford (until removed by the Puritans) and Bishop of Lincoln at the Restoration in 1660, puts quite clearly the implications of this Divine Right to all who possess it, in his 'First Sermon to the Magistrates, preached at the Sessions at Grantham, Lincolnshire, on the 11 June, 1623, on the text of Job chapter 29.verses 14–17':

> I put on righteousnesse, and it cloathed mee: my judgement was as a robe and diadem. I was eyes to the blinde, and feet was I to the lame. I was a father to the poore: and the cause which I knew not I searched out. And I brake the jawes of the wicked; and plucked the spoyle out of his teeth.
>
> Princes and Judges, and Magistrates were not ordained altogether, nor yet so much for their owne sakes, that they might have over whom to beare rule and dominiere at pleasure; as for the Peoples sakes, that the people might have to whom to resort, and upon whom to depend for helpe and succour, and reliefe in their necessities: and they ought to remember, that for this end God hath endued them with that Power which others want; that they might by their power helpe them to right, who have not power to right themselves. . . . This is the very thing, wherein the preeminence of Princes, and Magistrates, and great ones above the ordinarie sort singularly consisteth, and wherein specially they have the advantage, and whereby they hold the title of Gods, that they are able to do good, and to help the distressed, more than others are. For which ability how they have used it, they stand accountable to him from whom they have received it; and woe unto them, if the accounts they bring in, be not in some reasonable proportion

answerable to the receipts . . . and the mighty ones, if they have not done a mighty deale of good withall, shall be mightily tormented.[14]

This is hardly the language of the sycophant. It is unfortunate that little notice has been taken of the authority of pulpit proclamation in this vein by divines of the period. They sometimes generally have been judged to have been one of the main obstacles of the reform of the monarchy and the social *status quo*, and, indeed, aiders and abettors of excesses in the name of right and divine appointment.

Andrewes had complained sharply about the misuse of Law and the formulating of laws not in accordance with Common Law and good order. In his 'Sermon Preached at St Maries Hospital on the Tenth of Aprill, being Wednesday in Easter weeke, 1588' on the text of I Timothy, 6:17–19 – 'Charge them that are rich in this world, that they be not high minded' – he notes that

> The *Lawes* are like *Cobwebs*: that they hold fast the silly *flies*, but the great *Hornets* breake thorow them, as oft as they list. And as there are *Cobweb-lawes*, which exempt mightie men; So, the same Corruption, that was the cause thereof, would also make *Cobweb Divinitie*.[15]

In the same vein he speaks of Westminster Hall laws, which have no relation to the laws of God.

> What care men for *sinne*, if there be no action at the Common Law for it? None but *Westminster-hall sins* do men care for. God saw it would come to this; Men learne no more duty, than *penall Statutes* did teach them.[16]

To return to his 1621 sermon at the opening of Parliament, he uses the imagery of the human body to describe this Congregation called by God to fulfil its divinely appointed duties. It is 'a Congregation of Lawgivers'. It gathers together, all the constituent parts of it, the veins, the arteries, the sinews, to protect the heart, which is the nation. King and Parliament, in this high office under God, are 'the Scepter in Judas hand . . . the Lawgiver betweene his feet, even with Jacob'. They have the duty of bringing 'into course that is out, to set the foundations fast'. Like Sanderson, he reminds them of their accountability. In the place where they are gathered, there are many monuments to the mighty of time past who have gone into their dust and grave. By this means he stresses the contingent quality of the power and authority they wield, for they have in all things to yield it to God who grants it for a time to them. He compares them to the God who has done this, and who stands in the midst of this Congregation of human Gods.

> God *stands* . . . But *you shall fall*. A *standing* God; He who onely *stands*, and will *stand*, when they *all shall fall*, and *fall* even to *dust*, every *God* of them. And this could not be told us in a fitter *place*: the place where we stand, is compassed about with a *Congregation* of these *fallen Gods* . . . with *Monuments* of the *mortality* of many a great *Elohim* in their times. And let me tell you this, that in the Hebrew tongue the *Grave* is called a *Synagogue* as well as the *Church*. *All shall bee gathered*, even the *Gods*, even the whole *Synagogue of* them, into this *Synagogue* at last. So this first shewes them, *Their Godships* give them no *immortality. Gods*: but *mortall*, and *temporall Gods* they be.[17]

The second point he makes to them in this vein, is that of God's judging them, as He stands in their midst.

> When they have done *judging* others, they shall come to be *judged themselves* . . . *Gods* that shall *fall*, *Gods* that must come to *judgement*. From neither of these shall their Godhead excuse them.
>
> These two then, sever them from the first God; the *AEternall* God, and the *Soveraigne Judge of all*. And shew (the one, their *judging*) that their *Glory* is no *equall*; the other (their *falling*) that their Majesty is not *co-eternall*, that so they may understand themselves aright.[18]

(It may be noted that the choice of phrase is that of the language of the so-called Athanasian Creed.) So Andrewes severs King and Parliament from any delusions of their divinity, for the distinction he makes between them and the God who bestows authority and power and places them in these seats, is clear and determined.

Their duty, as King and Parliament, is to see that every deliberation, decision and action, is tested against the presence of the God who so stands and judges in their midst. In other words, their statutes and bills, are to stand the test of God's decrees. Laws formulated and promulgated, are to be in accord with the foundation of all law, and that means, of course, a constant regard for common law stemming from natural law as the attempt to administer the decrees of God for all things that are. This is done by Andrewes's further observations on the text:

> [God] while He *stood*, He *stood attentive*: He *stood* not like an *idoll*: was all the while no *idle stander* by, or *looker on*, but as the *Writing was on the wall*, [Daniel, chapter 5:25] *Mene, Mene*, He *told* and *numbered*; and *Tekel, Stetit cum statera, He weighed and pondered well, every motion* that was made, every Bill that was read, every *Consent* or otherwise passed upon it: And weighed withall, whence every of them proceeded, whether from a *dutifull regard of him* and *his* presence; or otherwise, for some *by-respect* of our owne.[19]

Andrewes ends the sermon by advice concerning their conduct and composure under all this knowledge.

This same principle of contingent authority, and all the implications of that which we have now set out, was applied by the Caroline Divines to every area and aspect of human society and existence. They applied it to monarch, parliament, and those set to execute the laws so made, the magistrates. In all this and in all these, there is stressed the sense of vocation in the decrees of God as fulfilled in Christ. It is this, and the concept of contingency which is carried through by way of uniform application, to every standing of every individual. Each person, in a sense, is a monarch, or a God, in his or her own domain and calling, in his or her estate and vocation.

Here the two aspects of the 'one body politick' converge. What is true of the temporal under God is true of the ecclesiastical. There is an ordering of the Church, within which the estate and vocation of persons is grounded in the proclamation, sacraments and worship of the church, and the order which is provided for the ministration of these. Here the knowledge of the order which God is and which He decrees is found. In this, canon law is rooted. This means that there are, with regard to the ordering of the Church, certain unchangeable and essential things. Canon law can only clarify these. There are also other considerations which are *indifferent* or inessential, but which, nevertheless, require to be stated for the best interests of the Church as it seeks to express the Christian faith to a particular people in a particular place at a particular time. These are also a matter of canon law. But just as statute law bears an inseparable and subservient relation to common and natural law, so canon law, which, like statute law is focused on the one head of the one body politic, and is indeed itself part of statute law, must bear that same relation. The Church requires codification of things inessential, so that there is no confusion of a multiplicity of practices and interpretations of customs. But these must be both in keeping with common law and seen to be but of a convenient nature. They may be altered or repealed from time to time, as Church and monarch see fit in changing situations.

There is a distinction in canon law between essentials and inessentials, as there is in the whole theological method of 'classical' Anglicanism dealing with theological beliefs and interpretations. Order, which is stable and unchanging, in its relation to God's *oikonomia* and the way that this is expressed in society, and order which is of temporary expediency, but nevertheless in harmony with the nature of that *oikonomia* and its expression, is the distinction which is the gist of Mason's sermon. But the whole sequence of argument set out above is followed through. There has to be realized a distinction in things inessential, which distinction is concerned with the view of each nation as a free, sovereign state. What may be expedient for the Church ministering to and in one particular nation with its history, ethos and character, is not necessarily valid for another nation where such circumstances are different. Things inessentially, but expediently, ordered for the Church of one country, cannot necessarily be transposed and forced upon the Church of another land. This would give a false and anthropocentrically contrived essential nature to such ordinances.

It is here, according to the Laudian Divines, that the estate and vocation of monarchs come into focus with regard to the Church, for in administering order for the welfare of the body politic of their respective kingdoms, they know what is most expedient for their particular peoples. In England, in consultation with the Church, canon law is promulgated concerning inessentials, by the monarch and his or her assisting Parliament, with the totality of the one body of the nation and its full welfare in mind. Yet nothing is passed contrary to common law – or should not be so passed.

In the sermon concerning *The Authoritie of the Church in Making Canons and Constitutions*, Mason is safeguarding against two stresses which could warp this proper balance and observation. First, that decrees or canons should not be passed which are contrary to things essential, or which artificially elevate things inessential to the status of the essential. Secondly, that those inessentials which are expedient elsewhere than England should not be imported and, for partisan reasons, construed as being binding on the English Church and people. He therefore is precise and meticulous about his definitions in the development of his argument.

First, the explication of the text. Mason examines the words of the text. It is a text concerning Church order. 'All things' refers to a general application to the Church's life. It refers to:

a generall conclusion comprehending not onely praier, thankesgiving, and prophecying, but moreover the ministration of the holy Sacraments, consecration to holy orders, and universally the publike discharge of such sacred and reverent duties: concerning all which, the spirit requireth that they be done, first you would say, after a good fashion, consisting in time, place, apparell, and other things required for the due and decent administration. They must have an honest decencie, and a decent honestie; they must be comely to the eie, and referred to a godly end, that is, the advancement of God's glory and the edification of the Church, not giving (just occasion of) scandall to Jew or Gentile, or to the Church of God. For if these ends must be duly respected in matters of common life, how much more reverently and religiously should they bee regarded in the solemne service of Almightie God?[20]

What is of import here is how Mason lays the same quality of honesty upon the matters of common life, for the same ends, though, obviously these are more specific and heightened in the service of God within the Church's life. He continues:

And as all things must be decent and honest before God and men, so it is required in the second place, that all things be done according to order. Which order, requireth authority with godly wisdome in the publike disposer, and cheerfull, obedience with gracious humilitie in such as are subject to those publike constitutions.[21]

Order, for Mason is a matter, not only of the form, but of the disposition of the administrator and the observer of order. Act and being, sign and thing signified, form and substance, are bracketed together. Order is a matter not of surface form only, but of existence in its totality. The implicit parallel is to God as the God of order in His existence and in His acts.

Secondly, Mason goes on to consider 'The general use of this text'. He begins with a statement of the significance of the text.

So this text is a Canon of Canons for all such Church government, and all Ecclesiasticall Canons must be cast in this moulde: Indeed it is a golden Canon or* [*in margin: Regula est ad quam omnia qua ad externam politiam spectani exigere convenenit. Calvinus ibid. (Calvin, Commentary on I Cor. XIV:40)] rule, whereby all Christian Churches must be ruled, an exquisite touchstone whereat all ceremonies must be tried: the beame of the Sanctuarie whereupon all Church orders and constitutions must be weighed and ballanced.[22]

We are concerned here with a basic principle which was widely appreciated in the late sixteenth and early seventeenth centuries. And that is that everything in Church life, with which the various Canons or constitutions of Churches are concerned, all pivot round the central fact of faith. They are pointers to it, and their value lies in this, their paradigmatic nature. That all things are to be done honestly and in order is an Apostolic charge concerning this very point – 'honestly' (or 'decently') refers to correspondence with the nature of Truth, and 'in order' to the setting out of the nature of that Truth by way of witnessing to it. Therefore this Apostolic charge is the test against which all practices, customs and ecclesiastical directives of whatever nature, are to be balanced.

Mason makes the familiar distinction here between things essential and things inessential. He outlines the way in which this distinction between necessary, or essential, and things indifferent or inessential, is arrived at:

> Necessarie I call that which the eternall God hath in his word precisely and determinately commanded or forbidden, either expresly or by infallible consequence. . . . Whatsoever God hath in his Word precisely commanded, so farre as it is commanded is necessarie to be done, for the not doing ofit is a sinne.
>
> Whatsoever God hath forbidden, so long as it is forbidden, is necessarie to bee left undone, for the very doing of it is a sinne. . . . Some things were everlastingly commanded, as to feare God, and keepe his commandements: everlastingly forbidden, as all sinne and wickednesse.[23]

Not only are these essential or necessary elements clearly set out in scripture; they are also correspondingly in that natural law, which is the creative intent of God as to the true nature of all things.

> For some things are correspondent to the Law written in our hearte, that is, the Law of humane nature, which considered in the originall beautie and brightnesse is the same in substance with the Law Morall, and these are in their owne nature good and everlastingly to bee embraced: some things are repugnant to it, and these are in their owne nature evill and everlastingly to be abhorred.[24]

Natural Law, it should be emphasized is not construed in terms of something natural within mankind as it is. The law of human nature is to be considered in its original beauty and brightness – that is, as it is seen in Christ, God's man.
Mason calls

> Indifferent, which the Lord hath not so commanded nor forbidden, but is contained in holy Scripture, rather potentially than actually, comprehended in general directions, not precisely defined by particular determinations. . . . Whatsoever is neither commanded nor forbidden, that (whether it concerne Churche or common-wealth) is left to the Lords viceregents upon earth, who, according to the exigence of the state, may by their discretion command it to be done, or to be left undone, and both without sinne.[25]

Likewise, things inessential have their correspondence in Natural Law: 'Some things the sacred Law of our nature hath left arbitrary, and these in themselves and of their owne nature indifferent.'

But these things inessential as far as the natural law is concerned, may for a time and place, by Divine command, become necessary. Mason instances such Old Testament ordinances as the eating of swines' flesh – as a meat indifferent in its nature and use – yet expressly forbidden by the ceremonial law for a season. But when that law ceased, the eating of such resumed its indifferent status. Again, implicit in this is the paradigmatic nature of such ordinances. Things may be used, which by nature are indifferent, as essential signs for a time. Others, however, by nature indifferent, by the law of God are used as essential signs for all time. The supreme instance here is the drinking of wine.

> Likewise, to drinke wine, or to abstaine from it, is a thing in nature indifferent, but being sanctifyed by our Lord Jesus to a sacramentall use, it is not in the power of man to cancell or disannull the holy institution of that heavenly Lawgiver.[26]

There is another element which gives authority for things to assume a status of things essential:

> And heere it must be considered, that there are some comely rites and decent orders whereof we finde not precise commandement in the holy Scripture, which notwithstanding the Scripture rectifieth to have beene very precisely observed by the Apostles and apostolicall men; and are of such nature, that they agree to all places and ages: in which respect, they may aptly be reduced to things necessary: because the holy Ghost so exquisitely recording the exact observation of them by the blessed Apostles, may seeme to have pointed them out to all posteritie, as a patterne to be unchangeably followed. This is the judgement of M. Calvin* [*in margin: Cal.inst. lib.4.3.16] concerning imposition of hands in the consecrating to holie orders. Although (saith he) there be extant no certaine precept of imposition of hands yet because we see that it was continually used of the Apostles, that their so exact observation should be to us in place of a precept.[27]

So it is with the transfer of the Jewish Sabbath to the first day of the week.

Order is viewed as that which exists in various levels or fields. But all these fields are related to the fundamental order which is the order of all things in Christ. There are various fields of the nature and exercise of order. Some are essential, being expressly laid out as such in Scripture. Some are essential only for a time – the span of their validity in pointing to Christ, until they are superseded in the dispensation of God. Others are essential because of Apostolic practice and the tradition of 'apostolicall men' and are for all time and every place. Yet others are inessential, but necessary for the particular ethos and nature of a kingdom, in which case, the monarch, God's vice-regent, with the welfare of the whole commonwealth under common law as one body politic as to its ordering, will rule on the matter accordingly. We have, then, the concept of interwoven and interrelating orders, all contingent on the fundamental order which is Christ Himself. In their respective and related natures, order itself is firmly embedded in the temporal and spatial realities of created existence, which moves according to the reality it is in Christ embodying, as He does, the new humanity, the new time, the new creation. It is a kaleidoscopic concept of apparently different and jumbled shapes of order, but when properly viewed in the light of Christ, and with respect to the nature of the various orders, falls into a true and coherent pattern – a unity of rich yet compatible diversity.

The next observation Mason makes concerns the question implied by the statement 'Let all things be done decently – who shall be the judge of decency?' This too is a matter of order, for the means of judging God has decreed:

> Now in this variety of opinions (concerning things indifferent), who shall be the judge? who shall governe and swaie the matter? Surely, they whom the Lord hath made Church governors. If private men will make publike orders, and require us to accept of them, they must shew their commission: Otherwise we must take that for decent in things indifferent, which seemeth decent in the eie of publike authoritie. And verilie for private men to range without the compasse of their calling, and upon their private opinions, to controle the publike judgement of the Church, in a matter of decencie, is in my opinion a matter very undecent. Likewise, seeing the spirit hath said, Let all things be done by order; therefore doubtles in the Church of God there must be an order. But who shall

appoint this order? shall every man doe what he list? that were disorder. Shall private men make publike constitutions? that were against good order. Therefore it remaineth that they onely have authoritie to make Church orders, whom the Lord hath made Church governours.[28]

Then comes Mason's appeal to the estate and function of the monarchy in this respect. Not only order itself, but the order of dispensing order, is therefore involved. Order, therefore, is a matter of the involvement of human existence and vocation and office, and not a matter of disinterested and detached imposition and acceptance of principle. This implants very fundamentally the concept of order into the whole nature of being itself. Lancelot Andrewes exhibits this outlook of the Jacobean and Caroline Divines clearly in various sermons. His 'Sermon Preached at St. Maries Hospital in 1588', in which he outlines the place and vocation of the rich in the dispensation of God, suggests that the principle of monarchy, that is, the 'orderer' under God of a particular domain, is applicable to every individual in his or her circumstances. The rich, for example, have an estate from God, but are answerable to God for the exercise of that office. In other words, vocation is the operative principle here.

> Lazarus in a rich man's bosome [John.12.], is a goodly sight in heaven; and no less goodly in earth. And there shall never be a rich man with Lazarus in his bosome, in heaven, unlesse he have had a Lazarus in his bosome here on earth. . . . This know; that *God* hath not given sight to the eye, to *enjoy*, but to *lighten* the members; nor *wisdome* to the *honourable* man, but for us men of simple shallow forecast; nor *learning* to the *divine*, but for the ignorant; neither *riches* to the *wealthy*, but for those that want relief.[29]

Each individual is a monarch responsible for order in his or her own field, each with their particular dispensation to administer order – the craftsman at his bench, the judge in his circuit, the teacher in his school, the captain on his ship, the farmer in his fields, the parents in their home. All human existence and authority is disposed and called to witness to that order declared in Christ.

The general application of the principle of monarchy throughout every level of society, demonstrates a concern for the status of every individual. This concern is expressed by the seventeenth-century divines in terms of God's apportionment. This apportioning of gifts by God to every individual has to be acknowledged, appreciated and acted upon. Part of the responsibility of every Christian is to assist their fellow in this, in ways appropriate to the assister's apportionment by God of His own gifts and in ways appropriate to the potential of the one receiving such assistance.

Here there is perhaps a sense of 'equality' – but not in terms of a 'levelling', so that all are deemed to be absolutely and mechanically equal. Rather, equality is based on God's apportionment – that is, the fact that it is God who gives and bestows. Because individuals are all receivers of God's largesse and bounty, they have respect and place, and in their particular callings and skills and places are to be regarded with the same respect as all others because they are the recipients of God's dispensation. If this is a correct reading of the attitude of these divines, then 'equality' for these divines means 'respect in diversity and variety'. It does not mean the setting aside of diversity and variety.

The concept of 'human rights' therefore (if this is not too an anachronistic term to use) would, on this view, mean the right of the person to be what he or she should be in the dispensation of God, and the encouragement of that person to pursue this end. This idea seems to be quite clearly stated in the whole drift of Lancelot Andrewes's sermon preached to the merchants of the City of London at St Mary's Hospital in 1588. The drift of his argument is that a responsibility for such an encouragement of others is laid on all in the ways which they are able to undertake this and pursue it on behalf of others.

'Human rights' are not something which exist independently and naturally – rooted in a concept of humanity as an entity separate from the dispensation of God and the relation of humanity to the Being and acts of God. The good ordering of society can only be, on this view, achieved by first acknowledging the creative intent and ordering of God for the individuals which compose society, and whose varying and different gifts and activities build up the quality of that society.

For these divines, natural law in this respect is firmly based on the value of the individual viewed within that *oikonomia* of God, not on the individual as an entity in, for and by himself. It consists of the acknowledgement that order is in diversity and in all the relationships, dependencies and inter-workings within that variety of persons, for this is the way that the Personal God personally acts towards and in human persons. Order is not a theory, based on mechanical or philosophical principles, to be imposed. It is the human counterpart of the order which is the creative intent of God wherein there is 'one glory of the sun, and another glory of the moon, and another glory of the stars; for one star differeth from another star in glory',[30] and both the created counterpart corresponding in their temporal and spatial dimensions, variety and harmony, to the glory which God is in Himself in the unity of His diversity as Father and Son bound in the bond of Eternal Love, the Holy Spirit.

Notes

1   William Barlowe: quoting the King in *The Sum of the Conference*, 1625 edn, p.36.
2   James VI of Scotland (James I of England): *The True Law of Free Monarchies* (published anonymously, 1598), quoted in J.R. Tanner: *Constitutional Documents of the Reign of James I*, Cambridge University Press, 1930, p.9. Cf. Francis Bacon: *Of the Proficience and Advancement of Learning*, Book II, 1778 edn, pp.97, 98, where he makes mention of this work.
3   Quoted in Tanner: *Constitutional Documents of the Reign of James I*, pp.12ff.
4   Ibid., pp.14ff.
5   Francis Mason: *Authoritie of the Church in Making Canons and Constitutions, etc.*, 1605 edn, p.11.
6   Lancelot Andrewes: *Ninety-six Sermons*, 'Sermon on the Right and Power of Calling Assemblies', 1635 edn, pp.B99ff.
7   Ibid., p.103.
8   Ibid., p.103.
9   Ibid., p.103.
10 Ibid., p.106.

11 Lancelot Andrewes: *Ninety-six Sermons*, 'Sermon Preached at the Opening of the Parliament 1621', 1635 edn, pp.B143ff.
12 Ibid., p.146.
13 Ibid., p.146.
14 Robert Sanderson: 'Sermon 3 Ad Magistratum', *Sermons Preached*, 1627 edn, pp.163, 164.
15 Lancelot Andrewes: *Ninety-six Sermons*, 'Sermon Preached at St. Maries Hospital, 1588', 1635 edn, p.B1.
16 Lancelot Andrewes: *Ninety-six Sermons*, 'Sermons of the Gowries – Sermon Preached before the Kings Majestie at Burleigh neere Okeham on the 5th of August, 1616', 1635 edn, p.847.
17 Lancelot Andrewes: *Ninety-six Sermons*, 'Sermon Preached at the Opening of the Parliament 1621', 1635 edn, p.B151.
18 Ibid., p.151.
19 Ibid., p.153.
20 Francis Mason: *Authoritie of the Church in Making Canons and Constitutions, etc.*, 1607 edn, pp.3, 4, 5 (4 and 5 are wrongly numbered 12 and 13).
21 Ibid.
22 Ibid.
23 Ibid., p.5 (wrongly numbered 13).
24 Ibid.
25 Ibid.
26 Ibid.
27 Ibid., pp.5 (wrongly numbered 13) and 6.
28 Ibid., pp.8, 9 (wrongly numbered 16, 17).
29 Lancelot Andrewes: *Ninety-six Sermons*, 'Sermon Preached at St. Maries Hospital, 1588', 1635 edn, pp.B20, B16; cf. p.B22.
30 I Corinthians 14:41.

Chapter 8

Order, Uniformity, Preaching and Sacraments

In the sermons and writings of most of the Caroline Divines, doctrine, the worship of the Church and the morality required of Christians, are inextricably interwoven. There seems to be no concept of Christian Ethics or Moral Theology being in a department of its own, as though it could be arrived at and studied and practised in isolation from all other considerations of the Christian faith. The same is true of Liturgy and Doctrine. These are not regarded as subjects which can be entered into, in, by and for themselves. The underlying binding factor is the concept of order – again, that order which God eternally is in His own internal relations, and the nature of the order of the created sphere and its relation to the Divine order. Liturgy and Moral Theology are but particular expressions of a practical nature evoked by that concept of order. Doctrine, therefore, as that which is man's obedient interpretation of order, is primary to Liturgy and Moral Theology, in that it sets out the concepts of order to which these two respond visibly and actively in their particular ways. They are the inseparable and boon companions of Doctrine, and, indeed, are the practical handmaids of it. Order is expressed, as man's 'Amen' to God's decree of order, in all Christian activity, in the intellectual field, in matters of behaviour and conduct, and in worship.

That important exponent of uniformity, Archbishop William Laud has undoubtedly suffered an undeserved reputation. The view of some historians[1] is that he imposed a strict and stern uniformity upon the Church to the exclusion of all other possibilities of worship and practice. A reading of the *Relation of the Conference* would soon disabuse people of that fallacious notion. His *Private Prayers*, too, soon dispel this. For both reveal in fact a generous mind – something which was common to all the great names of the 'Laudian' school. It simply is not true that Laud imposed upon the Church the liturgical equivalent of what Edward Thomas, the poet, has used to describe Laud's Statutes for the University of Oxford – 'A many-tailed whip'.[2] Laud, in common with most of his 'Laudian' contemporaries, was well aware of the Patristic dictum by St Cyprian that 'the coat, though seamless, has many colours',[3] and this was his, and their, view of the Church.

What Laud was concerned with was the underlying concept of order to which the Christian Church witnessed, and which it was called to express in its own practice. This did not mean a drab sameness of practice and a refusal to allow individual emphases. Behind this lies the distinction between *essentials* and *inessentials*, so characteristic of 'classical' Anglicanism. On essentials of the faith there could be no dispute and no variety, but on inessentials, shades of opinion and practice were permissible. The main objective of uniformity was to set out the unchangeable truth and the order expressed in that. There is therefore an insistence on collective obedience yet also, hand in hand, individual insight. Provided the truth was not changed in its various expressions in the Church, uniformity was deemed to be upholden.

Laud sets out his arguments in *The Relation of the Conference*, emphasizing first scripture and tradition. Laud has much to say in the preface about the nature of truth. He speaks of the Jesuit Fisher making

> a great Protestation of seeking the *truth* only, and that for it selfe. And certainly, *truth*, especially in *religion* is so to be sought, or not to be found.[4]

Laud is concerned with truth for truth's sake – truth which speaks for itself, and truth which is to be objectively perceived. It is not, he warns, to be sought with the preconception of any bias, Roman or otherwise. In the margin of the Preface, he notes that

> One of these *biasses* is an Aversion from all such Truth as fittes not our ends. . . . And 'tis an easie Transition, from a man that is *averse* from, to become *adverse* to the Truth.[5]

Laud is emphasizing the freedom, majesty and authority of the truth, which confronts the mind, and to which the mind must be disciplined in obedience to the nature and autonomy of that truth. The perception of Christian truth through and in and by scripture and the tradition of the Church of the first five centuries, is a matter of the constant reformation of the mind to the truth so disclosing itself. In speaking of the Church of England's position *vis-à-vis* both Rome and the Puritan tendency, Laud remarks that :

> while the one faction cryes up the *church* above the *scripture*: and the other the *scripture* to the neglect and Contempt of the *church*, which the *scripture* it selfe teaches men both to honour, and obey: They have so farre endangered the *beliefe* of the One, and the *authority* of the Other, as that neither has its *due* from a great part of Men. Whereas according to *Christ's institution*, The *scripture*, where 'tis plaine, should guide the *church*, And the *church*, where there's Doubt or Difficulty, should expound the *scripture*; Yet so, as neither the *scripture* should be forced, nor the Church so bound up, as that upon Just and farther Evidence, Shee may not revise that which in any Case hath slipt by Her.[6]

He is criticizing on the one hand the then Roman view of tradition, which means the magisterial authority of the Church (not just of the first five centuries, but of all time) to determine truth, in such a way that scripture is subordinate to the Church, and on the other, the Puritan view which dismisses all tradition and relies on individual interpretation. On the one hand the final authority is the collective mind of Rome, and on the other final authority resides in the supposed autonomy of the individual to perceive and judge. In both instances, human reason becomes the absolute arbiter of the truth, and the truth subservient and subordinate to the mind.

The Caroline position, which Laud later elaborates in the *Conference*, is that Christian truth is a matter of scripture, tradition (that is the direction of the Ecumenical Councils of the undivided Church – which Councils are thereby truly ecumenical, and not just Roman) and reason. But not these three as separate and independent categories. The Caroline emphasis is on scripture, tradition and reason in their relation one to another. Scripture and tradition have a common *scope*, and that is Christ Himself. All Scripture points paradigmatically to Christ as its inner content, nature and goal. This is purely Athanasian in its understanding and application. Likewise, tradition, particularly in the historic Creeds of the Church, distils scripture, so that its essential essence becomes available, and is used as the catalyst to interpret scripture according to its scopic nature. Christ Himself, as Eternal Truth made flesh, is therefore the common *scope* of scripture and tradition, and this is what binds them inseparably but unconfusedly together.

Reason, the third factor, however, falls into a slightly different category, yet is bound in the same way to scripture and tradition, as has already been stated. These inform the mind, and the mind must follow the pattern which truth takes to reveal itself through these. In other words reason must be obedient to the nature and way of truth as declared in scripture and through the Church's tradition. Reason operates by letting the truth declare itself, and not by imposing its own ideas upon it. As such, the mind is the servant of scripture and tradition, not the master, and is bound to them by the *scope* common to each – Christ as Self-giving Truth. Laud does not make the mistake of limiting the truth, and the rational perception of the truth, to the Church of England. He is concerned with the majesty of the truth, which cannot in any way be confined.

He likens both Romanists and Puritans to the Donatists, who believed themselves to be the only ones whom Christ would judge as having true faith, and he warns against any such tendencies:

> The *Catholike Church* of Christ is neither *Rome*, nor a *conventicle*. Out of *that* there's no Salvation, I easily confess it. But out of *Rome* there is, and out of a *conventicle*, too; *salvation* is not shut up into such a *narrow conclave*. In this ensuing Discourse therefore I have endeavour'd to lay open those *wider-gates* of the *Catholike Church*, confined to no *age*, *time*, or *place*; Nor knowing any *bounds, but that faith, which was once* (and but once for all) *deliver'd to the saints, S.jude 3*. And in my pursuite of this way, I have searched after, and deliver'd with a single heart, that *truth* which I professe. In the publishing whereof, I have obeyed *your majesty*, discharg'd my *duty*, to my power, to the *Church of England, given account of the hope that is in me*; And so testified to the world that *faith* in which I have lived, and by God's blessing and favour purpose to dye.[7]

Such is the breadth of truth. But at the same time, that Truth is to be visibly demonstrated. It is to be made visible as well as audible. Here Laud deals with the liturgy and worship of the Church, and the question of uniformity. This uniformity is no imposing of a narrow and ungenerous practice on the Church. Worship, too, has that self-same scope as scripture, tradition and reason. The liturgy is the witness to the nature of that scope, Christ Himself. True theology is expressed in decency of worship.

> And this I have observed: That no One thing hath made *conscientious men* more wavering in their owne mindes, or more apt, and easie to be drawne aside from the sincerity of *religion professed in the Church of England*, then the Want of *uniforme* and *decent order* in too many Churches of the *kingdome*. . . 'Tis true, the *inward worship* of the Heart, is

the *great service of God*, and no Service acceptable without it: But the *externall worship of God* in his Church is the *great witnesse* to the World, that Our heart stands right in that *service of God*. Take this away, or bring it into Contempt, and *what light is there left to shine before men, that they may see our devotion, and glorify our father which is in heaven?* And to deale clearely with *your majesty*, These *thoughts* are they, and no other, which have made me labour so much, as I have done, for *decency* and an Orderly settlement of the *externall worship of God in the Church*. For of that which is *inward* there can be no *witnesse* among men, nor no *example* for men. Now no Externall Action in the world can be *uniforme* without some *ceremonies*. And these in *religion*, the *ancienter* they bee, the better, so they may fit *time* and *place*. *Too many* Over-burden the *service* of *God*; and *too* few leave it naked. And scarce any Thing hath hurt *religion* more in these broken Times, then an Opinion in too many men, That because *Rome* had thrust some Unneccessary, and many Superstitious Ceremonies upon the Church, therefore the *reformation* must have none at all; not considering therewhile, That *ceremonies* are the *hedge* that fence the *substance of religion* from all the Indignities, which *prophanenesse* and *sacriledge* too Commonly put upon it.[8]

Here the Caroline distinction between essentials and inessentials in the matter of the faith, is implicit, in Laud's note of things 'Unneccessary'. That which is necessary and essential, both in doctrine and in worship, is the clear statement of Christological Truth. Opinions may be held, and some practices indeed permitted, concerning inessentials. But these are not to be elevated to dogmas, and expression of them laid as mandatory on the worship of the Church. Reason and Liturgy together serve Scripture and Tradition, in making the Word audible and visible, yet leaving that truth in all its autonomous majesty and freedom, as that Lord, whom human words and actions can only, even in their obedience, inadequately serve. It is faithful adherence to the truth which marks the antiquity and continuity of the Church. It is not, as in Rome's case the age-long perpetuation of error regarding the truth – error embedded for such a span that it has come to be the standard of judgment:

They which speake for the *truth*, though it be farre *older*, are ordinarily challenged for the Bringers in of *new opinions*. And there is no *greater absurdity* stirring this day in *christendome*, then that the *reformation of an old and corrupted church*, will we, nill wee, must be taken for the *building of a new*. And were this not so, we should never be troubled with that idle and impertinent *question* of theirs: *where was your church before* Luther? For it was just there, where their's is now. *One*, and the *same* Church still, no doubt of that. One in *substance*, but not one in *condition of state and purity*; Their part of the same Church remaining *in corruption*: and Our part of the same Church under *reformation*. The same *naaman*, and he a *syrian* still, but *leprous* with them, and *cleansed* with us; The same man still.[9]

The question of uniformity loomed large in the conscious efforts of the Caroline Divines to settle and ground the Church firmly as the servant of truth, essentials and inessentials considered. But it is a uniformity which springs naturally out of a consideration of the nature of the Truth of God as it is in Christ. Uniformity in the Church's life is that which corresponds to the nature of the truth in that it faithfully and appropriately to the truth displays the truth visibly. It is not a devised plan into which the Truth has to be squeezed irrespective of its nature. The Church is reformed by reference to that truth in Christ, against which it must be constantly tested. And it is by the testing of that same referring that liturgy and worship is deemed seemly and appropriate. This is also true of orders of ministry in their relation to that Truth.

Laud's observations on the Episcopate in the *Conference*, demonstrate the zeal for Truth and Order as primary, and how all things must serve that secondary but necessarily, if they are deemed to be 'valid'. He points out that the Episcopate is by no 'bare succession'. The laying on of hands is but the sign of the transmission of 'verity of doctrine', and without the latter then the succession is useless and those so appointed are 'strangers' to the true succession, which, of basic necessity, concerns the truth of Christian doctrine.

> Succession, as it is a Note of the true church, is neither a Succession in place only, nor of Persons only, but it must be of true and sound Doctrine also . . . Sound Doctrine is indivisible from true and Lawfull Succession.[10]

Holy Orders must express this. Laud also remarks in the Preface that ceremonies are 'the hedge that fence the substance of religion'.[11] Liturgy, too, must express Truth.

Francis Mason in *The Authoritie of the Church* likewise, speaks of ceremonies and liturgy in the same manner:

> Ceremonies depend upon the doctrine, especially of the free grace of God and the merits of Christ. So long as this doctrine is preserved pure, the ceremony is pure; when the doctrine declineth, the ceremonie is perverted. . . . When the doctrine was corrupted, no manner if the ceremonie was defiled.[12]

All worship and liturgical observance gathers round, and is the expression of, the essential which is the truth. Indeed, when the Carolines speak of *essentials* in all matters other than the truth itself, they are doing so by way of second-hand usage. There is, strictly speaking, in their view but one essential, and that is the truth which is Christ and the order which that truth demands by its very nature. That truth and that order are the essential business of liturgy and worship. There may be permitted inessentials besides the essentials in liturgy and worship, which do not contradict or cloak the nature of truth and order, but are convenient to serve truth and order in a particular place for a particular time.

All things were to be done decently and in order. There is a great awareness in the Divines of the period that worship is undertaken at the point where heaven is bent down to earth and earth stretched up to heaven. It is the worship of the whole Church, militant here in earth, and triumphant in the heavenly places, gathered round the victorious Christ, with which they were concerned. Reverence, dignity, solemnity and great gladness are thus the characteristics of worship. All the God-given skills of art and craft and heart and mind are to be employed in this, the highest activity of man.

Francis Mason speaks eloquently of the worship of the Church and its relation to God's Order. Worship must be undertaken:

> First, honestly, that is, (as was before declared) in decent sort, with relation to the glorie of God, and the edification of the Church, without scandall. Secondly, according to

order, for God is the God of order, and not of confusion. Now if all things in the Church must be done decently, then nothing may be established which is base or beggerly: The ceremonies of the Church though they cannot alwaies be costly, yet they must alwaies be comely. . . . If. all. things must be one to the glory of God, then nothing may be established in superstitious or idolatrous maner, for that were repugnant to the glorie of his majestie; then nothing must be established contrarie to the Scripture, for that were repugnant to the glorie of his wisedome; then things indifferent must be established as indifferent, not as meritorious or satisfactorie, not as necessary to divine worship, to justification or salvation; for this were repugnant to the glorie of his grace. If all things must bee done to edification, then the ceremonies of the Church must not be darke, but so cleereley set foorth, that every man may know what they meane, and to what use they serve. . . . If all things must bee done in order . . . that no marvell, seeing the whole fabricke of the World, both the celestiall orbes and the globe of elements are framed and upholden by an order. . . . Order proceedeth from the throne of the Almightie, it is the beautie of nature, the ornament of Arte, the harmonie of the world. Now shall all things be in order, and the Church of God onely without order? God forbid. The Church is a Garden inclosed, and a garden must be in order.[13]

Here there is linked the eternal order which God is in Himself, the order of creation contingent to and from Him, proceeding from His throne and giving creation its own beauty and identity, and Church order. It is by Church order that thanksgiving and glory is returned to God on behalf of all creation, and the Word and Order of God proclaimed and set forth. It is significant, too, that Mason uses the symbol of the garden for Church order. This is constantly used in the period to designate that order, harmony and peace which God has eternally decreed for all creation in Christ. The usual use of this symbol is to describe the estate of man in the creative intent of God in Eden, and man's re-creation in the sufferings of Christ as the Passion intensifies from Gethsemane onwards, fulfilled in the Garden of the Resurrection.

But the unitary view of order is the emphasis here. Mason penetrates to the heart of the matter. He is speaking of his text, I Corinthians, 14:40, 'Let all things be done honestly and by order':

And as all things must be decent and honest before God and men, so it is required in the second place, that all things be done according to order. Which order, requireth authority with godly wisedome in the publike disposer, and cheerfull, obedience with gracious humilitie in such as are subject to those publike constitutions. So this text is a Canon of Canons for all such Church government, and all Ecclesiastical Canons must be cast in this moulde: Indeed it is a golden Canon or rule whereby all Christian Churches must be ruled, an exsquisite touchstone whereat all ceremonies must be tried: the beame of the Sanctuarie whereupon all Church orders and constitutions must be weighed and ballanced: And therefore let us search a little deeper, into this golden mine: For the better understanding whereof, it must bee observed, that some things are necessarie, and some things indifferent [that is, essential and inessential].[14]

Mason concludes this part of the extended sermon:

Things necessarie God hath reserved to Himselfe, no men, no Angels have authoritie to alter them: but things indifferent being of a variable nature, are referred to the discretion of the Church, as may appeere by the words of my text. Wherein the spirit speaking to the Churches, willeth all things to be done after a good maner: not defining what manner, but reffering all to the discretion of the Church, so things be ordered in an honest and decent maner.[15]

Not only Church order in its liturgical and administrative aspects, but even the ordering of the building itself is meant to serve to the witnessing of Divine and Divinely appointed order. George Herbert in his *Priest to the Temple* has these general instructions to offer:

The Country Parson hath a special care of his Church, that all things there be decent, and befitting his Name by which it is called. Therefore, First he takes order, that all things be in good repair; as walls plaistered, windows glazed, floor paved, seats whole, firm and uniform, especially that the Pulpit, and Desk, and Communion Table, and Font be as they ought, for those great duties that are performed in them . . . as following the Apostles two great and admirable Rules in things of this nature: The first whereof is, Let all things be done decently, and in order; The second, Let all things be done to edification, I Cor.14. For these two rules comprize and include the double Object of our duty, God and our neighbour. So that they excellently score out the way, and fully and exactly contain, even in external and indifferent things, what course is to be taken.[16]

Order and decency have their language – they point beyond themselves to the virtues and qualities of God's order. Thus Herbert again in one of his poems, 'The Church Floor'

Mark you the floor? that square and speckled stone
Which looks so firm and strong,
        Is *patience*:
And th'other, black and grave, wherewith each one
Is checkered all along,
        humility:
The gentle rising, which on either hand
Leads to the Choir above,
        Is *confidence*;
But the sweet cement, which in one sure band
Ties the whole frame, is *love*
        And *charity*.[17]

And the same on 'The Church Windows':

    But when thou dost anneal in glass thy story
    Making thy life to shine within
The holy Preachers – then the light and glory
    More reverend grows, and more doth win,
Which else shows waterish, bleak and thin.
Doctrine and life, colours and light, in one
When they combine and mingle, bring
A strong regard and awe; but speech alone
Doth vanish like a flaring thing,
And in the ear, not conscience, ring.[18]

An analysis of Herbert's works show that these are a poetic way of expressing Caroline theology. He is entirely concerned with this concept of order, and if he stresses the art and craft and skill of man, and the emotions so evoked, he is not entering the realms of a nebulous mysticism, but is still entirely within the context of rational order. He has the ability to understand the orderly significance of ordinary things – seeing them as pointing beyond themselves to where their true significance lies in that which gave them being and form, the eternal Truth of God Himself. This is how images and statues and all that adorned churches were regarded.

This is very far removed from the iconoclasm of the extreme Puritan. Such iconoclasm was born out of that attitude which read immediate truth out of the words of Scripture. For the Puritan, the very words themselves were that divine truth – all dualistic thought eventually confusing the things it separated – God and creation, the eternal and the temporal – in a compensating, artificial framework of its own devising, to bridge the gap. Thus, for the extreme Puritan, all images were superstitious. They were the thing pointed to. This is also another curious contradiction in dualistic thought, that it is highly selective in its approach, even to the extent of contradicting itself. They could not see the paradigmatic nature of words and images, nor could they see that in rejecting images as superstition, in thinking that the image was confused with that which it images, they were passing judgment on their own scriptural fundamentalism. All words, and images beautifying churches and teaching people visually, were pointers to that One who is Himself the Word, and is that which He images as the true Image of God, Christ Himself, and the truths attendant on Christ.

Robert Sanderson's 'Second Sermon to the Clergy, At a visitation at Boston, Lincolnshire, on the 24. April, 1611', deals in part with this very point. His text was Romans, 3:8, 'And not rather, (as we be slanderously reported, and as some affirme that we say,) Let us do evill, that good may come: whose damnation is just.' He was preaching, as Archdeacon, in that part of the country noted for its Puritan sympathies, and these sympathies had lately expressed themselves in typical iconoclastic action. He uses the example of the state of the Church in which the Clergy were gathered for this Archidiaconal Visitation. He divides the 'doing of evil' of his text into 'sins of commission and sins of omission'. He has an example of sins of commission at hand. This is worthy of a lengthy quotation for it reveals the mind and reasoning of one confronted with the work of iconoclasm and how he deals with an assessment of the mentality behind such a work. The balanced and reasoned temper of his argument in which he contains both anger and sorrow, should be noted.

> The sinne of Commission wherein I would instance, is indeed a sinne beyond Commission: it is the usurping of the Magistrates Office without a Commission. The Question is; whether the zealous intention of a good end may not warrant it good, or at least excuse it from being evill, and a sinne? I need not frame a Case for the illustration of this instance: the inconsiderate forwardnes of some hath made it to my hand. You may read it in the disfigured windowes and wals of this Church: Pictures, and Statua's, and Images; and for their sakes the windowes and walles wherin they stood, have been heretofore, and of late pulled downe, and broken in pieces and defaced: without the Command, or so much as

leave of those who have power to reforme things amisse in that kind. Charitie bindeth us to thinke the best of those that have done it: that is, that they did it out of a forward (though mis-governed) zeale; intending therein Gods glory in the farther suppression of Idolatry, by taking away these (as they supposed) likely occasions of it. Now in such a case as this, the Question is, whether the intention of such an end, can justifie such a deed? And the fact of Phinehes, Numb.25. (who for a much like end, for the staying of the people from Idolatrie, executed vengeance upon Zimri & Coshi, being but a private man, and no Magistrate; seemeth to make for it.

But my Text ruleth it otherwise. If it be evill; it is not to be done, no not for the preventing of Idolatry. I passe by some considerations otherwise of good moment; as namely first, whether Statua's and Pictures may not be permitted in Christian Churches, for the adorning of God's House, and for civill and historicall uses, not only lawfully and decently, but even profitably? I must confesse, I have never yet heard substantiall reason given, why they might not: at the least, so long as there is no apparent danger of superstition. And secondly, whether things either in their first erection, or by succeeding abuse superstitious, may not bee profitably continued, if the Superstition be abolished? Otherwise, not Pictures only, and Crosses, and Images; but most of our Hospitals, and Schooles, and Colledges, and Churches too must downe: and so the hatred of Idolatrie should but Usher in licentious Sacriledge, contrary to that passage of our Apostle in the next Chapter before this, Thou that abhorrest Idols, committeth thou Sacriledge? And thirdly, whether these forward ones have not bewrayed somewhat their owne selfe-guiltinesse in this Act, at least for the manner of it, in doing it secretly, and in the dark? A man should not dare to do that, which he would not willingly either bee seene when it is a doing, or owne, being done. To passe by these; consider no more but this one thing onely, into what dangerous and unsufferable absurdities a man might run, if hee should but follow these mens grounds. Erantinullus terminus: Errour knoweth no stay, and a false Principle once received, multiplieth into a thousand absurd conclusions. It is good for men to goe upon sure grounds, else they may runne and wander in infinitum. A little errour at the first, if there bee way given to it, will increase beyond beliefe; as a small sparke may fire a large City, and a cloud no bigger than a mans hand, in short space overspread the face of the whole Heavens. For grant, for the suppression of Idolatrie, in case the Magistrate will not doe his office, that it is lawfull for a private man to take upon him to reforme what he thinketh amisse, and to doe the part and Office of a Magistrate (which must needs have been their ground, if they had any, for this action:) there can be no sufficient cause given, why by the same reason, and upon the same grounds, a private man may not take upon him to establish Lawes, raise Powers, administer Justice, execute Malefactors, or doe any other thing the Magistrate should doe; in case the Magistrate slacke to do his duty in any of the premises. Which if it were once granted (as granted it must bee, if these mens fact be justifiable;) every wise man seeth, the end could bee no other but vast Anarchie and confusion both in Church and Commonweale: whereupon must unavoidably follow the speedy subversion both of Religion and State.[19]

Here was the Anglican position regarding images, statues, pictures and the general adornment of churches. Such things were not to be of superstitious regard. The truth did not reside in these things in and by themselves. They too, in their proper regard, were paradigmatic. They pointed away from themselves, in their form, their beauty, their art and craft, to that truth to which they were the witnesses. For that they were to be treasured and revered. Craftsman's skill and music's pleasure all combined to point to that Holiness which is God's alone. They were the work of men's minds and hands, through God given skills, and as such, in the use to which they had been put, and for which they had been created, were truly pious. Such barbaric iconoclasm, which smashed such things in pieces, and the manner in which this was done, struck, as Sanderson saw, at the very roots of truth itself and at the order and harmony of human existence dependent on that truth.

The concept of holiness and the reverence which this called forth was the well-spring of the Caroline attitude to worship, too. As 'holiness becometh the house of God',[20] so reverence in the worship of that God was paramount. All things were to be done to the glory and honour of God, and the edification of the people in the things of God. Regard to Divine order and Divinely appointed order, as revealed in Christ, was the first principle, nothing more, nothing less. If that was the first principle, and no other consideration was allowed to intrude, then all else would fall into place, and all other by-products of worship would follow on naturally.

The weight of things done decently and in order was laid, and the greatest care was taken, in the matter of the sermon and of the celebration and administration of the Sacraments. Andrewes's sermons are an outstanding example of careful and scrupulous preparation. His scholarly exegesis of his texts, on the basis of Hebrew or Greek, his great skill in languages, his critical faculties and his oratorical abilities, his sense of occasion and the need to feed the minds of the people, are all in abundant evidence. But he does not stand alone in recognizing the importance of the instruction of the sermon. His famed contemporaries, according to their various gifts, were all in the same mould, and they were all concerned that preaching should be given its due place. If the Carolines did not tolerate slovenliness in ceremonial, they equally did not care for it in the matter of preaching.

The sermon is, in Andrewes's view, a sacramental institution. It is a matter of not only being a hearer of the Word, but a doer of the Word. Andrewes preached in 1607 on this text from the 'Epistle General of St James, 1:22'.[21] He points out that the text stresses the necessity of hearing the word. The Apostle does not take away the necessity of hearing for the sake of doing. Before one can do anything, what to do must be made clear. It is a matter of not being a hearer *only*. Preaching itself, as a sacramental institution, gathers round that Sacrament of Godliness which is the manifesting of the Word in the Flesh. Here Andrewes uses the word 'Godliness' in its proper and prime meaning, that is, 'God-ness', the essential Being of God the Eternal Son in the Flesh. And so the Sacrament of Godliness refers in the first instance to Christ's Incarnation. Preaching follows the pattern of the Incarnation, and points to that Incarnate Christ, who is the Scope of all preaching. In the second instance it refers, derivatively, to the status of the faithful hearer and doer of the Word, who then may be described as 'Godly'.

In 'Sermon 10 Of the Sending of the Holy Ghost, preached before the Kings Majestie at Haly-rud House, in Edinburgh, on the 8. of June, 1617, being Whitsunday', he has some advice for all preachers regarding the order and authority of the sermon. This sermon was preached on the text of Luke, 4:18,19 – which is the text from Isaiah which Christ took for His first sermon at Nazareth. Here then is a model sermon.

> Christ . . . tooke a Text, to teach us thereby, to doe the like. To keepe us within; not to flie out, or preach much, either without, or besides the booke.[22]

All preaching is to be on a text from the Bible. No extraneous authorities are allowed. Preaching is therefore firmly grounded, and the text is itself the bounds or horizon of the particular sermon.

Andrewes, like all his 'Laudian' contemporaries, emphasizes the primacy of the scriptures in the matter of the knowledge of God. Any thought of preaching on something outwith scripture was entirely abhorrent to them. The Scriptures were the Royal Law, the Lively Oracles, of God. They were the mirror of Christ, and as such were to be looked into as the source of the light of that knowledge of God in the face of Jesus Christ. The gaze was not to be averted elsewhere for inspiration. That would have been disorder in the theological method, and but the projection of man's fancy into a supposed knowledge of God. He speaks of the necessity of Scripture:

> What that necessity is He tels us, when He cals it the *key of knowledge*. That there is a door shut; this is the *key*: no opening, no entrance without it; none at all. . . . For it should be *the Word*, we *heare*. Words we heare every foot: but I dare not say, *the word*, alwayes. Much *chaffe* is sowne, in stead of *right graine*. Many a *dry stick ingrafted*, in stead of a *Siene* with life and sap in it.[23]

In this sermon on James 1:22, this is how Andrewes sees the place and nature of preaching:

> To bee a *Doer* of the *Word*, is (as Saint *Gregory* saith well) *Convertere Scripturas in operas*, To *change* the *Word* which is audible, into a *Worke* which is visible: the *Word* which is *transient*, into a *Worke* which is *permanent*.
>
> Or rather, not to change it, but (as Saint *Augustine* saith) *Accedat ad verbum*, unto the *word*, that we *heare*, let there be joyned the *Element* of the *Worke* (that is) some reall *Elementall deed* . . . and so shall you have the great Mysterie or *Sacrament of Godlinesse*. For indeed, *Godlinesse* is as a *Sacrament*: hath not onely the Mysterie, to be knowne, but the exercise to be done, not the *Word* to be heard, but the *worke* also to be performed: or else, if it be not a *Sacrament*, it is not true *godlinesse*.
>
> Which very *Sacrament of godlinesse* is there said to be the *manifesting of the Word in the flesh*: which it selfe is lively expressed by us, when we are *doers* of the *Word*; as it is well gathered out of our *Saviour Christ's* speech, to them which interrupted Him in His *Sermon*, and told him, his *mother was without*: Who is my mother (saith He?) *These* here, *that heare and doe my words, are my mother*: They *travell* [travail] *of me till I am fashioned in them. Hearing*, they receive the *immortall seed of the Word*; by a firm purpose of doing, they *conceive*, by a *longing desire*, they *quicken*; by an *earnest endeavour*, they *travell* with it; and when the *Worke* is wrought, *Verbum caro factum est*, they have *incarnate the word*. Therefore to the womans acclamation, *Blessed bee the wombe that bear thee*; true (saith *Christ*) but that blessing can extend onely to one, and to no more; I will tell you, how you may be blessed too; *Blessed are they, that so incarnate the written word by doing it*, as the *Blessed Virgin* gave *flesh*, to the *eternall word*, by *bearing it*.[24]

Here the preaching of the Word is directly linked to the incarnation of the Word, the order of preaching being contingent on the dispensation of God in the Incarnation. Although the sermon is the making of the Word audible, it is not divorced from the making of the Word visible. This latter is the sacraments primarily, and certainly for Andrewes, preaching and sacrament are the two indispensable sides of the one dispensation. But here the making of the Word visible is the effect which the sermon has on those who hear aright. The Word is made visible in the good works which result from their faithful hearing of the Word.

Here is a 'high' doctrine of preaching indeed. It is firmly rooted and grounded in the fact and process of the incarnation. The Word is both audible to the ear and visible to the eye. In the matter of the Word made visible, that is in the sacraments, Andrewes shows the same reverence and regard. As to the number of the sacraments, Andrewes is positive of the nature and identity of baptism and the Eucharist, but seems to leave open and unanswered the question as to Orders, etc., being sacraments. He speaks of baptism and the Eucharist in 'Sermon 13 of the Sending of the Holy Ghost':

> These are (not *two* of the *Sacraments*; so there might be more, but) the *twin-Sacraments* of the Church. So, but *two* of that kind; *two famous memorialls* left us.[25]

Again in 'Sermon 9 of the Sending of the Holy Ghost', in speaking of the bestowing of Orders in the Church by the breathing of Christ upon His assembled Apostles after His Resurrection, he says:

> Which act is here performed, somewhat after the manner of a *Sacrament*. For here is an outward Ceremony (of *breathing*) *instar elementi*; and here is a *Word* comming to it, *receive ye the Holy Ghost*. That some have therefore yeelded to give that name or title [Sacrament] to *Holy Orders*. As (indeed) the word [*Sacrament*] hath been sometime drawne out wider, and so *Orders* taken in: and other some, plucked in narrower, and so they left out; as it hath pleased both the old and the latter Writers. And, if the Grace here given had been *gratum faciens* (as, in a *Sacrament*, it should:) and not (as it is) *gratis data*, but in *office* or function: And againe, if the outward *Ceremony of breathing* had not been changed (as it hath plainely) it had been somewhat. But, being changed after into *laying on of hands*, it may well be questioned. For we all agree, there is no Sacrament but of Christs owne *institution*: and that, neither *matter* nor *form*, He hath *instituted*, may be changed.[26]

Again, however, in 'Sermon 6 of the Sending of the Holy Ghost',[27] Andrewes notes that the Schoolmen, the theologians of the middle ages, numbered seven sacraments, as the seven seals.

This then is not a clear-cut issue. That Andrewes emphasizes the two Dominical Sacraments is without dispute. As to the others, if sacraments they be, he leaves that open to question. It would appear to be a permissible opinion, but not more than such, to regard them as Sacraments. The important thing is to understand the nature of the two Dominical Sacraments.

The context of the Eucharist is the life of men in its relation to the life of the Triune God. In speaking of the sending of the Holy Spirit, he says in 'Sermon 7 of the Sending of the Holy Ghost':

> The *end* now, why all this. *Hominibus*, for *men*, that God *may dwell among men*, God, that is the whole *Trinitie*, by this *Person* of it [the Holy Spirit] . . . It is for love, even . . . for His *love* of *men*, that makes Him desire thus to *dwell* with us.[28]

Christ dwells with us, in and by and through and with the Holy Spirit. Throughout his sermons on the Holy Spirit, Andrewes emphasizes the fact that the Spirit is the Spirit of the Word. It is the role of the Holy Spirit to take the things of Christ, even Christ Himself, and apply them to men. The Spirit is therefore anchored in the Word, and cannot be separated from Him. Andrewes continues with the dwelling of Christ and the Holy Spirit:

> What shall we doe then? Shall we not yeeld to Him thus much, or rather, thus little? If He have a minde to *dwell in us*, shall we refuse Him? It will be for our benefit: we shall finde a good neighbour of Him. . . .
>
> And, in *us*, He will *dwell*, if the *fruits* of His *Spirit* be found in us. And, of His *fruits*, the very first is *Love*. And the *fruit* is, as the *tree* is. For, He Himselfe is *Love*, the essentiall *Love*, and *Love-knot* of the *undivided Trinitie*.
>
> Now, to work *love* (the undoubted both signe and meanes of His *dwelling*) what better way, or how sooner wrought, than by the *Sacrament of love* . . . when Love descended with both His hands full of *gifts*, for very *love*, to take up His *dwelling* with us?
>
> You shall observe: there ever was and will be, a neere alliance, betweene . . . The *Gifts* He sent, and the *Gifts* He *left* us. He left us the *gifts* of *His* body and *bloud*. His *body broken*, and full of the characters of *love*, all over. His *bloud shed*, every drop whereof is a great drop of *Love*. To those which were sent, these which were left (*love, joy, peace*) have a speciall con-naturall reference, to breed and to maintaine each other. His body, the Spirit of strength; His *bloud*, the *Spirit* of *comfort*. Both, the *Spirit* of *Love*.[29]

It is impossible in Andrewes's view, to separate the earthly elements of bread and wine from that which they convey – the body and blood of Christ. And that which is conveyed bears a special relation to the Holy Spirit. 'Sermon 9 of the Sending of the Holy Ghost':

> And there is no better way of celebrating the Feast of the receiving of the *Holy Ghost*, than so to doe, with receiving the same *body* [that is, Christ's body] which came of it [that is, the Holy Ghost] at His *birth*, and that came from it now at His *rising* againe.
>
> And so *receiving* it, He that *breathed*, and Hee that *was breathed*, both of them vouchsafe to *breathe* into those holy *Mysteries* a divine power and vertue; And make them to us the *bread of life*, and the *Cup of Salvation*, *God* the *Father* also sending His blessing upon them that they may be His blessed meanes of this thrice blessed effect.[30]

The whole awareness here is that the Eucharist is so caught up in the eternal existence of God, in the Incarnate Son and His work, to which is united the sending of the Spirit, that the end and significance of the sacrament is clear. It is the meeting place of earth and heaven, the trysting place of Christ with us:

> Will ye now heare the end of all? By this meanes God shall *dwell with us* (the perfection of this life:) and He dwelling *with us*, we shall *dwell with Him* (the last and highest perfection of the life to come.) For, with whom God *dwelleth* here, they shall dwell with him there, certainly. . . . So, the *Text* comes round about. It began with an *ascension*, and it ends with one: began with *Christs*: ends with ours. *He ascended*, that God *might dwell with us*; that, God *dwelling with us*, we might, in the end, *ascend* and *dwell with God. He went up on high*, that the Spirit might *come downe* to us below; and, that *comming downe*, make us goe the same way, and come to the same place, that He is. *Sent Him downe to us*, to bring us up to *Him*.[31]

Baptism, too, is regarded with all awe and reverence. Andrewes's teaching on baptism makes a basic distinction between the baptism of John the Baptist, and Christian baptism. This is to heighten the fact that we are baptized into Christ, and that through this sacrament, our life stands in a particular relation to His incarnate, dying, risen and ascended existence, and thereby to the life of the eternal, Triune God. The baptism of John stands on the horizon where Law and Gospel, Old Covenant and New Covenant, Israel and the Church, meet. It is God's ordinance which Christ submits to, in order to declare His identity with sinful flesh standing under the judgment of God, and in need of repentance. Thus, the baptism of John to which He submits in His identification to us, merely points to the nature of the baptism of which He Himself speaks which He is to undergo – His own baptism of His incarnation, life, passion and death. His incarnation was a baptism – it was His identification with flesh standing in need under the judgment of God:

> First *baptised* (as I may say) in so many millions of sins, of so many millions of sinners (in so foule a puddle). . . . And so was He *baptised*. And He had *trinam mersionem*: One in *Gethsemane*, One in *Gabbatha*, and a third in *Golgotha*. In *Gethsemane*, in His *sweat of bloud*. In *Gabbatha, in the bloud*, that came from the *scourges* and *thornes*: and in *Golgotha*, that which came from the *nailes* and the *speare*. Specially, the *speare*: There, met the two streames, of *water and bloud*, the true *Jordan*, the bath or *laver*, wherein we are *purged from all our sinnes*. No sinne, of so deepe a die, but this will command, it and fetch it out. This in *Jordan*, here now, [Christ's baptism by John] was but an undertaking of that, then; and in vertue of that, doth all our *water-baptisme* worke. And therefore, are wee *baptised* into it: not into His *water-baptisme*, but into His *Crosse-baptisme*; not into His *baptisme*, but into His death.[32]

Baptism is a making of a new creature – it is re-creation in the Incarnate Word, the Word by whom all things were made, and who, the self-same in the flesh, re-creates all things:

> There is not . . . a childe a day old, but needs . . . the Baptisme of the Church, if it be but for the baptisme, it had in the wombe. [Andrewes is here speaking of the sinful and needy state of each from his or her origin – man standing from his conception in need of the grace of God]. Let the people then be baptised in Gods name: good and bad, men and children and all.[33]

Baptism is only to be administered once. To repeat baptism is to scorn the grace of God, and is to be regarded as a heinous sin.

As Baptism is once, and only once administered, so we need strengthening in that new creaturehood in Christ with which we are clothed at that Sacrament. For this reason, the Communion of Christ's Body and Blood is instituted and given. Andrewes speaks of the difference between the two Dominical Sacraments:

> Onely this difference betweene them. . . . That, where the one *Seale*, (the *Seale of Baptisme*) can be set to but once, and never repeated more; this other should supply the defect thereof, as whereby, if we have not preserved the former figure *entire and whole* [that is, if we have not lived up constantly and daily to our Baptism], we might be (as it were) *new signed* over againe. And that, not once alone, and no more; but, that it should be *iterable* . . . God therein providing for our frailenesse.[34]

Moral Theology was not regarded as a department in its own right. It was the expression of doctrine, and as such, the practical expression of that order which God has re-created in Jesus Christ. In the sacraments above all, man was given to be incorporated into that new humanity in Christ – God's humanity – and to taste the powers of the age to come which is a present reality in Christ, in whom is recapitulate the new creation. By preaching and through the sacraments, man was both informed and strengthened in that order, and finds his true estate, vocation, dignity and responsibility, there – 'God . . . providing for our frailenesse'. That is the sum and total of Caroline Moral Theology. The joyous awe before the God of order, love and grace, Who had drawn man into communion with Himself in Christ, and set Him in Christ in the heavenly places, called forth that reverence and beauty of holiness which characterized seventeenth-century appreciation of and obedience to the things of eternal truth, which by grace, they claimed, their hands handled, their eyes saw and their ears heard.

Notes

1 Cf. C. Hill: *Change and Continuity in seventeenth Century England*, 1979; L. Stone: *The Causes of the English Revolution, 1529–1642*, 1972.
2 Edward Thomas: *Oxford*, Hutchinson, re-published 1983, p.51.
3 Cyprian: *De Catholicae Ecclesiae Unitate*, 7.
4 William Laud: *Relation of the Conference*, 1639 edn, 2nd page (without number) of Preface.
5 Ibid.
6 Ibid., 17th, 18th pages (without numbers) of Preface.
7 Ibid., 21st, 22nd pages (without numbers) of Preface.
8 Ibid., 18th–20th pages (without numbers) of Preface.
9 Ibid., 16th page (without number) of Preface.
10 Ibid., pp.383, 384.
11 Ibid., 20th page (without number) of Preface.
12 Francis Mason: *Authoritie of the Church in Making Canons and Constitutions, etc.*, 1607 edn, p.52.
13 Ibid., p.9 (wrongly numbered 17), p.11.
14 Ibid., p.4 (wrongly numbered 12).
15 Ibid., p.8 (wrongly numbered 16).
16 George Herbert: *Priest to the Temple*, 1701 edn, pp.47ff.
17 Quoted by A.L.Rowse: *Reflections on the Puritan Revolution*, 1986, p.54.
18 Ibid., p.55.
19 Robert Sanderson: *Sermons Preached*, 1627 edn, pp.50ff.
20 Cf. Psalm 93:5
21 Lancelot Andrewes: *Ninety-six Sermons*, 'Sermon of the Doing of the Word', 1635 edn, pp.B129ff.
22 Lancelot Andrewes: *Ninety-six Sermons*, 'Sermon 10 of the Sending of the Holy Ghost', 1635 edn, p.698.
23 Lancelot Andrewes: *Ninety-six Sermons*, 'Sermon of the Doing of the Word', 1635 edn, pp.B132, B134.
24 Ibid., pp.B136–B137.
25 Lancelot Andrewes: *Ninety-six Sermons*, 'Sermon 13 of the Sending of the Holy Ghost', 1635 edn, p.738.

26   Lancelot Andrewes: *Ninety-six Sermons*, 'Sermon 9 of the Sending of the Holy Ghost',
     1635 edn, p.687.
27   Lancelot Andrewes: *Ninety-six Sermons*, 'Sermon 6 of the Sending of the Holy Ghost',
     1635 edn, p.660.
28   Lancelot Andrewes: *Ninety-six Sermons*, 'Sermon 7 of the Sending of the Holy Ghost',
     1635 edn, p.671.
29   Ibid., pp.671, 672.
30   Lancelot Andrewes: *Ninety-six Sermons*, 'Sermon 9 of the Sending of the Holy Ghost',
     1635 edn, pp.696, 697.
31   Lancelot Andrewes: *Ninety-six Sermons*, 'Sermon 7 of the Sending of the Holy Ghost',
     1635 edn, pp.672, 673.
32   Lancelot Andrewes: *Ninety-six Sermons*, 'Sermon 8 of the Sending of the Holy Ghost',
     1635 edn, p.677 and p.678.
33   Ibid., p.676.
34   Lancelot Andrewes: *Ninety-six Sermons*, 'Sermon 6 of the Sending of the Holy Ghost',
     1635 edn, p.660.

Chapter 9

Order, Natural Calamities and Evil

The question of evil is not one which the Laudian Divines dwelt upon. As to the origin of evil, they give no precise theory. Rather, they shun such penetration into such matters. Their theology is positive. It emphasizes light and truth and love and holiness. It speaks of the acts of God in correspondence with His Being – an eternal existence of light and truth and love and holiness. The acts of God are acts of His grace, creative acts which correspond in the ordering of creation in the dimension of time and things and the existence of humanity, to His eternal existence. In this ordering God does not accord a place to evil.

But they were realistic in their theology. They recognized that evil does exist within the created order, though not as either a creation of God or as co-eternal with Him. There is no dualism of thought here. The *fact* of evil they recognized; the *how* of evil they refused to examine. They were quite clear, however, that evil's activity centres on humanity, the crown of God's creation, and that that activity is determined to thwart the good purposes of God.

It has not been possible to discover extant sermons preached by Anglican divines on the theological and moral question of the outbreak of the plague in 1603, save one in the collection of Lancelot Andrewes's published sermons. No doubt in time of such outbreaks the normal processes of writing and publishing were in disarray, more immediate considerations leading to the temporary suspension of such activities. This sermon of Lancelot Andrewes is certainly one which is a most profound work dealing with the question of evil, and one which certainly delves deeply into the cause of the rise of evil. It is the sermon preached by him in the time of plague on 21 August 1603. The text was Psalm 106:29–30 –

> Thus they provoked Him to anger with their owne inventions, and the Plague was great (or brake in) upon them. Then stood up Phinees, and prayed (or, executed judgement) and so the Plague was ceased (or, stayed).[1]

This sermon is short against Andrewes's normal measure of length. This is hardly surprising taking into account the circumstances in which it was preached. The text is of plague, and Andrewes sets himself the task of delving into the causes of the pestilence then raging in London.

For him, the hand of God is not absent even in this situation. The terrifying spectacle of the outbreak of the plague bears a relation to the dispensation and ordering of God – albeit a negative relation. It is in the outlining of this relation that the substance of this sermon lies. He notes that a plague is mentioned in the Book of Numbers (35:9):

And we complaine of a *Plague* at this time. The same *axe* is layd to the *root* of our trees. Or rather, because an axe is long in cutting downe of one tree, the *Razor* is *hired for us*, that sweeps away a great number of haires at once (as Esay calleth it) or a *Scithe* that mowes downe grasse, a great deale at once. ... Now *whatsoever things were written aforetime, were written for our learning*, and so was this Text. Under one, to teach us how the *Plague* comes, and how it may be *stayed*.[2]

He then examines the question of cause in a detailed fashion. Andrewes is a realist. He notes the physical, medical and hygienic aspects of the plague and the social consequences. These were the external causes and subsequent effects. But he goes on to penetrate to what, for him, were the root causes. These latter lie in the people's relation to, and conduct before, God:

That there is a *cause* (that is) that the *Plague* is a thing causall, not *casuall*; comes not meerely by *chance*, but hath somewhat, some *cause* that procureth it.[3]

He approaches this theme of the causality of the plague from the starting point of the providence of God in His dispensation and economy of creation:

Sure, if a *Sparrow fall not to the ground without the providence of God, of* which *two are sold for a farthing*; much less doth any *man*, or *woman*, which are *more worth than many Sparrowes*.[4]

He goes on to say that the Hebrew and Latin words for 'plague' (deber) and 'plaga' necessarily infer a cause. The Latin 'plaga' is properly 'a stroke', and behind that there must be one who strikes. God striking is God judging. So Andrewes arrives at the judgment of God in the matter.

There are two dimensions to the question of cause. There is a human level of cause. The physician will say that the cause is in the contagion of the air:

The *Aire* is infected; the *Humours* corrupted: the *Contagion* of the sick, comming to, and conversing with the sound. And they may all be true causes.[5]

But citing Luke 13:11, Andrewes notes that there is both a bodily infirmity and a '*Spirit of infirmity* ... something *spirituall* there is, in all infirmities; something in the *soule* to be healed.' Behind the plagues of Egypt, the plague of Sennacherib's camp and the plagues of Israel under David, there is not only the earthly fact of the pestilence, but a destroying angel.

No man looketh deeply enough into the *Cause* of this sicknesse unless he acknowledge the finger of *God* in it, over and above any causes naturall. ... [There is] some worke for the *Priest*, as well as for the *Physician*, and more, then (it may be).[6]

This 'more, then (it may be)' is significant. It sums up the dimensions of the problem of evil as Andrewes sees it. There is the level of the physician; there is the level of the priest; but there is the third factor against which both of these are conjoined in a relation of cause. That is, there is a temporal or earthly cause; there is a spiritual and moral cause; but the significance of both in their relation is found only in the 'more than', that is, God Himself. The question of the cause of evil has to be worked out with this formula of reference in mind.

The root cause is not the decree of God simply. It is the anger of God. But God's anger has itself a cause. God cannot contradict His own Being and Nature. He is righteous and judges righteously. Therefore, if His judgment is a judgment of anger it is because His righteousness has been slighted and contradicted – the cause behind God's judgment. But we can also say that, since, if God was not righteous there would be no judgment, the very fact that He is righteous is itself the cause also.

The plague comes not by chance, casually, but by God's judgment, and therefore causally, the cause being our sin which provokes His anger. In saying all this, Andrewes is asserting quite clearly that God is in control of the movement and fortune of all human affairs. There is no aspect of these which is divorced and hidden from the scrutiny and action of God. But that control is not to be construed as the working of God as a simple, bare and immediate cause in the matter of evil befalling humanity. It is the interaction of His righteousness and our sin which is the cause.

Here it is necessary to be careful in the apportionment of primary and secondary causes in Andrewes's argument. God does not create or directly cause evil. The cause of the plague does not lie primarily or at the root in Him. In a sense, He may be described as the secondary cause, for this secondary causality is the result of His unwavering and constant righteousness. The primary cause is humanity's disobedience, inevitably shattering itself in judgment when it clashes with and opposes this righteousness. The hand of God holds all things constantly in order, in that state in which they can alone truly exist as the handiwork of God. But humanity, disrupting that order because of its disobedience to the precepts of God's good order for it, breaks itself against the constant and unyielding goodness of God.

> There is a cause in God, *that hee is angry*. And there is a *Cause*, for which he is *angry*. For he is not *angry* without a *Cause*. And what is that cause? For what is God *angry*? . . . And this is the very *Cause* indeed. As there is *Putredo humorum*; so there is also *Putredo morum*. And *Putredo morum*, is more a *Cause*, than *Putredo humorum*. The *Corruption* of the *soule*, the *corruption of our wayes*, more than the *corrupting of the ayre*. The *plague of the heart*, more than the sore, that is seene in the *body* . . . *And as the Balme of Gilead*, and the *Physician* there, may yeeld us helpe, when *God's* wrath is removed: so, if it be not, no *balme*, no *medicine* will serve. Let us with the Woman in the Gospell, *spend all upon Physicians, we shall be never the better*, till we come to Christ, and he cure us of our sins, who is the onely *Physician* of the diseases of the *soule*. And with Christ, the *cure* begins ever *within*. for, *Sonne thy sinnes be forgiven thee*; nand then after, *take up thy bed and walke*. His *sins be* first, and his *limbes* after.[7]

In this way Andrewes penetrates into causality, and makes clear its movement. The sequence of enumeration of the causes of the plague is:

1 the corruption of humanity in its disobedience to the good ordering of God, as the root or primary cause.
2 Then, because God is constant in the determination of His decrees of good order by which creation and humanity is sustained and redeemed, the shattering

of humanity in its disobedience against that ordering – which result is ascribed to, and designated, the wrath of God's judgment, the secondary cause.

Andrewes then lists the specific sins which were the cause of this and of Biblical plagues:

1   Fornication, as that of Zimri with a daughter of Moab (Numbers 25:6,14).
2   Pride, as David's in numbering Israel (I Chronicles 21:14).
3   Blasphemy, as Sennacherib's plague came from Rabshekah's blasphemy (Isaiah 37:23,36).
4   Neglect of the sacrament, either in refusing to come to it, or in coming unworthily – the cause of the plague at Corinth (I Corinthians 11:30).

All these sins are called 'inventions' – they are men's imaginings. They are primarily concerned with the faith. We imagine that we can do better than God in the matter of ordering ourselves:

> Out of the old disease of our *Father Adam* . . . thinke it a goodly matter to be *witty*, and to *find out* things our selves to *make our selves*, to be Authors, and inventors of somewhat, that so we may seeme to be as wise as *God*, if not wiser: and to know what is for our turnes, as well as he, if not better.[8]

Man had forsaken the good ordering of God in things temporal and ecclesiastical, then and now, in Andrewes's view. In the matter of the worship of God there is still the 'devising new tricks, opinions and fashions, fresh and newly taken up, which their *Fathers never knew of* '. The same attitude spoiled all in common life too –

> The *wanton invention* in finding out new *meats* in diet, in *inventing* new fashions in *apparell*, which men so dote on . . . as *they even goe a whoring with them*, with *their owne inventions*, and care not what they spend on them. And know no end of them: but as fast as they are weary of one, a new *invention* is found out; which, *whatever it cost*, how much soever it take from our *Almes*, or *good deeds*, must be had, till all come to nought. That the Psalmist hath chosen a very fit word, that *for our inventions*, the *plague* breakes in among us: for them, as for the *primarie*, or first moving cause of all.[9]

So, Andrewes claims, by turning to the trivialities of the imaginings of the mind, the whim and passing fancy, the whole good order of things ecclesiastical and temporal is overlooked and overturned. This is the cause of the evil of the plague.

As to the cure for the plague, that lies in prayer. Such a cure is evident in both Old and New Testaments, and Andrewes cites examples. Prayer is like incense, purifying the air:

> For, as the *Aire* is infected with *noisome sents* or smels, so the *infection* is removed by *sweet odours*, or *incense*: which *Aaron* did in the *Plague put sweet odours in his Censer*, *and went betweene the living and the dead*. Now there is a fit resemblance betweene *Incense* and *Prayers: Let my Prayer come before thy presence, as the Incense*. And when the *Priest* was within, burning Incense, *the people were without at their prayers*. And it is expressly said, *that the sweet odours were nothing else, but the prayers of the Saints*.[10]

Phineas's prayer, David's, Hezekiah's, all for the removal of the plague, are instanced by Andrewes. He points out that part of the good ordering of God is the place and office of the priest with regard to prayer. As the office and place of the Sergeant is to make arrests, and those of the Notary to make acts, and these functions fulfilled by them are more authentical than the same performed by common people, so too, in this matter, the prayers of the priest are specifically called for by God. In this, Andrewes is pointing out the necessity of faithful duty by the Church to observe and pray for that ordering of God's goodness over all things.

But because the root cause of the plague is disregard of that order over and in all aspects of life, more than prayer is required by God if cure is to be effected. The order of God is concerned with the physical and the spiritual qualities of life.

> For, though *God* be a *Spirit*, and so *in Spirit* to be *worshipped*; yet, inasmuch as He hath given us a *body*, with that also are we *to worship Him*, and *to glorifie him in our body and spirit*, which both *are Gods*: and *to present* (or offer) *our bodies to God, as a holy and acceptable sacrifice, in the reasonable service of Him.*[11]

Andrewes here begins to elaborate on what he had said earlier regarding inventions in common life. We are to present our bodies, and therefore our whole physical life, decently before God so that it is acceptable to Him. He begins by emphasizing the physical aspect of worship. Decent carriage in Church is necessary as an expression of the devotion of the whole man to God, and an acknowledgement of the involvement of the whole being of man in the ordering of God's economy for creation. Slovenly attitudes at prayer are criticized, and he appeals to Tertullian[12] – that to sit praying or pray sitting is against the order of the Church. There is a seemly discipline in the matter.

But that decency which is acceptable to God is of wider concern than behaviour and attitudes in Church. It is required in all areas of life: '*Unreverent, carelesse, undevout behaviour, pleaseth Him not.*' It is by our daily carriage, behaviour, conversation and conduct of ourselves that we please God

In this setting out of primary and secondary causes of evil manifested in the present plague, Andrewes exhibits a mode of thought parallel to that of Calvin, particularly in the latter's observations on the question of predestination. At this point it must be emphasized that Calvin's doctrine of predestination is not a matter of double predestination – that is, that God from all eternity has decided who is to be elected and who rejected. Calvin's whole argument here, set out at length in *De Aeterna Praedestione Dei*[13] centres round a setting out of primary and secondary causes in election and rejection. In brief, his thesis is that predestination is in Christ – indeed, is Christ. He is the goodness and the righteousness of God, and therefore the point where making or breaking of salvation occurs. The primary cause of our election is that grace of God in Christ. The secondary cause is our response to this Personal act of God in the Incarnation, Crucifixion, Resurrection and Ascension of the Word made Flesh. That response, however, adds nothing to the full and sufficient accomplishment of Christ, but is rather our 'Amen' to it – our thankful acceptance under the compulsion of the graciousness of God confronting us in Christ. In the question of rejection, the causes are reversed. Our rejection is caused by our refusal to bow to the grace of God, and this refusal becomes the primary cause of our rejection. But the secondary cause of our rejection is that grace, which, by virtue of being there, must be a cause as it is that against which we rebel.

The parallel to Calvin's thought in Andrewes's observations about the cause of the plague is significant. It is to be deduced that evil itself has a negative relation to the grace of God, and in that sense plays a part in God's dispensation and economy. But it has no positive place. It is there, and Andrewes is quite clear that it is used by God, despite itself, to bring about repentance and obedience. It is clear from the sermon preached by Andrewes at St Mary's Hospital in 1588, where he mentions Calvin[14] as the best of the new writers, that he was familiar with the works of Calvin. Calvin's work – *Institutes of the Christian Religion*[15] – was well known by that time, and widely read, and this discussion of causes is also set out in this.[16]

It could be objected that Andrewes's reference to Calvin was an argument *ad hominem* – that is, using Calvin merely as an objection to Calvin's supporters. Yet both this parallel to Calvin's thought, and Andrewes's well known good disposition towards displaced Calvinist scholars from the continent, would suggest that there is a deeper appreciation of Calvin than is generally recognized or admitted.

As to the origin of evil, there is little speculation and more silence in the works of the Laudian Divines. Fallen angels, in their dogmatic dress, are a Miltonian exaggeration. Where such things are mentioned, the important point is disobedience to God's good order. Certainly in Andrewes and his Anglican contemporaries with a like concern for good order, the main drift of the question is centred on humanity as the crown of God's creation, and its disobedience to His economic decrees. But even here, the grace of God much more abounds, and is set out as making even the wrath of man redound to His praise, and to a greater awareness of the maintenance of good order in correspondence to that Divine order, in all matters, ecclesiastical and temporal, spiritual and common. Order and grace are inseparable, and not even evil and the resultant work of men's chaos are outwith the scrutiny and working and utility of that God.

Notes

1 Lancelot Andrewes: *Ninety-six Sermons*, 'Sermon Preached at Chiswick in the Time of Pestilence, August 21, An. Dom. 1603 – Sermon 11 of Certain Sermons Preached at Sundry Times upon Severall Occasions', 1635 edn, pp.B159ff.
2 Ibid., p.B159.
3 Ibid., p.B160.
4 Ibid.
5 Ibid., p.B161.
6 Ibid., pp.B161, B162.
7 Ibid., p.B162.
8 Ibid., pp.B163, B164.
9 Ibid., p.B164.
10 Ibid., p.B165.
11 Ibid., p.B166.
12 Tertullian: *De Orat.* 12.
13 John Calvin: *De Aeterna Praedestione Dei* (*Concerning the Eternal Predestination of God*), James Clarke and Co., 1961.

14   Lancelot Andrewes: *Ninety-six Sermons*, 'A Sermon Preached at St. Maries Hospital, 1588', 1635 edn, p.B8.
15   John Calvin: *Institutes of the Christian Religion*, trans. H. Beveridge, Eerdmans, 1979.
16   Ibid., Chapter 24, pp.239ff.

Chapter 10

Order and the Nature of Political Unrest

Christopher Hill in his preface to his book *Change and Continuity in Seventeenth Century England*, quotes with approval the French Historian, R. Mandrou on 'the crucial significance of the English Revolution'. He quotes:

> The leading political power of Europe in the first decades of the eighteenth century is also the society which has broken with traditional principles, rejected divine-right monarchy, absolutism and arbitrary government. . . . England has overcome the internal crises of the seventeenth century and represents not only a specific political force, but also another sort of society, victorious because different.[1]

What is of significance here is the assumptions underlying the analysis. These assumptions are skilfully laid out in all that follows in Christopher Hill's book, namely that 'social attitudes' underlay all that resulted in the Civil War, and 'the radical critique of the three traditional professions, divinity, law, medicine'.[2] He points out that:

> in chapter 3 I suggested ways in which protestantism, the religion of the heart, made advocacy of social change easier . . . just as protestant theologians by denouncing, often in crude materialsitic terms, the miracle of the mass, helped to create a mental climate more favourable to the rise of rational science.[3]

The assumption that social attitudes were formed by emotion and the rejection of what some would call superstition, is curiously selective and superficial. In all that Christopher Hill says in this book, there is no appeal to sources other than Puritan material. For example, his second chapter entitled 'Arise Evans: Welshman in London', which is an examination of this person's writings is a curious main source of authority to which appeal is made on the basis that this lets us know what the common man of the seventeenth century was thinking. (The 'Common man', in any case, is usually a convenient figment of imaginary mass authority.) Christopher Hill's own words tend to detract from this authority:

> Endearing though Arise Evans is, he was clearly mentally abnormal. But we can learn from him perhaps something about the (relatively) common man and his attitudes towards religion, the Bible, politics, at one of the very few times when we can hear him speaking in his own voice.[4]

It may be that the London Street Ballads, with their lampooning of so much of what the 'common man' of Puritan persuasion thought, by 'common men', are in greater proximity to popular thought than the writings of an admittedly somewhat deranged Welshman. But there is no appeal to such sources, or to the political and social comment of the Divines of the Church by Law Established – or indeed, to any of the Roman Catholic literature of the time.

Christopher Hill seems to let the anachronistic concern of egalitarianism sway his judgement in such matters, and his thesis is therefore selective. The works of the Laudian Divines are quite clear that the root cause of unrest and disorder in the nation was of theological concern. Social issues were seen in the context of theological grounding, and any *radical critique* of religion, law and medicine, was by way of viewing their validity or otherwise within the framework of God's economy for creation, humanity and nations. There is no more radical critique of these things than in the sermons of Andrewes, and a penetrating social comment, unparalleled in the time, is offered in his sermon preached at St Mary's Hospital in 1588, outlining, as it did, the ills of the day and the ground of all that follows. What Christopher Hill has failed to grasp, seemingly, is that the issue on both sides was not primarily social concern, but the theological reasons undergirding the shape of society. The rift was over the method of theological interpretation. This is what lies at the heart of the ensuing strife; it was essentially a theological struggle.

The other point on which Christopher Hill may be criticized here is that of his claim that the protestant rejection of the miracle of the mass tended to give the necessary mental climate for the rise of rational science. This is simplistic. A more dispassionate view would reveal that the very way of thinking advocated by the Anglican Divines, where objective reasoning disciplined to the nature of the object, or class of objects being studied, where objective truth was allowed to reveal itself without alien presuppositions being forced upon it by the thinking subject, was the necessary climate for the rise of natural science. There has always been a link between theological discipline and its way of thinking, and natural science. The scientific academies of fourth-century Alexandria are a case in point, with the interaction there between the Nicene mind and scientific endeavour. The work of Grosseteste and Duns Scotus in the Middle Ages, particularly with the former's understanding of the principles of light in the creation narratives, again pushed natural science on. In the seventeenth century, the impetus, inspiration and legacy of the Anglican theological method is surely the catalyst which inspired, through the contribution it made to the general endeavour of thought in that time, to the rise of the Royal Society later. Francis Bacon's device, for example, of transferring the way of dealing with 'the Books of God' to the way in which 'the Books of Nature' were to be studied, is a case in point, and this his essays demonstrate more than adequately.

We have here the confrontation between a concept of order arrived at by the theological method of the use of scripture, tradition and reason in their relation one to another, and that which was arrived at by an essentially private interpretation of scripture, the divisive nature and results of which were seen internally in the factions of what is generally labelled 'Puritanism'.

The former was a unitary way of thinking, in which God and man, Creator and creation, eternity and time, matters ecclesiastical and matters temporal, were bracketed together, inseparably yet unconfusedly. All these things were viewed from the vantage point of the incarnate Christ, the scope of the scriptures, of tradition and of reason disciplined to the nature of that revelation. The latter by and large represented a dualistic way of thinking, imposing its own preconceptions of a philosophical framework on all things – including God ultimately – and using scripture as a justification for an outlook already arrived at on the basis of other idealistic considerations. When to artificial idealism there is added the means of efficiency and practical skills, then points of view are hammered home – religiously, politically, socially – regardless of the consequences to the proper and intrinsic nature of things and of humanity.

The Laudians were quite clear that this was the age-old sin of Adam, and they saw this Adamic stance as the loss of the dignity, estate and vocation of humanity, the exploitation and misuse of the gifts of creation, and society as a factious gathering at variance within itself. They did not confine this to the Puritan tendency, but were critical of those within the Church whose attitudes of indifference and exploitation led to the same results.[5]

The Puritan Revolution was not something new. Milton, at least somewhat perceptively critical among Puritans, saw this partially when in his aptly titled *New Forcers of Conscience*, he wrote: 'New Presbyter is but Old Priest writ large'.[6] Without a doubt there was misuse of the office and calling of priest, born of the same attitude of mind which brought the new presbyters to the fore, and the Laudians were not slow to point out such abuses either contemporary or past.

Behind the Puritan attitude particularly, there was a hinterland of like ecclesiastical and political views, and resulting upheavals, stretching back to the fourteenth century and the days of John Wyclif and the Lollards. It can be seen from two of his works especially (*De Dominio Divino, De Dominio Civili*) that Wyclif operated with a dualistic mode of thought. This separated the eternal, ideal realities from the visible, temporal, realities on earth. The latter did not have any authority save that which derived from the former. All temporal and ecclesiastical authority depended on grace, and if the holders of office, particularly the priesthood, were not in such a state of grace, they were to be deprived. This view depends on the assumption that Wyclif had immediate and full understanding of the eternal virtue of grace. His theory of 'dominion', indeed, in the last resort, saw authority residing in the individual, derived directly from God. He argues on that basis that there is no need of a hierarchy in either the secular or the ecclesiastical domains, for all are equal. All dualistic thought eventually confuses those things which it had originally separated, and we have here a confusion between the supposed right of the individual and that authority which is God's alone. The translation of the Bible into English undertaken by Wyclif, was to give the individual direct access to the things of God.

What all this does is to cut across any idea of a contingent estate or vocation held from and to God, with subsequent right and responsibility. It is the failure to understand the principle of contingency which leads to a misinterpretation of the Divine Right of Kings and its corollary, the Divine Responsibility and Answerability of Kings – and indeed to a misrepresentation of the true nature and quality of any authority under God, whether secular or sacred.

In close company with Wyclif were the Lollards. They had every sympathy with Wyclifian views, which gave some academic standing and justification to the revolution which they wished to perpetrate in reorganizing a society which had suffered the upheaval of the Black Death with its subsequent chaos throughout the Feudal System. One of the foremost Lollards was Sir John Oldcastle with a history rooted in the Parish of St Giles-in-the-Fields, London. He was arrested in 1413, the indictment against him and other Lollards being: that they had plotted the death of the King and his brothers together with the prelates and other lords of the realm, the transference of the religious to secular employment, the spoilation and destruction of all Cathedrals, Churches and Monasteries, and the elevation of Oldcastle himself to be Regent of the nation.

Oldcastle was charged with raising an insurrection – the contemporary account, whether by exaggeration or by slip of the pen, remarks that 20,000 Lollards were to gather in St Giles Fields. Such an insurrection did take place, but was easily put down, the king having been forewarned and appropriate action taken to prevent the London Lollards joining with those from the country areas. After arrest, escape from the Tower of London and eventual recapture, Oldcastle was brought to the place of his crime – probably the corner of the present Shaftesbury Avenue with Princes Circus – as was the custom, and hanged and burnt both as an outlawed traitor and as a convicted heretic.[7] Social upheaval, iconoclasm and individual interpretations of the scriptures are the ingredients here.

In this can be perceived the seeds of later thought and event. Puritanism, with its emphasis on the individual's right to interpret the Bible, of individual inspiration, and of a confusing of the Kingdom of Heaven with the rule of the saints (that is the Puritans) on earth, is embryonic here. Stone, in his *The Causes of the English Revolution, 1529–1642*, writes:

> The independence of moral judgment about the religious and political hierarchy, and later the development of sectarian pluralism, arose from the process of individual interpretation of the vernacular Bible, the free access to which was regarded by Hobbes as one of the principal causes of the revolution. He complained that 'after the Bible was translated into English, every man, nay every boy and wench, that could read English thought they spoke with God Almighty, and understood what He said' (Hobbes: *Human Nature*, p.21).[8]

It is only partly true that the availability of the Bible in the vernacular led to individuals elevating their opinions into dogmas. The Laudians, too, had the accessibility of the English Bible. What is at stake is the means of interpretation of the Bible – that is, in the Puritan case, the guidelines of tradition and reason disciplined to the way of doctrine setting out the Incarnate Word, were missing.

It is not surprising to find that there was no such thing as a united body of people called 'Puritans'. That title is merely an umbrella under which sheltered a medley of sects. The Puritan Presbyterians were Federal Calvinists and besides them there were Independents, Fifth Monarchy Men, Millenarians, Levellers, Soul-Sleepers, Muggletonians, Ranters, Diggers, and many more. One of the London street ballads (surely a product of Christopher Hill's 'common man') ridiculed the idea that any of the Puritan factions could command majority rule in and by the Commons:

> Now thanks to the Powers below
> We have even done our do,
> The Mitre is down and so is the Crown,
> And with them the Coronet too. . . .
> There is no such thing, as Bishop or King

Or Peer but in name and show.
Come clowns and come boys, come hobbledehoys,
Come females of each degree,
Stretch out your throats, bringing in your votes,
And make good the anarchy. . . .
We are fourscore religions strong,
Then take your choice, the major voice
Shall carry it, right or wrong;
Then let's have King Charles, says George,
Nay we'll have his son, says Hugh,
Nay, let's have none says jabbering Joan,
Nay, we'll all be Kings, says Prue.[9]

This divisiveness was a characteristic of the Puritan tendency. It is also not surprising that Oliver Cromwell only managed to gain and keep control by the use of like-minded members of the Army – removing all Levellers and others in dispute with him from its ranks. The question may well be asked what the essential difference was between an apparent military dictatorship and that supposed absolute tyranny which the Puritans claimed to have removed? Certainly Cromwell gradually assumed the trappings of an absolute monarch, except (reluctantly) the title. Butler, in 'Hudibras' sums it up:

Such as do build their Faith upon
The holy text of Pike and Gun;
Decide all Controversies by
Infallible Artillery;
And prove their Doctrine Orthodox
By Apostolic Blows and Knocks[10]

Seventeenth-century Puritanism had its antecedents. It was a growing tendency throughout the sixteenth century, but it is to be noted that neither then, nor in its seventeenth-century heyday, was it representative of anything other than a minority of the people, and that minority split within itself. It may be asked if this is a constant throughout all revolutionary movements – that their shape is determined by the few, and that they throw up a new and artificial elite who generally exercise a tyranny comparable to what they claim is the tyranny they have overthrown. Accompanying this may be an iconoclasm of the symbols and images of all that opposed and opposes their interpretations of the truth.

Such signs were long noted by the Anglican Divines. Laud, imprisoned since his accusation of high treason by the House of Commons in 1640, wrote in his *Private Prayers*:

Nov. 1.1644. I received a summons to appear in the House of Commons next morning. [date and first sentence is in the margin]. O merciful Lord, I have had a long and tedious trial. . . . Lord, continue all thy mercies toward me, for the storm gathers and grows black upon me, and what it threatens is best known to thee. After a long trial I am called to answer in the House of Commons, and that not to evidence, but to one single man's report of evidence, and that made without oath. What this may produce in present or in future, thou knowest also. O Lord, furnish me with patience and true Christian wisdom and courage, to bear up against this drift, and send not thy storms to beat upon me also; but look comfortably upon me to my end.[11]

That storm and drift which now concentrated upon Laud, and was about to be felt by the king, had long menaced. In 1625, Laud had warned:

> They, whoever they be, that would overthrow Sedes Ecclesiae, the seats of ecclesiastical government, will not spare (if ever they get power) to have a pluck at the throne of David.[12]

Here, the dictum of King James VI and I – 'No Bishop, No King' – is seen to be an astute weighing up of the situation. Laud saw well that heresy meant social unrest, and that unbridled opinion about fundamental truths meant civil chaos.

Bearing in mind the king's estate as the upholder of all order in the body politic, Laud issued certain instructions to his Vicar-General, Sir Nathaniel Brent, to see to the Church of Boston, Lincolnshire – which was in the heartland of Puritanism. During an Archiepiscopal Visitation, he ordered the walls of the church to be

> adorned with devout and holy sentences of Scripture . . . divers of which sentences shall tend to the exhortation of the people to obedience to the King's most excellent majesty.[13]

On one such text, Lancelot Andrewes had preached on the anniversary of the Gunpowder Plot in 1605, before the King at Whitehall (Proverbs 8:15, 'By me Kinges reigne'). Andrewes asks who the *me* of the text is, and answers:

> *Wisdom* it selfe made this *sermon*. And wee may bee bold to preach, what *Wisdome* preacheth. . . . Specially, this *Wisdome*; the essential *Wisdome* of God; which upon the point, will prove to be none other, but *Christ*.[14]

The *by* of the text is 'Christ's preposition, this (ever)'. He is the One by whom all things were made. Here Andrewes makes clear the contingent, personal nature of kingship, linking it to the doctrine of the Person of Christ:

> And by Him, most properly: for, in that He was to be Man, all the benefits which were to come from *God*, to *man*, were to come by him. He, the *Per*, of all: among which, this one of *Regall Regiment* is a principall one.[15]

Then comes a statement of the nature of kingship so held in and by Christ, bringing the doctrine of Recapitulation into focus – the gathering up of all things in time and space in Christ, so that all order throughout time and space is by Him:

> By Him, againe . . . Because He is *Wisdome* (which I reckon worth a note) that the *per* of *Kingdomes*, whereby they consist, is not *Power* so properly (the Attribute of the first [that is, the Father, the first Person of the Trinity] as *Wisdome* (the Attribute of the second Person:) they stand rather by *Wisdome* than *force*. Besides, *Sapientis est ordinare* (saith the great Philosopher) the proper work of *wisdome* is to *order*. And what is *Anarchie*, but a disordered *Chaos* of Constitution? Or what is Rule, but . . . , a setting and holding of all in good order. . . .

By Him, yet againe, because on Him hath the *Father* conferred all the kingdomes of the Earth; we reade it *Psal.II*. We see Him *Apoc.XIX, with many crownes oon His head.* . . . Meet then it was, that the Kings of the severall quarters of the Earth, should be by Him, that is *Rex universae terrae*. That the Kings of the severall Ages of the world should be by Him, who is *Rex Saeculorum*, whose Dominion endureth through all ages.[16]

Andrewes gathers up the nature of kingship, and shows its foundation in personal contingency, rooted in the doctrine of the Person of Christ, and in that, in the doctrines of Recapitulation and the Trinity. It is by Christ, and Christ alone, that kings rule and exercise their office. Likewise, he appeals to natural law as to the holding by kings of their office:

By Him, and by none *but by Him*, they be; *By Him*, and by none *but by Him*, they cease to be. In Nature, every thing is dissolved by the same meanes, it came together. In Law, *Institution* and *Destitution*, belong both to one.[17]

Only He who makes Kings, and He by whom they reign, can unmake Kings. The warning note is creeping in. Andrewes refers to that incident where the people of Israel demanded Kings from God: 'The people importun'd God, and Hee yeelded with much adoe.' But God's reluctance is caused by the fact that the people saw kingship as residing in their will for a king; kingship was a matter, for them, of their demand and toleration:

They would have Kings to be, by *Toleration* only; and so, by that *Per*, are all the evils and mischiefes in the world. And, are not Kings much beholden to these men, thinke you?[18]

Andrewes asks the question sarcastically; but it was a real question in view of the growing Puritan attitude that it was by the people, and only by desire of the people, that Kings reigned. And that which permits can also forbid.

While his immediate subject is the late Gunpowder Plot, Andrewes warns of the constant danger of such attempts to remove the throne:

For, here comes all the danger; there is much heaving and lifting at them [that is, kings] after they bee in; such thrusting force, such undermining with fraud; So many *Per me's*, *Per Me Clement, Castell, Catesby*; and they againe so many *Per's, Per knives, pistoll, poyson, powder*, all against this *Per* of continuance.[19]

In the sixth sermon on the Plot, preached in 1614, Andrewes also speaks in warning tones. The text was Proverbs, 24:21–3, 'My Sonne, feare thou the Lord, and the King; and meddle not with them that are given to change.' Andrewes speaks of fear properly lying in regard to God and God's appointments. Having dealt with the Gunpowder Plot conspirators and their lack of this fear, he speaks of others whose fear of God has been transformed into fear of men. The crowd, the mob, has usurped God's place:

They feare *the face of man*. And thus, with their new *feare of God*, they put out of countenance the *feare of the King*. . . . This for conjunction [the word 'and' in the text] which (I wish) we may endevour by all meanes to maintaine. For, besides the offence to God and *His feare*, it is a preparative to the *change* (which here followeth) to sever God from the *King*, or the *King* from the *Kingdome*; to force them one from the other, that God hath so straightly united together: hath Himselfe, and would have us doe the like.[20]

Here the sense is of a unitary way of thinking, where Kingship – as all else – is held in its contingency to and from God. The meddling and change, of which Andrewes warns, is concerned with breaking this contingency, with separation, and therefore with that severance at the base of all dualistic thought. The end of such thought, paradoxically, is the confusion of the things separated. It is the people who eventually become God, and are feared. Andrewes continues, concerning the Puritans:

> What say some other ... ? You shall *change* for a *fine new Church-government*: A *Presbytery* would doe much better for you, than a *Hierarchie*; And (perhaps) not long after, a government of *States*, than a *Monarchie*. Meddle not with these *Changers*.[21]

What was at stake here, in Andrewes's view, was not a surface political or social change, but the change of that fundamental theological view of the relation of God, creation and humanity, on which the genuine identity, character and nature of humanity rested. The preservation of this was the insistence of the Laudians, and their support of institutions and their ordering which pointed beyond themselves in an appropriate way to that relationship, was to further this and safeguard it against all intrusions of human devising. The *oikonomia* of God for creation, and the contingent relation of that creation to and from God, with humanity as its crown, was their concern in all their writing and proclamation.

Notes

1   C. Hill: *Change and Continuity in Seventeenth Century England*, Preface, p.ix (quoting R. Mandrou, *Louis XIV et son temps, 1661–1715*, Paris, 1973, p.544).
2   Ibid., Preface p.x.
3   Ibid., p.282.
4   Ibid., p.58.
5   Cf. Lancelot Andrewes: *Ninety-six Sermons*, 'A Sermon Prepared to be Preached on Whitsunday, 1622', 1635 edn, pp.755ff; 'Sermon 6 of the Gun Powder Treason', 1635 edn, pp.945ff; Robert Sanderson: *Sermons Preached*, 1627 edn, pp.147ff.
6   John Milton: *New Forcers of Conscience under the Long Parliament*, from Poems Upon Several Occasions, 1673, p.130 line 20.
7   Gordon Taylor: *History of St Giles-in-the-Fields* (pamphlet, n.d.).
8   L. Stone: *The Causes of the English Revolution, 1529–1642*, 1972.
9   London Rump Songs, 17th cent. MS.
10   Samuel Butler: 'Hudibras' (quoted, A.L. Rowse, *Reflections on the Puritan Revolution*, 1986, p.188).
11   William Laud: *A Summarie of His Devotions*, ed. J.H.Parker, Oxford, 1838 edn, p.176.
12   William Laud: *Private Devotions*, ed. J.H.Parker, Oxford, 1888 edn, p.176.
13   William Laud, 'Sermon On the Opening of Parliament, 6 February, 1626'; *Sermons*, ed. J.W. Hatherell, London, 1829, pp.91–3.

14 Lancelot Andrewes: *Ninety-six Sermons*, 'Sermon 5 Of the Gun Powder Treason', 1635 edn, p.933.
15 Ibid., p.936.
16 Ibid., pp.936–7.
17 Ibid., p.939.
18 Ibid., p.937.
19 Ibid., p.940.
20 Lancelot Andrewes: *Ninety-six Sermons*, 'Sermon 6 Of the Gun Powder Treason', 1635 edn, pp.949–50.
21 Ibid., p.951.

Chapter 11

Order: The Knowledge and Being of God and Humanity

This survey of some of the works by several of the Laudian Divines has concentrated so far (though by no means exclusively) on the *noetic* aspect of Order – that is, the knowledge of God and humanity's understanding of Order in the light of that knowledge. It has been impossible, however, to isolate the noetic and treat it solely as a consideration by itself. This is because theology can never sunder act from being or knowledge from existence. God is as He acts and acts as He is: there is no disjunction or contradiction between what God is and what God does: His works express His being consistently. In the same vein, to know God is to know Him in His Self-revelation and the knowledge of God to which we come concerns not just intellectual assent but, radically, the totality of our being.

The knowledge of God primarily is the knowledge which God has of Himself as He exists as Father and Son bound in the bond of divine love, the Holy Spirit. His Self-revelation, the person, acts and words of the Word made flesh is the revelation of this Triune God, God as He exists *in se*. Our knowledge of God is therefore not, in essence, knowledge about God, as though God were a disinterested object, but rather our participation in that self-knowledge of God as the Word brings our existence to bear on His existence and gives us to share in it in His assumption of our flesh and nature, which, of course, includes the human mind. This relation between God and humanity in Jesus Christ is the ground of our knowledge of God. The *noetic* therefore is anchored in the *ontic* – the existence of God being brought to bear on humanity in the Word made flesh and the way in which our existence is related to God in, through, by and with that self-same Word in his incarnation.

This inseparability and this mutual interpenetration of the noetic and the ontic are hallmarks of the thought and works of these divines. They were well aware that in the matter of the knowledge of God, 'deep calls unto deep' – the depths of the Being of God to the depths of humanity's existence in the depths of the dereliction of Christ on the cross, and that this involves the totality of the human being and the iron necessities and concrete circumstances in which that being lives and moves, acts and speaks and knows. This has been touched explicitly upon already in, for example, the discussion of preaching and sacraments in Chapter Eight, but implicitly elsewhere in every other consideration of the various aspects of order.

Light and life, revelation and reconciliation, are bracketed together in the Laudian mind. This is abundantly clear in the sermons of Lancelot Andrewes on the Holy Spirit. In order to redress the balance between the noetic and the ontic considerations so far in this survey and to make clear that order is not just a conceptual matter but an integral truth about the totality of human existence in its relation to the divine existence, these sermons should be considered as part of the whole panorama of order. For in this particular area of Lancelot Andrewes's preaching, the basic truth of the oikonomia of human existence as that which is truly human in the eyes of God, God's humanity, and the way of being brought to that, are set out as the basis of all true order in every dimension and quality of created existence. This way and this truth and this life rest on the Word made flesh who is the Way, the Truth and the Life, Order himself, and on the role and work of the Holy Spirit in relating humanity to this Word.

We face here again the difficulty in assessing doctrine in the works of the Laudian Divines – that is that they were not systematic in setting out a clear corpus of any one doctrine. The formulation of any doctrine in its Laudian setting is a matter of a general survey and (as far as possible) a systematic assessment made from this. To do this is, in a measure, somewhat contrary to the Laudian approach to doctrine which tends to be open rather than definitive. That is not to say that there is no interest in clear doctrine; rather, there is a reluctance to define and to circumscribe God within a definition.

Andrewes's sermons *Of the Sending of the Holy Ghost* concentrate variously on aspects of the doctrine of the Holy Spirit as demanded and controlled by the exegesis of the particular text on which he was preaching on a specific Whitsunday. As with the other groupings of his sermons – *Of the Incarnation, Of the Resurrection*, etc. – the fact that his Pentecost sermons are gathered together do at least make the task of gleaning a doctrine of the Holy Spirit somewhat easier.

There is, however, another more general problem in piecing together such a doctrine. This centres around the historical reluctance of the church to formulate a clear doctrine of the Spirit. Such reluctance stems from: first the sheer difficulty of the subject, since the Spirit, according to our Lord, speaks not of Himself but is self-effacing; the neglect of the subject by and large after some attempts in the early church to clarify the matter (which attempts, such as Basil's work on the Spirit to instance but one of great value for the Church's understanding, were indeed laudable and significant); the problem of disentangling objective and subjective elements in attempting to delineate a doctrine of the Spirit with the attendant danger of a confusion between the Holy Spirit and the human spirit as has been instanced in several periods of Christian thought. In the seventeenth century in particular, claims of familiarity with the Spirit and inspiration by the Spirit abounded – a presumption dreaded by Andrewes and his like-minded contemporaries. We may instance again his abhorrence of what he and they regarded as impudent prying with the deep things of God which the Spirit alone searched and knew.

This sounding the depths of His *Judgements* with our line and lead; too much presumed upon by some, in these days of ours ... (Saith the Psalmist) *His Judgements are the great deepe*. St. Paul, looking downe into it, ranne backe, and cried, *O the depth!* the profound depth! not to be searched, past our fadoming or finding out. Yet there are in the world that make but a *shallow* of this great deepe: they have sounded it to the bottome. God's *Decrees*, they have them at their finger ends, can tell you the order and number of them just, with 1, 2, 3, 4, 5. Men that (sure) must have beene in God's *Cabbinet*, above the *third heaven*, where Saint *Paul* never came.[1]

For these reasons it would not be in keeping with the thought of the Laudian Divines to attempt to cut out and paste together a definitive doctrine of the Holy Spirit which then may be labelled 'Laudian'. Such a doctrine, for them, must always remain open, for it is only under the guidance of the Spirit that the human mind may begin even to think about God and this guidance is a constant movement which never reaches a destination until that day when the thinker is called into the nearer presence of God and sees him face to face. It is therefore better to take a corpus of writings on the Holy Spirit, examine these and let them speak for themselves. To this end the sermons of Lancelot Andrewes on the Holy Spirit have been chosen, for he, above all others, manages to capture in his writings the fullness of Laudian thought.

There are certain interlinking broad strokes that may be penned regarding emphases in Andrewes's writings on the Spirit as indications of his consistent way of thinking throughout these sermons. These emphases are locked together, however, and tend to merge into one another in his thought, but they may be disentangled even if partially. They are: the 'Person and work and communion of the Holy Spirit'. The totality of creation is ordered, adorned, governed and upheld by the Holy Spirit. The Spirit in his creative work is none other than the presence of God Himself towards His handiwork. It is the dominical presence of God – but not in separation from the Word of God by whom all things are created, for whom they are created and in whom they consist. There is, in Andrewes's thought the underlying Patristic mode of thinking (particularly from Irenaeus) of the Spirit and the Word as the two hands of God – that is, God in all his Godness in his work *ad extra*. The Word and the Spirit are not to be regarded as mere instruments of God, but rather God personally present, both distinct from the Person of the Father and the Word distinct from the Person of the Spirit and the Spirit from the Person of the Word, yet both proceeding personally from the Father, the Spirit also proceeding from the Son. All this is in the unity of the one God. The Spirit, both in the internal and eternal relations of the Godhead and in the work of God towards His creation is God in all His Godness and majesty and dominion.

Andrewes is a firm advocate of the *filioque clause*. Nowhere is the Spirit divorced from the Word; there is no independence of the Spirit in the sense that the Spirit has His own agenda in isolation from the Word and the Father. He is supremely the Spirit of the Word and of the Father. Thus there is in Andrewes's thought, in common with his fellows, the awareness that there is a correspondence between the Being of God *in se* and the action of God *ad extra*. Act and being are one: God is as He acts and acts as He is.

The Spirit, as with the Word, is not regarded as some sort of immanent principle within creation. Rather, while both Spirit and Word operate within and with the temporal/spatial realities of creation, they are the power and action and presence of God the Creator impinging upon, interacting with and lovingly embracing creation in a personal and transcendent fashion and without compromising, changing or discarding their essential divinity. It is never as other than God that the Spirit acts towards us and is present with us. While there is relation between the Spirit and us there is no question of confusion in that relationship, but rather a communion of the two in which the integrity of both – the uncreated quality of the Creator and the very different quality of that which is created – is preserved.

It is the role of the Spirit to bring about this communion between Creator and that which is created. This work of God the Spirit *ad extra* is in exact correspondence to his role *in se*, within the Godhead. There he is the *vinculum caritatis*, the bond of divine love between the Father and the Son and the Son and the Father. It is ever the work of the Spirit to be the communion, the bond. Thus the filioque clause is emphasized in Andrewes's thought, for the Spirit's propriety within the Godhead is to be the communion of the father with the Son and the Son with the Father. The communion which the Spirit bestows upon creation is communion with the Triune Being of God. But this has direction.

The direction of God towards creation, in the totality of the act of creating, in upholding and in redeeming creation, is that of the Word, the Word by whom all things without exception are created, the very Word by which God upholds all things and the self-same Word who became flesh for the sake of all things.

In all of Andrewes's observations on the subject, he makes it clear that the Spirit is also present in this Word-orientated and focused direction which God takes towards creation. Throughout his sermons – not only those specifically preached at the feast of Pentecost – he makes it clear that the Holy Spirit companies with Christ in every aspect of his Person and work. It is by the power of the Spirit that the patriarchs journey by faith in the faithfulness of God's Word, that prophets in their warnings and exhortations utter the Word of God, that kings in the righteousness and wisdom of their rule point to Christ's kingship and kingdom, that priests offering the sacrifices of the Temple foreshadow the cost of redemption by the sacrifice of Christ on the cross, that the Blessed Virgin conceives and the Word becomes incarnate, that by the Spirit Jesus is anointed at His baptism by John, that by that Spirit Jesus performed miracles as by the finger of God, that through the Spirit Jesus offers Himself to the Father as a spotless sacrifice, that according to the Spirit of holiness He was raised from the dead. It is the same Spirit which our Lord bestows upon His church after His ascension, and it is by that Spirit that we receive adoption as children of God through the Son, the Word made flesh, our brother, and whereby we may cry 'Abba, Father'. By that Spirit we are able to participate in all that Christ has done for us in His Person and perceive Christ as the Self-revelation of God. Thus the Spirit gives us life and light by bringing us into communion with Christ and therefore with the divine life of the Triune God, restoring us through the Word made flesh to the Father.

All this may be deduced from an examination of Andrewes's and his fellows' sermons, their important view of the Spirit being that it is His proper work to establish our communion with Christ, Christ present with us and we with Christ, so sealing Christ's complete and sufficient and once-for-all work of revelation and reconciliation by making it actual in us when He so unites us to Christ. And underlying this, for the Laudians, is the fundamental truth that it is the Spirit's office and estate within the Triune Being of God to be the bond of love and communion of the Father with the Son and the Son with the Father. The Spirit's role and work towards creation and us is consistent with His Being and role within the Godhead.

Nowhere do the Laudians treat the outpouring and presence of the Holy Spirit as if the incarnation had never taken place. God is not Spiritless; but neither is he Wordless. The Spirit is firmly linked to the Word and considered in no other context – for there is none other. The Spirit does not exist apart from and independent of the Word or the Father. The direction of the Spirit is to the Father through Christ, just as His direction to us is from the Father through the Son from whom, therefore, He also proceeds. But just as that Son or Word has become flesh, so it is from the incarnate Word that the direction is taken from God towards us and from us towards God.

What is of great significance, particularly in the sermons of Andrewes, is the emphasis on the relation between Spirit, incarnation and all creation. This may be summarized briefly by the following discussion.

When humanity in the person of Adam falls, not only is there an expulsion from the garden, that is the break in relationship between humanity and its environ and context, but the ground itself was cursed for man's disobedience. The order of creation in which Adam holds a pivotal role is broken and fragmented because the primary bond in all creation in the *oikonomia* of God for His handiwork, the bond between God and humanity at the heart of creation, is shattered by that disobedience of man.

In the old covenant the various elements, personages and institutions in the whole epic of Israel, the law itself, the precepts and rituals and content of liturgy, the prophets, priests, psalmists, judges and kings, all have a paradigmatic role; they point beyond themselves to the fullness of God's revelation, reconciliation and restoration of all creation. These are moved by the Word and Spirit, but not by the fullness of their abiding presence endowing these things with an once-and-for-all significance and effect. The status of these institutions and personages is that, while moved and empowered by God, they nevertheless witness to the 'distance' at which God holds Himself from fallen creation and fallen creation from Him.

Thus the Word and the Spirit bring God's judgement to bear upon creation in the existence of Israel and the content and substance of its history, yet in such a way that fallen creation is not consumed, but maintained by his gracious patience until the fullness of reconciliation provided by God comes and effects its work in and by and through and as the Word made flesh. When the issue between God and humanity and creation has thereby been resolved and reconciliation effected, then and only then, when the Word in all His Godness has come and in the incarnation accomplished His once-and-for-all and sufficient work, the Spirit in all His Godness and fullness can be poured out on all flesh without consuming all things in the fire of his righteous judgement.

The restoration, or as Andrewes calls it the 'palingenesis', the 'new genesis', of all creation is not only a matter of the Word assuming flesh and, as the One by whom all things were created, for whom they were created and in whom they hold together, recapitulating all things in Himself and restoring them in Himself. It most certainly is this, but, as Andrewes though clearly indicates, it is this as one side of the one deed, the other side being the outpouring of the Spirit upon all flesh by the Word made flesh in His accomplishment of this restoration in its declaration at his resurrection and ascension. The Holy Spirit is the *seal* of the legacy of Christ's accomplished work.

It is this unity of thought concerning the twofold work of Word and Spirit as two aspects of one work which characterizes Andrewes's approach to order – the ordering of creation and re-creation. It is on this unity of thought that all order depends.

But because we still await the disclosure of the new heavens and the new earth, the Spirit, while poured out upon all flesh is poured out in such a way that distance is still maintained between God and creation and nature. The creation still groans and travails, waiting for the eventual disclosure of its redemption accomplished in Christ. But its crying and striving is paradigmatic, pointing to that resurrection accomplished for it in and by Christ for which it longs.

The Holy Spirit, and therefore Christ and his benefits, is poured out upon the Church, creating and sustaining it, in a particular way and for a particular purpose in the midst of creation. It is the trysting place of God with humanity in the Word and through the Spirit. Here is the place in the midst of the created realities of actualization of the reconciliation of God, for it is the place of communion with Christ where we participate in, and taste, the powers of the age to come.

Thus the Church is at the heart of creation, and it is the place where the light and life of that order which the *oikonomia* of God is grasped in that community of union with God in the power of the Spirit through and by the Word. It is the place where the Royal Exchange is effected, where the Word, having adopted Himself to our body, has adapted us to His Spirit, and thus it is the place where the creation can be interpreted and understood in the light and life of the Word made flesh through the drawing and inspiration of the Spirit, as the theatre of God's glory to which all its groaning and travailing points. It is the place where order is perceived and grasped – not because it is the Church, as though the Church were an institution in and by itself which ministers the things of Christ and the Spirit – but because the Church is the firstfruits of the new creation, planted, watered, cared for and gathered by the Word and Spirit.

All order therefore, is to be understood by us as we are conjoined to Christ by the enlightenment and enlivening of the Spirit, as Christocentric. It is that enlivening and enlightenment, and therefore with the basis of our understanding of Order, with which Andrewes's sermons *Of the Sending of the Holy Ghost* are concerned.

The above points which have been set out are the framework, generally constructed from the whole of this corpus of sermons, to which the particular parts of them which are instanced should be understood. The specific emphases of the doctrine of the Holy Spirit which Andrewes places in particular sermons have this framework as their context and no one of them should be singled out as determinative of the whole. Andrewes has, in fact, a very consistent doctrine of the Holy Spirit, which, while it certainly contains such differing emphases, is not contradictory, but complementary within itself. Again, however, it must be emphasized not only that these emphases should be seen to point beyond themselves to that mystery of the Being of God which is beyond the grasp of human circumspection, understanding and apprehending, but also that what doctrine may be gleaned from this harvest of Andrewes's sermons can never be regarded as a satisfactorily rounded-off and definitively concluded doctrine of the Spirit. Andrewes would never have ventured on such, but himself would be satisfied to point beyond himself to that lively, living and life giving Spirit, in whom we live and move and have our being, from which all order and adornment and harmony of creation, church, society and the individual flows. and who may be comprehended but never apprehended.

In the following consideration of some of these sermons return by reference has to be made to themes already set out or mentioned in passing – for example, the incarnation, the sacraments and prayer – but from this different aspect of a concentration on the Holy Spirit. All the themes so treated, whether additional or already dealt with under different emphases, are aspects of the well-spring of Order, the Person or work of the Spirit who is the light in which we see light, the well of life drawing from which we live and move and have our being.

The doctrine of the Holy Spirit as expressed by Andrewes stands at the heart of the question of order. In it the relation between God and humanity, the community of union which the latter has with the former, is seen as the very bond of order. For here that order which is natural and proper to creation becomes visible and possible. This is because the order in which creation is held in that community of union, as the double contingency of creation to and from God (its utter dependence upon God for its beginning, its upholding and its purpose – its contingency to God, and yet its own quality, nature and identity which God wills it to have within that contingency to Him – its contingency from God), is perceived here and comprehended and may be practised. And that heart of the question of order is the Godly, natural man – not the man of nature, for this is Adamic, fallen, judged man – but man as he is naturally, humanity as it is found in right relation with God, being bound in the Holy Spirit in the Word to the Father – God's man, the proper man.

It is to that binding at the heart of order in the sermons of Lancelot Andrewes on the Holy Spirit that we now turn.

Notes

1 Lancelot Andrewes: *Ninety-six Sermons*, 'Sermon 15 Of the Resurrection', 1635 edn, p.548.

Chapter 12

Order: The Holy Spirit
and the Centre of Human Existence

The first 'Sermon of the Sending of the Holy Ghost, Preached before the King's Majestie at Green-wich, on the VIII of June, AD1608, being Whitsunday', on the text of Acts 2:1–4,[1] is concerned largely with the significance of the feast of Pentecost in relation to all that had gone before. The descent of the Spirit is described as one of the

> *Magnalia Dei* (as they bee termed after in the XI.*Verse*;) One of the *great* and *wonderfull Benefits* of *God*; Indeed, a *Benefit*, so *great* and so *wonderfull*, as there were not *tongues* enow, upon earth, to celebrate it withall, but there were faine to bee more sent from heaven, to helpe to sound it out throughly: Even a fresh supply of *tongues from heaven*.[2]

Andrewes raises the question as to whether or not this sending of the Holy Spirit may be treated as a benefit in itself. Is it an additional gift of God independent of all else that is bestowed, or is it to be regarded as the finale of a series of benefits and in a particular relation to those preceding it? Does it stand by itself, or is it the last of Christ's benefits? He notes that the Apostle Paul makes a distinction with regard to this sending of the Spirit, saying in one verse (Galatians 4:4) that '*God sent His Sonne*', and in another (Galatians 4:6) '*God sent the Spirit of His Sonne*'.[3] Yet this distinction does not mean the disjunction of the two sendings. The ascension of Christ, while it concludes the incarnation is not the completion of Christ's benefits. For there remains the bestowal and pouring out of all that has been accomplished from the incarnation to the ascension.

> We may . . . make this the last of Christ's Benefits: For, *Ascendit in altum*, is not the last; there is one still remaining, which is *Dona dedit hominibus* (Psalm LXVIII:18) . . . all in one gift, the gift of the *Holy Ghost*.[4]

All the feasts of our Lord

> though all of them be great, and worthy of all honour in themselves; yet to us, they are as nothing, any of them, or all of them (Even all the Feasts in the *Calendar*) without this Day, the Feast, which now we hold *Holy* to the sending of the *Holy Ghost*.[5]

The words 'to us' are to be noted here, for Andrewes is not dismissing the objective reality and validity of all that Christ accomplishes from the incarnation to the ascension. They do not fall, as accomplishments in themselves, without this further

141

benefit. His point is that these are made accessible 'to us' by this benefit of the sending of the Holy Spirit. Here is their application to us. Objective as they are, they become subjectively real, for by this sending, the Spirit conjoins us to all that Christ has once-and-for-all and sufficiently accomplished for us. This is the import of the 'to us'.

To elucidate the particular significance of Pentecost, Andrewes describes the descent of the Spirit in terms of the legal transaction of a will and testament. The Holy Spirit is Christ's Solicitor to us. He is in His descent the

> *Seale* or *Signature* (cf. Ephesians IV:30) . . . A *testament* we have and therein many faire legacies; but, until this day, nothing administered; *The administrations are the Spirits* (I Corinthians XII:4). In all these of Christs, there is but the *purchase* made, and payd for; and (as they say) *Ius ad rem* acquired: But, *Ius in re, Missio in possessionem, Liverie,* and *seizin*; that is, reserved till this day: For the *Spirit* is the *Arrha*, the *earnest* or the *investiture* of all, that Christ hath done for us.[6]

For Andrewes, then, the distinction of Pentecost and the uniqueness of the descent of the Spirit lie in the fact that nothing new is added to the acts of God in the Word made flesh, in the sense of an addition to what may have been lacking in the incarnation and atonement, but rather that all that has been accomplished from incarnation to ascension is here given to humanity in a novel and unique way. Pentecost is the handing over and signing of a legal document, the fair legacies of Christ, humanity's redemption, the purchase of which was made at the incarnation, paid for in crucifixion and declared in resurrection and ascension.

Comparisons as to the relative importance of the giving of the Word in the incarnation or the giving of the Spirit at Pentecost, are odious – 'We will not compare them: they are both above all comparison'. It is useless to ask which is the greater –

> That of the *Prophet, Filius datus est nobis* (Isaiah IX:6); Or that of the *Apostle, Spiritus datus est nobis* (Romans V:5): the *ascending of our flesh*; or the *descending of His Spirit: Incarnatio Dei,* or *Inspiratio hominis*; The mystery of *His incarnation,* or the Mystery of *our inspiration.* For, *Mysteries* they are both, and great *Mysteries of Godlinesse* both: and, in both of them, God *manifest in the flesh*: In the former by the *union* of *His Son*: in the later, by the *communion of His blessed Spirit.*[7]

Both the incarnation and the sending of the Spirit are concerned (1) with the actual Being of God in all his Godness, and (2) with the actual human situation of earthly and earthy reality. Both follow the same pattern therefore, which is God meeting the flesh in that reality. There is no room for gnosticism in Christology and no place for it in the doctrine of the Holy Spirit either. The realities of both God and man and the relation between them are clear in both incarnation and the outpouring of the Holy Spirit. In both of them we have to do with none other than 'God *manifest in the flesh.* . . . He, *clothed with our flesh* and we *invested with His Spirit.*' Andrewes conceives both these mysteries, the incarnation of the Word and the sending of the Holy Spirit, as a movement from God and back to God. By Pentecost, the 'royall exchange' is complete. As Christ took our nature, so here by the Holy Spirit we are made partakers of His.

The coming of Christ and the complementary coming of the Spirit bring to fulfilment a previous programme of the acts of God. The coming of Christ is the fulfilment of the whole movement of the history of Israel and of the Old Testament promise. The coming of the Holy Spirit fulfils the New Testament promise that we should be partakers of the divine nature. Here Andrewes cites Tertullian: '*Christus, Legis; Spiritus Sanctus, Evangelii Complementum*. The comming of Christ was the *fulfilling* of the *Law*: The comming of the Holy Ghost, is the *fulfilling* of the *Gospel*.'

This fulfilling of the fulfilment of the Old Covenant is emphasized by Andrewes's appeal to four of the early Fathers of the church – Cyprian, John Chrysostom, Augustine and Cyril of Alexandria.[8]

1   Cyprian: who emphasizes that the choice of the day of Pentecost was deliberate in order to hold and demonstrate the harmony between the two testaments, the old and the new. Christ's death was at the Feast of the Passover; he is the fulfilment of the Passover lamb of the old covenant. From the dating of the Passover in that old covenant, there were 50 days until the Israelites came to Sinai, where there was established the Feast of Pentecost in the event of the giving of the Law. So here there are 50 days between Christ our Passover sacrificed for us dying and dead on the cross, and the day of Pentecost, the giving of the new law in the descent of the Holy Spirit. This new law is the Gospel, sealed and delivered to humanity, the Royal Law of Christ the King.[9]

2   Chrysostom: who remarks that under the feast of Pentecost in the old covenant, it was then that men put the first sickle to the harvest. So here, the feast of Pentecost under the new covenant, is the time when those who were the chosen, called witnesses to Christ first put the sickle to every nation under heaven.[10]

3   Augustine: who notes that the number indicated by the name 'Pentecost' – fifty – is the number of the year of Jubilee under the old dispensation, the time of forgiving and cancelling debts and restoring estates and belongings and rights to persons previously dispossessed of them.[11]

4   Cyril: who applies Psalm 54:30 – *Emitte Spiritum tuum et creabuntur, et renovabis faciem terrae* – to the feast of Pentecost. Here is the second coming of the Spirit. His first coming concerns the work of creation; now this second coming is with regard to the work of re-creation. It is the same Spirit who works both. Just as at the first coming of the Spirit, order and harmony is established for creation, so now order and harmony in the work of the restoration and the renewal of humanity in Christ is established not only for humanity but for all creation.[12]

Here, then, Andrewes emphasizes the Holy Spirit as the Spirit of re-creation and restoration under the new covenant. He does so in the context of the Order of the working out of God's design of redemption, stressing the continuity of God's acts towards humanity and His creation in the old covenant and into the new, and the constancy of the Order of the ways of God in so doing. Behind this Order of God's way towards creation, lies that Order which God eternally is in Himself as the Triune God, that is, the Order of God's Being.

This foundational theme of Andrewes's view of order is then applied to the subjective disposition of the Apostles in the receiving of the Spirit – 'How Hee found them framed, and fit to receive such a Guest.'[13] As there is an order of the Divine being and acts, so there should be a corresponding order of the existence and circumstances of those called into relation to the Being of God expressed in His acts and to receive such benefits. As he expounds this, Andrewes is careful to show constantly the parallel between the disposition of the apostles and the disposition of God. This disposition of the apostles is categorized by Andrewes into:

1   unanimity
2   uniformity and
3   longanimity.

Regarding unanimity, no spirit, notes Andrewes, can vivify a natural body if its members are dismembered.

> Can any spirit *animate* or give life to members dismembered, unlesse they be first united and compact together? It cannot: *Unitie* must prepare the way to any *spirit*, though but *naturall*. A faire example we have, in *Ezekiel, Chap.XXXVII.* A sort of scattered dead bones there lay: They were to be *revived . . . and then, when they were thus united, then and not before, called Hee for the Spirit from the foure winds, to enter them and to give them life.* No Spirit, Not the ordinary, *naturall Spirit* will come, but where there is a way made and prepared by *accord* and unitie of the bodie.[14]

Having taken this exemplar from Ezekiel, Andrewes immediately removes his thought into the interior life of God and the role of the Holy Spirit there. Just as swiftly he moves on to the role of the Holy Spirit in the incarnation of the Word and straight on from there to the work of the Spirit towards the church. In all this there is a parallelism exhibited and the constancy of order, both uncreated order which the Being of God is, and its correspondent created order reflecting this and in harmony with it in its own created quality and nature, is stressed:

> Now then take the *Holy Ghost*, the Spirit of all *spirits*, the *third Person in Trinitie*: He is the very *essentiall Unity, Love,* and *Love knot* of the two Persons, the *Father* and the *Sonne*; even of God with God. And He is sent to be the *Union, Love* and *Love-knot* of the two *Natures* united in Christ; even of God with man. And can we imagine, that He will enter (Essentiall unitie) but where there is unitie? The *spirit* of *unitie*, but where there is *unitie* of *spirit*? Verily there is not, there cannot possibly be a more proper and peculiar, a more true and certaine disposition, to make us meet for Him, than that qualitie in us, that is likest His nature and essence, that is *unanimitie*.[15]

But this disposition of the recipients of and partakers in the Order of the Being and acts of God, is not created by human endeavour, however: 'Faith, to the Word; and Love to the Spirit, are the true Preparatives.'

This faith and this love are not our achievements. Andrewes's theology as to faith in and love towards God, as instanced in, for example, his sermons on Prayer (which will be examined later), is abundantly clear that these two virtues are the work of sheer unmerited grace. In the second sermon on the Holy Spirit, he is also clear that the Holy Spirit had been operative before in the existence of Israel and towards the apostles themselves. Because of this prior operation they were in this fit state to receive the Spirit further and in more permanent abundance. No thought that some human working and achieving of these virtues are the necessary prerequisites before God can act and the Spirit descend, is present in Andrewes's mind and proclamation. It is a matter of human working and achievement that the opposites – 'discord and dis-united mindes' – are a 'fatall or forcible opposition to His entrie'. Andrewes treats the phrase 'of one accord' in his text from the Acts of the Apostles to mean 'unanimity, of one mind'. This of itself is needful, but not enough. So he passes to his second point which he stretches to fit the characteristic pattern of the Laudian preoccupation and passion for uniformity, namely the uniformity is demonstrated by the fact that the apostles were all gathered together under one roof.

Uniformity is the necessary outward seal and the essential evidence of inward unanimity:

> God's will is, wee should be, as upon one foundation, so under one *roofe*: That, is His doing, *Qui facit unanimes*, etc. (Psalm LXVIII:6) *Hee that maketh men of one minde to dwell in one house.*[16]

Again we may see Andrewes's theological assertion that this uniformity is not achieved by human will and activity, but is *God's doing*.

The practice of the early Christians as evidenced in the Acts of the Apostles is cited here to show the disposition towards uniformity. The apostles –

> where they pray, *they prayed altogether (Acts IV:24)* When they heard, *they heard all together (Chapter VIII:6)* When they *brake bread*, they did it *all together (Verse 46.) All together*, ever; not, in one place, some; and some in another: but . . . all in one and the selfe-same *place*. For, say what they will, *Division of places* will not long be without *division of mindes*. This must be our ground. The same *Spirit*, that loveth *unanimitie*, loveth uniformitie; unitie even in matter of *circumstance*, in matter of *place*. Thus the *Church* was begun; thus it must be continued.[17]

Beside the points of unanimity and uniformity, Andrewes notes that the Fathers of the early church laid a third – longanimity, the patience of the apostles in waiting the 50 days for the promised outpouring of the Holy Spirit. This he deduces from the first part of his text: 'When the Day of Pentecost was come (or, when the fifty days were fulfilled)'.

He seizes on the fact that while this feast had various names before this time,

> the *Feast* of the *Law*, the *Feast* of *harvest*, the *Feast* of *Pentecost*: We may put to a fourth (out of *Deut. 16:9.*) It is there called the *Feast of Weekes*. It is not *houres* will serve the turn, nor yet *dayes*: it must be *weekes*, and as many weekes as be *dayes* in a weeke, to make it *Pentecost* (that is) *fifty dayes*. This long they sate by it (as it is in the next verse) and tarried patiently the Lord's leisure, till He came unto them, *Qui crediderit ne festinet* (saith the Prophet *Esay*) *He that beleeveth, let him not be hastie*: And, *si moram fecerit, expecta Eum* (saith *Abacuk*) *If He happens to stay, stay for Him*. And so we shalle, if we call to minde this, that He hath waited for us and our conversion, more yeares, than we doe dayes for Him.[18]

The patience which is laid upon us corresponds to the patience which God has with us: 'We are called to a stance whereby we find ourselves tarrying the Lord's leisure.' Again this underlines Andrewes's insistence that the initiative in matters of faith lie with God, for our faith, it is clearly implied, rests not on our achievement, but on God's faithfulness.

In these three interdependent and interrelated stances of unanimity, uniformity and longanimity, Andrewes must not be interpreted in any way as saying that the Holy Spirit is dependent upon how humanity disposes itself. The sending and work of the Holy Spirit is not determined by a precedent human work.

He touches explicitly on this question in the second sermon *Of the Sending of the Holy Ghost*.[19] One particular point at issue dealt with in this sermon is the estate of the apostles before Pentecost, compared with their estate after the event. He is clear on the fact that in order to think, speak and act aright, men must be filled with the Spirit first, and this is the Holy Spirit, not some affectation taken up and exhibited. The Holy Spirit came in 'wind' and 'tongues' – 'spirit and speech' – and came to 'helpe our infirmities':

> *Spirit*, because *speech* without *spirit*, is but a dead *sound* like the *tinckling of a Cymball* (I Cor. 13:1). *Speech*; because *spirit* without *Speech*, is but as the *spirit* which Christ cast forth, (Luke 11:14) and *illud erat mutum*, a *dumbe spirit*, none the better for it. Which made the Holy Ghost come in *spirit* and *speech*. . . .
> But in *spirit* first, and then *speech*. So is the order. The Holy Ghost begins within, *a centro*, and worketh outward: alters the *minde*, before it change the *speech*: giveth another *heart*, before another *tongue*: workes on the *spirit*, before on the *phrase* or utterance: ever, so. It is preposterous, and all out of order, to have the *tongues* come, before the *wind*; where they doe, it commonly falls out in such, all their religion is in common *phrases* and *termes* well got by heart, and nothing else. This for their *joyning*, and for their *order*.[20]

This order of the Spirit descending and working upon human existence is the fundamental of order. Before any perception, any word, any deed, there must be this inspiring context of the Spirit's order.

There are those who misinterpret the Spirit and confuse their hot and zealous spirits or humours for the Holy Spirit and His operation. Indeed there are those possessed with that which is manifestly not the Spirit and His Wind, but with another individualistic

> *windie humour* proceeding from the *spleene*, supposed to be this *Wind* here, and they that *filled* with it (if no bodie will give it them) taking to themselves the *style* of the *godly brethren*. I wish it were not needfull, to make this observation. But, you shall easily know it, for an humour: *Non continetur termino suo*; It owne limits will not hold it. They are ever mending *Churches, States, Superiours*; mending all, save themselves: *alieno, no suo*, is the note to distinguish an humour.[21]

Andrewes thus underlines his constant theme that the disorder which lies at the heart of church, state and society is caused by a disjunction between the human spirit and the divine Spirit. Conversely, all order in church, state and society, is dependent upon the proper relation between humanity and the Holy Spirit, the

Creator Spirit, the Spirit of the Word and therefore the Spirit of Divine Rationality and Order bringing forth, building and upholding, inspiring and enlightening created order in correspondence to His Divine Order. The 'Wind' of the Spirit represents

> the *saving grace*, which all are to have (so to serve God, that they may please Him;) as necessary to all, and without which, we can be no more, in our *spirituall* life, than we can, without our *breath*, in our *naturall*. [22]

Andrewes then proceeds to demonstrate by an examination of the respective estates of the apostles before and after Pentecost, that there is a total dependence on, and no intrusive question of human achievement in, the operation and order of the Spirit. Before the sending of the Spirit at Pentecost, the apostles 'were not emptie or void of the Spirit, before this comming'. Christ after his resurrection had breathed on them and bidden them so to receive the Spirit. This shows, says Andrewes, that there are portions or measures of the Spirit given, as is paralleled in Elisha's request (I Kings 2:9) for a double portion of Elijah's spirit. It is the same Spirit who comes twice to the apostles, but now in a new way in this second coming at Pentecost:

> That, as there are degrees in the wind, *Aura, ventus, procella*; a *breath*, a *blast*, a *stiffe gale*: so there are in the *Spirit*. One thing, to *receive the Spirit*, as on *Easter-day*; another, as on *Whit-sunday*. Then, but a *breath*: now, a *mighty wind*: then, but *received* it; now, *filled with it*. *Sprinkled* before, as with a few drops, *Ezekiels stillabo Spiritum*; but now comes *Joels Effundam spiritum* (which very Text is alleged at the XXVIII. *verse* after by Saint *Peter*) *powred out plenteously*, and they *baptized* (that is) *plunged* in it. *Imbuti Spiritu*, covered with some part of it; so were they before: here now, they bee *induti Spiritu*, clothed all over with *power from above*, as Christ promised (*Luke* XXIV:XLIX.) To conclude: the Holy Ghost came here (saith Leo) *cumulans, non inchoans; nec novus opere, sed dives largitate*: rather, by way of *augmenting the old*, than *beginning a new*. Though (to say the truth) both wayes Hee came here. The rule of the *Father* is (*Hierome* and *Cyrill* have it) where the Holy Ghost was before, and is said to come againe, it is to be understood, one of these two waies: Either of an *increase* of the former, which before was had; or of some *new* not had before, but sent now for some new effect. *Breath* they had before: *breath* and *wind* are both of one kinde: differ only *secundum magis et minus*: to be *filled*, is but to *receive* only in a *greater measure*: therefore greater, because their worke was now greater. Before, but to the *lost sheepe of Israel*: now to all the stray *sheepe* in all the *mountaines* of the whole earth.[23]

Andrewes is insistent that the difference in the various sendings and comings of the Spirit lies not in the quality of that Spirit – it is the same Spirit always – but in the measure which is apportioned. There is an *oikonomia* of the Spirit whereby the Spirit is measured to the particular task and need for the fulfilling of the task.

The novelty of Pentecost is that the Spirit comes, certainly in a fullness not hitherto, or ever thereafter to be, experienced, but also in a 'new form'. What the Holy Spirit imparts essentially is not something novel. Part of the *oikonomia* of the Spirit is the constancy of his Being and acts. But Pentecost stands out from all other outpourings and sendings of the Spirit for it is

Christs *Coronation day*, the day of placing Him on His *Throne*, when He *gave these gifts unto men*. That day, all *magnificence* was shewed, the like not to be looked for ever after.[24]

Here Andrewes emphasizes certain factors in the doctrine of the Holy Spirit.

1   The Spirit is Christ's gift – the largesse of a triumphant and newly-crowned monarch.
2   In this form, the sending of the Holy Spirit is a never to-be-repeated experience. Just as the sacrifice of Christ is full, sufficient and once for all, so too, the sending of the Spirit of Christ, conveying all that Christ has accomplished to humanity and bringing humanity into communion with Christ, is once and for all, sufficient and full. The Spirit now abides with the church always, and with Him and in Him and by Him, Christ's promise to be with us always even till the end of the ages, is fulfilled.
3   The Spirit is firmly anchored in his relation to the Word made flesh and all that the incarnate Word has accomplished for the redemption of humanity and creation.

The munificence of the gift of the Spirit on this day was in measure to the greatness of the task before the apostles. The scope of their work – all the world – and the necessities for the undertaking and fulfilling of this work, is set out by Andrewes as he examines the significance of their being filled, and the fire and the tongues which came upon them. That they were so filled and endowed was 'happie for the world'. Creation and redemption are here brought together by Andrewes:

Whereby, as the *line of the Creator* is said to have gone *into all Lands* (*Psal.* 19:4.) so is the *sound* of the *Apostles* said likewise to have gone as farre (*Rom.* 10:8) The one, to proclaime the *creation*; the other, the *redemption* of the *world*.[25]

The apostles were *ambassadors* to the whole world and the novel gift of Pentecost was to enable them to fulfil their embassage by witnessing in a new and more potent way to that which they already knew – the truth of Christ with whom they had companied, whose signs they had seen, whose words they had heard and whose death and resurrection and ascension they had witnessed.

The universal scope of the apostles' task is set out in context of the Spirit's *oikonomia* as the ground whereby the truth of Christ is proclaimed and practised. In other words the order of creation and redemption in the purpose of God's acts in the involvement of His Being in and by His Word and Spirit towards and in His handiwork, is that into which the apostles are grafted in the *oikonomia* of the Spirit.

That *oikonomia* of the Spirit in what was previous to Pentecost and, in turn, what was previous to the incarnation, in its relation to the *oikonomia* of Pentecost itself is set out in the first sermon *Of the Sending of the Holy Ghost*, to which sermon reference is now made again. The particular section of this sermon[26] which requires attention here is the exposition of that part of the whole text (Acts 2:1, 2, 3 and 4), 'There came . . . the sound' (Acts 2:2). This section of this sermon can be deemed very involved and obscure – unless detailed attention is paid to the exact wording.

The first point to be noted is that, according to Andrewes's interpretation, the sound of the wind heard by the apostles at the descent of the Spirit, is not the Spirit himself but his 'fore-runner'. Andrewes has pointed out already that the Holy Spirit in the signs of wind and fire accommodates Himself to the human senses:

> To the *eare* and the *eye* both . . . To the *eare* which is the sense of *faith*: To the *eye*, which is the sense of *love*. The *eare*, that is the ground of the *Word*, which is audible: the *eye*, which is the ground of the *Sacraments*, which are *visible*.[27]

(We may note how the Spirit is related here primarily to the Word, and secondarily to the Word made audible in the church's proclamation and the Word made visible in the church's sacraments.)

But as to the sound accompanying the Spirit's descent: this shows that the Spirit is:

> no *dumbe Spirit* but *vocall*. And so it is: the *sound thereof* is not only *gone into all Lands*: but hath beene *heard, in all ages*. Before the *Floud* it sounded in *Enoch* a *Prophet*, and *Noe a Preacher of righteousnesse*. All the *Law* long, it *sounded* in them, by whom *Moses was preached every Sabbath day*. The very beginning of the *Gospell* was with a *sound, Vox clamantis*: and but for this *sound* Saint *Paul* knoweth not, how we should doe; *How should they beleeve* (saith he) *in Him, of whom they have not heard?* and without a *sound*, there is no *hearing* (Rom. 10:14).[28]

There is a continuity of the Spirit and his work, for his sound encompasses and embraces the old and the new covenants. But it is in Andrewes's description of this sound that the obscurity lies. He notes that the word used here for sound is echo, and immediately goes on:

> you know, what sound an *Echo* is: a *sound* at the *second hand*, a sound at the rebound. *Verbum Domini venit ad nos; the Word of the Lord commeth to us*: there is the first sound, *To us*: and ours is but the *Echo* the *reflection* of it to you. God's first, and then ours second. For, if it come from us directly; and not from Him to us first, and from us then to you (*echo*-wise) it is to be suspected. A *sound* it may be; the Holy Ghost commeth not with it: His fore-runner it is not; for, that is.[29]

From this, the second point is to be deduced that the human word, of itself and by itself, has no authority. Authoritative human words witnessing to the truth of God must be derived from God. Only then can truth be conveyed from human individual to human individual. Here then we have a twofold 'echo' – from God to us and from individual to individual. Both are the sound of the Spirit, for, rightly grounded by the Spirit on the Word of God uttered by the Spirit, and called forth from the Word of God by the Spirit, then the true echo of this will be heard from one human mouth to another's human ear. An echo is a sound at rebound. The sound of the Holy Spirit is not a new word from God: it is a new way of conveying the Word which God has once and for all uttered in Christ, the incarnate Word.

Following on this is the third point that the unanimity, uniformity and longanimity of the apostles were evoked already by the Word of God who had confronted them in the flesh, by Jesus Christ the bearer of the Holy Spirit, to whom the same Spirit had borne witness in ages past – the hinterland of the incarnation which is the epic of Israel, out of the womb of which the Word became incarnate – by prophets, psalmists, priests, judges and kings in Israel. That same Word now sends the Spirit in full measure to empower and expand that which had been created already in the apostles, standing as they did within the inheritance of Israel and standing as they had in the company of the One who was the fulfilment of that inheritance.

The fourth and full and determinative point is the relation between Word and Spirit and the involvement of the apostles in the light of that relation. This is continued by Andrewes in his exposition of the figures of the wind and the tongues of fire in which the Holy Spirit came upon the apostles. By wind or breath we ourselves live: but by the tongue when added, we make others live too by communicating with that fiery tongue that knowledge which is life itself in the purpose and *oikonomia* of God.

It would no doubt be tempting to draw from all this that the apostles' disposition before they received the Holy Spirit at Pentecost is in the figure of the wind or breath – that is, the figure of wind expresses the Word who confronted them and with whom they kept company in His incarnate life on earth, and that the tongue stands for the Spirit who is now given to them to communicate that Word for all to have life and have it abundantly. But Andrewes is not guilty of such a facile application. The substance of the communication and the method of communication are not separable. As truth is, so is the way of truth. There is not such a distinction between Word and Spirit that they can be dealt with independently of each other. The Holy Spirit's role is to convey Christ to us and us to Christ. Therefore the whole Christ comes in the wind and the fiery tongues of the Spirit and those upon whom the Spirit is poured are conjoined in a community of union with the whole Christ. The wind and the tongues are the love and the grace of the Spirit, respectively, and as such they convey the love and the grace of the Word. While Andrewes seems to apportion the wind as a type to the Spirit and the tongue to the Word in this sermon, noting that the former serves the latter, yet no such neat or even hard and fast disjunction is implied in the context of this observation. Both wind and tongue, life and proclamation come from the Spirit to the one body, either of the individual or of the church. So, Andrewes can say that the tongue is the instrument of the Holy Spirit whereby Christ is set forth. It is in the whole operation of the Spirit that the whole Christ is present and proclaimed.

> So we have briefly the four properties of this *Wind*, and of the *Spirit* whose Type it is: That *it is sudden*, in the first comming; That it is *mightie* in proceeding; That it commeth *from heaven*; That it commeth *into the Church*; to fill it with the *Spirit* of *heaven*, and to carry it thither whence it selfe commeth. . . .
>
> This wind brought downe with it *tongues*; even *imbrem linguarum*, a whole shower of them, which is the next point, Of the *shew* which appeared, By which appearing, it appeareth plainly, that the *Wind* came not for themselves onely, but for others too beside: In that here is not only sent a *Wind*, which serveth for their own *inspiration*; but there be also sent *tongues* with it, which serve for *eloquution* (that is) to *impart* the *benefit* to more than themselves.
>
> It sheweth, that the Holy Ghost commeth and is given here, rather as *gratia gratis data*, to doe others good; than as *gratia gratum faciens*, to benefit themselves. *Charitas diffusa in corde* would serve them, Charity powred into their *hearts*; but *gratia diffusa in*

labiis, Grace *powred into their lips*, that is not needfull for themselves, but needfull to make others, beside them, partakers of the benefit. The *Wind* alone, that is to breathe withall; the *grace* of the Holy Ghost whereby our selves live: but, the *Wind* and *Tongues*, that is to speake withall; the *grace* of the Holy Ghost, whereby we make others live, and partake of the same knowledge to life. An union of the *Wind* and *Tongue* here on earth, expressing the unity of the *Spirit* and the *Word* in Heaven: that, as the *Wind* or breath in us is to serve the *Tongue*; so is the *Spirit* given, to set forth the *Word*, and the Holy Ghost to spread abroad the knowledge of Christ. . . .

But if we shall say to our tongue, as *David* did to his, *Awake up my glory* (that is) make it the glory of all the rest of our members; it can have no greater glory than this, to be the *Organ* of the Holy Ghost: to set forth, and *sound* abroad, the knowledge of Christ, *to the glory of God the Father*.[30]

So the figures applied to Word and Spirit in Andrewes's thought, while they are not mixed in confusion are variously applied. In this way the awareness of both the unity and diversity of the Triune Being of God is, perhaps unconsciously but intuitively, applied in his writings. Perhaps there is the application, not only here but throughout his sermons *On the Sending of the Holy Ghost*, of Gregory Nazianzen's observation that what is applicable to the Word is applicable to the Spirit save, of course, the assumption of the actual flesh.[31]

Behind this flexibility of application lies the twofold fact that Andrewes is careful not to erect an epistemology of the Spirit thereby not asking the abstract question 'How can we know God?' Rather, he is concerned only to relate that knowledge of God comes from the Father in the Word by the Holy Spirit – comes in the unique relation of the three Persons of the Godhead. Such is beyond human understanding, for God remains Lord over us and certainly over our theology. There can be no epistemology of the Spirit for Andrewes. If there could be this would mean that the knowledge of God is explicable from our side, that it could be reduced to our forms of understanding, and that ultimately some theory of knowledge would render the activity of the Spirit unnecessary.

The apostles were not, and we cannot be, concerned with

the crudities of their owne braine, idle, loose, undigested geere (God knoweth:) No, but pithy and wise *sentences*: those be *sicut dedit Spiritus*, such as the Holy Ghost gave them. It is after said (in the 11 verse) that by vertue of this, when they spake, they spake *Magnalia*: *Magnalia*, great and *high Points*; not *Trivialia*, base and *vulgar stuffe*, not worth the time it wasteth, and taketh from the hearer. Yet now, all is quite turned: and we are come to this, that this kinde of *speaking* is onely from the *Spirit* of God: and the other . . . is *studie*, or *affectation*, or I wote not what: but, *Spiritus non dedit*, that is certaine.[32]

Again this is touched upon in the first sermon *Of the Sending of the Holy Ghost*. The particular section dealing with this in this sermon concerns the nature of the wind from heaven. It is its source and direction which make this wind unique and it alone, unlike other winds, able to inspire with divine knowledge.

It came from Heaven. Winds (naturally) come not from thence, but out of the caves and holes of the earth: they blow not downward, but move laterally from one coast or climate to another. To come *directly downe*, not only *de sursum*, from above (so it may be, from the *middle region* of the *aire*) but *de caelo*, from Heaven it selfe; that, is *supernaturall*, sure: that, is a *Wind* out of God's *owne Treasury* indeed: that, points us plainely to Him, that is *ascended up into Heaven*, and now sendeth it downe from thence.

And therefore sendeth it *from Heaven*, that it may fill us with the *breath of Heaven*. For, as the *wind* is, so are the blasts, so is the *breath* of it: and, as is the *Spirit*, so are the *motions*, it useth; so are the *reasons*, it is carried by.

To distinguish this *Wind* from others, is no hard matter. If our *motions* come from *above*; if we fetch our grounds there, *de caelo*, from *heaven*, from *Religion*, from the *Sanctuary*; it is this wind: but those, that *come from earthly respects*, we know their *cave*; and that there is nothing but *naturall* in them. This *wind* came thence, to make us *heavenly minded, sapere quae sursum*, to *set our affections on things heavenly*, and to *frame the rules of our conversation agreeable unto heaven*. So wee shall know, what wind blowes; whether it be *de caelo*, or *de hominibus*: whether it be *defluxus coeli*, or *exhalatio terrae*; from *heaven* or of *men*, a *breath* from *heaven* or a *terrene exhalation*.[33]

It is to be emphasized that the whole tenor of Andrewes's sermons *Of the Sending of the Holy Ghost* is an ontological concern and not just (though this cannot be divorced from the other) a noetic one. What is primary is the Being of the Spirit and the Word and the Father, the relations which constitute the Godhead, and the relation of the Triune God through the Spirit and the Word with humanity and with creation. This latter relation concerns and affects the totality of the human being, the individual existence, the totality of the body of believers, the church, and indeed, the totality of creation. It is the relation by which and in which we live and move and have our being as God's humanity – not because we have this by nature, but because by the grace and loving kindness of the Word and the Spirit and by the will of the Father we are conjoined to the One who is God's man, clothed in that proper humanity which He has re-created in Himself from His incarnation to His ascension. So we, thus conjoined to Him by the Spirit, are brought to a community of union with the divine Life itself. This it is which is the ground of all Order in creation because it rests on the Order which God is in Himself and which He expresses in His work *ad extra*, towards creation. It is therefore the foundation of natural law, for it exhibits and makes possible the grounding and working of the created realities as they are intended to be in their true nature – what they are naturally in the sight and *oikonomia* of God.

The noetic aspects, our knowledge of God, of ourselves in His light and of this relation with him, are certainly part of this, but Andrewes is concerned principally here in these sermons with these living and determining relations of the uncreated existence of God with the created existence of his handiwork which relations are brought about by the Spirit proceeding from the Father and the Son.

Andrewes is clear that it is impossible to separate the work of any one Person of the Trinity from the work of the other two. He is equally clear that, whether in the act of creation or the work of re-creation, the whole Trinity is involved. This heightens the relation between the Order which God eternally is in Himself and the corresponding Order of His handiwork in its created dimension and quality. Thus he can say in his fourth sermon *Of the Sending of the Holy Ghost*:

absolute necessity it is; in both the maine principall workes of the Deitie, all three persons cooperate and have their concurrence. As, in the beginning of the *creation*, not onely *dixit Deus* was required, which was the *Word*; but *ferebatur Spiritus*, the *motion of the Spirit*, to give the *Spirit* of life, the life of Nature. As, in the *Genesis*, so in the *Palingenesie* of the world, a like necessity: not onely the *Word* should take *flesh*; but flesh also *receive Holy Spirit*, to give life, even the *life of grace*, to the *New Creature*. It was the Counsell of God, that every person in the *Trinitie*, should have his part in both; in one worke, no lesse than the other, and we therefore *baptized* into all three.[34]

Creation and the work of redemption are inseparable in Andrewes's thought, are so because the Trinity in its three Persons works in both. This is emphasized constantly. And not only in these two 'maine principall acts', but in the individual episodes of the work of redemption. For example, we find again in the eighth sermon *Of the Sending of the Holy Ghost*, preached on Luke 3:21–2, concerning the baptism of our Lord:

To looke into the Text, there is no man but at the first blush will conceive there is some great matter in hand. First, by the *opening of heaven*: for, that *opens* not, for a small purpose. Then, by the solemne presence of so great Estates at it: for, here is the whole *Trinitie* in person. The *Son in the water*, the *Holy Ghost in the dove, the Father in the voice*. This was never so before, but once: Never but twice, in all; in all the Bible. Once in the Old Testament, and once in the New. In the Old, at the *creation*, the beginning of *Genesis*. There finde we God, and the *Word* with God creating, and the *Spirit of God moving upon the face of the waters*. And now here againe, at Christ's *christening* in the new.[35]

In all the works of God the apostles were confronted with God in all His Godness. Andrewes notes that the knowledge of God was given to them because God was present with them and they were disposed in obedience to the compulsive presence and enlightenment. However, how that presence and revelation was brought to bear – the mechanics, so to speak of the Being of God as opposed to the mode of the expression of that Being and revelation – he refuses to investigate. The how of God he refuses to try to fathom. That, for Andrewes, would be utter presumption.

But the work of the Holy Spirit, through which the work of Christ is sealed and delivered, is not confined to one direction. The course the Spirit takes in conveying Christ to us is the same direction as that observed in Word made flesh. The Word descends and becomes flesh and ascends with the flesh back to the father, so that in the Being of God there is now incorporated our humanity. In the same way the Spirit descends, inspires, enlightens and empowers, and evoking and grasping our human words and actions to Himself, ascends to present us through Christ to the Father. Here we are concerned in Andrewes's writings with the epiclesis and paraclesis of the Spirit – the coming of the Spirit in this particular manner and movement.

The Spirit descends to us as He did to the apostles, but now through the proclamation and sacraments of the church. He puts into our mouth the Word of God made audible, and into our hands the Word of God made visible; He uses our mouths and our hands and empowers them with that which He has, which is nothing less than Christ Himself. It is not only a question of giving Christ to us, but of uniting us with the already completed and sufficient work of Christ in His incarnate, dead, resurrected and ascended humanity. We are given to participate in the once-for-all and sufficient work of Christ by the operation of the Holy Spirit. Therefore He not only descends *to us* but ascends *with us* – not only comes to bear upon us, but bears and carries us – and with us and our words and deeds returns to God, giving us to participate in the worship of heaven and in the everlasting communion of the Trinity.

Again in the figure of the 'wind' in the first sermon *Of the Sending of the Holy Ghost*, this direction of the Spirit is set out:

> So doth *Salomon* (Eccles.I:6) describe the nature of the *Wind*: That *it goeth forth*, and that *it compasseth round about*, and then last, *That it returneth, Per circuitus suos*: So doth this, it commeth *from Heaven*, and it bloweth into the *Church*, and thorow, and thorow it, to *fill* it with the *breath* of *heaven*: and as it came *from heaven* to the *Church*, so it shall returne from the *Church, into Heaven* againe, *per circuitus suos*: and whose sailes it hath filled with that wind, it shall carry with along *per circuitus suos*; even to *see the goodnesse of the Lord in the Land of the living*, there to live with Him and His *Holy Spirit* for ever.
>
>   So we have . . . That it commeth *from heaven*; That it commeth *into the Church*; to fill it with the *Spirit* of *heaven*, and to carry it thither whence it selfe commeth.[36]

In this way our words and worship, which by themselves are nothing but words, the lalia of humanity, are made to participate in what has been done already in and by the Logos, the Word of God, and are lifted up into conjunction with the worship of the heavenly host. We are not only given faith, but lifted up in faith to where the end of faith is, the beatific vision of God.

Here we are concerned with what the Greek fathers taught as *theosis*. This has nothing whatsoever to do with the deification or divinization of humanity, as though that which is intrinsically human should be dissolved and swallowed up in divinity. Andrewes is adamant that by the descending, companying and ascending of the Holy Spirit involves not the changing of our humanity into what it is not, but the establishment of our humanity in a community of union with the divine existence – through the fallen, judged, Adamic humanity which the Word assumed and re-created in and from the incarnation to the ascension. In this we are bound to the Word and therefore to the existence of the Triune God.

The sermons *Of the Nativitie* are clear in the matter of the Word assuming Adamic flesh and nature. The same theme of the 'Royall Exchange', so prevalent in the sermons *Of the Sending of the Holy Ghost*, is found not surprisingly in these sermons on the incarnation. The latter are at the beginning of the 'Royall Exchange': the former at the completion of it. We may instance a few such observations on this theme of the Word assuming needful, judged human nature. The underlying awareness behind this theme is the Pauline 'He who knew no sin was made sin for us'; that is, the Word assumes sinful flesh and nature but does no sin therein, thus cancelling the power of sin over our flesh and nature just as Adam had admitted this power into it and over it.

Preaching on the text of Hebrews 2:16, that the Word took the seed of Abraham and not the seed of angels at the incarnation, Andrewes observes:

> And, what is the *seed of Abraham*, but, as *Abraham* himselfe is? And, what is *Abraham*? Let him answer himselfe; *I am dust and ashes*. What is the *seed of Abraham*? Let one

answer, in the persons of all the rest; *Dicens putridini, etc. saying to rottennesse, thou art my mother, and to the wormes, ye are my brethren.* 1. They [the angels] are *spirits*; Now, what are we, what is the *seed of Abraham? Flesh.* And what is the very harvest of this *seed* of *flesh?* what, but *corruption*, and *rottennesse*, and *wormes?* That is the substance of our bodies. 2. They [the angels], *glorious spirits:* We, vile bodies (beare with it, it is the *Holy Ghosts* owne terme, *Who shall change our vile bodies.*) And not only base and *vile*, but *filthy* and *uncleane: ex immundo conceptum semine, conceived of uncleane seed:* There is the *metall.* And, the mould is no better: the *wombe*, wherein we were conceived *vile, base, filthy, and uncleane.* There, is our *quality . . .*

The *seed of Abraham*, with their *bodies, vile bodies, earthly bodies* of clay, bodies of *mortality, corruption*, and *death:* These Hee *tooke*, these Hee *tooke for all that . . .* And we (unworthy, wretched *men* that we are) above and before the *Angels*, the *Cherubim*, the *Seraphim*, and all the *Principalities*, and *Thrones*, in this dignity.[37]

Whereby, He, and we, become not only *one flesh*; (as *man* and *wife* doe, by *conjugall union*:) but, even one *bloud* too, (as *brethren*, by *naturall union*:) *Per omnia similis* (saith the *Apostle*, in the next verse after againe) *sin only set aside: Alike* and suitable to us *in all things: flesh*, and *bloud*, and *nature* and all.[38]

In the context of the Eucharist, the communion of the body and blood of Christ, Andrewes writes:

Now, *the bread which we breake, is it not the partaking of the body, of the flesh, of Jesus Christ* (I Cor. 10:16)? It is surely; and by it, (and by nothing more,) we are made partakers of this blessed union. A little before, (I Cor. 10:14) He said; *Because the children were partakers of flesh and bloud, He also would take part with them*; May not we say the same? Because He hath so done, taken ours of us, we also ensuing His steps, will participate with Him, and with His flesh which He hath taken of us. It is most kindely, to take part with Him, in that, which He took part in, with us; and that to no other end, but that He might make the receiving of it by us a meanes, whereby He might *dwell in us, and we in Him.* He *taking our flesh*, and we *receiving* His *Spirit*; by His *flesh*, which He tooke of us, *receiving* His *Spirit*, which He imparteth to us; That, as He, by ours, became *confors humanae naturae*; so we, by His, might become *confortes divinae naturae*, partakers of the Divine nature. Verily, it is the most streight and perfect *taking hold* that is. No union so knitteth, as it; Not *consanguinity; Brethren fall out*: Not *mariage; man and wife are severed.* But, that which is nourished, and the nourishment, wherewith, they never are, never can be *severed*; but remaine one for ever. With this Act then of mutuall taking, *taking of His flesh*, as He hath taken ours, let us seale our dutie to Him this day, for not taking *Angels*, but the *seed of Abraham*.[39]

Again and again through these sermons, the same theme sounds, the taking to himself by the Word of our Adamic flesh and nature at the incarnation.

Therefore, Hee became bound for us also, entred bond anew, tooke on Him, not onely our *Nature*, but our *Debt; our Nature* and *Condition* both. *Nature*, as men; *Condition*, as sinfull men.[40]

In the same way, the corollary of this, our partaking of the Divine nature is set out equally firmly in the sermons *Of the Sending of the Holy Ghost.* The transaction of and by and in the grace of God in Christ, His covenant with us and with His handiwork is complete. This 'Royall Exchange' is the establishment of a right relation of humanity with God, which relation is the ground and foundation of all Order and its perception and application, for it is the true centre of our existence.

One further note may be made: and this concerns the dynamic and lively way in which Andrewes (and indeed his Laudian contemporaries) approach the relation between our existence and the existence of God. The doctrine of the Trinity is no mere concept set out in abstract terms. We are related, in this 'Royall Exchange', to the Triune Being and action of God. The doctrine is never static. Rather, it is, to take but one example in the matter of the sealing of the covenant made by God with humanity in the outpouring of the Holy Spirit, of '*Filius orans; Pater donans; Spiritus consolans*. The *Sonne praying*; the *Father granting*; the *Spirit comforting*.'[41]

It must not be thought that the Laudian's trinitarianism was of the *economic* variety – that is, deducing a doctrine of the Trinity merely from a consideration of the acts of God *ad extra*. The instances of God's acts in incarnation, crucifixion, resurrection and ascension, and here in the outpouring of the Holy Spirit, make it abundantly clear that there is no separation or divide in the Laudian mind between the acts of God and the Being of God. God is as He acts and acts as He is. His acts are in strict conformity with the nature of His Being, and the quality of His acts in accordance with the mode of His Being, that is a Being of Love. It is here that the *noetic* and *ontic* considerations of doctrine above all are seen as interlocked and inseparable. The doctrine of the Trinity is a matter both, indissolubly, of revelation and reconciliation. As God reconciles so He reveals; and as He reconciles in sheer unmerited grace which far surpasses the expectation or merit of human standards, so He reveals himself as the God who is beyond comparison and who exists in a way which we can comprehend but never apprehend in the unity and diversity of His threefold Being.

The Laudians were quite well aware that the interaction of God with humanity in the incarnation and in the outpouring of the Holy Spirit, was essentially a mystery which was to be lived in and not thought out and explained. In the last resort the Trinity was to be acknowledged, adored and worshipped, not explained, formulated and encompassed. The living relation between humanity and God established by God by the Word and through the Spirit was theology in praise, not philosophy in speculation.

Notes

1   Lancelot Andrewes: *Ninety-six Sermons*, 'Sermon 1 of the Sending of the Holy Ghost', 1635 edn, pp.595ff.
2   Ibid., p.595.
3   Ibid., p.596.
4   Ibid.
5   Ibid.
6   Ibid.
7   Ibid. In passing it may be noted that this is one of the passages throughout Andrewes's sermons in which he delicately uses an alliterative contrast of words and terms in order to highlight the cohesion of what the respective words and terms substantially convey. By this literary device he highlights both the distinction and the unity of the acts of God. It also may be brought to attention here that his use of 'godlinesse' refers not to

human piety but to the Godness of God. The great acts of God are primarily acts which concern the Being of God, and not acts accomplished either by an agent or on any human response or achievement. They are acts of God's initiative and involve His Being. He is as He acts and acts as He is. As such they are acts of sheer grace dependent on nothing but God's good will and loving kindness.

8   Ibid., pp.597ff.
9   Cyprian: *Ser. de Spiritu.*
10 Chrysostom: *Hom. 4 in Act. Apost. init.*
11 Augustine: *Ep.* 119.
12 Cyril of Alexandria: *De Sanct. Trin. Dial.* 7.
13 Lancelot Andrewes: *Ninety-six Sermons*, 'Sermon 1 of the Sending of the Holy Ghost', 1635 edn, p.598.
14 Ibid.
15 Ibid., pp.598, 599.
16 Ibid., p.599.
17 Ibid., p.599.
18 Ibid., p.600.
19 Lancelot Andrewes: *Ninety-six Sermons*, 'Sermon 2 of the Sending of the Holy Ghost', 1635 edn, pp.608ff.
20 Ibid., p.609.
21 Ibid., p.610.
22 Ibid., p.611.
23 Ibid.
24 Ibid., p.612.
25 Ibid., p.613.
26 Lancelot Andrewes: *Ninety-six Sermons*, 'Sermon 1 of the Sending of the Holy Ghost', 1635 edn, pp.595ff.
27 Ibid., p.600.
28 Ibid., p.601.
29 Ibid., p.601.
30 Ibid., pp.603f.
31 Gregory Nazianzen: *Orationes.*
32 Lancelot Andrewes: *Ninety-six Sermons*, 'Sermon 2 of the Sending of the Holy Ghost', 1635 edn, p.614.
33 Lancelot Andrewes: *Ninety-six Sermons*, 'Sermon 1 of the Sending of the Holy Ghost', 1635 edn, p.602.
34 Lancelot Andrewes: *Ninety-six Sermons*, 'Sermon 4 of the Sending of the Holy Ghost', 1635 edn, p.632.
35 Lancelot Andrewes: *Ninety-six Sermons*, 'Sermon 8 of the Sending of the Holy Ghost', 1635 edn, p.675.
36 Lancelot Andrewes: *Ninety-six Sermons*, 'Sermon 1 of the Sending of the Holy Ghost', 1635 edn, p.603.
37 Lancelot Andrewes: *Ninety-six Sermons*, 'Sermon 1 of the Nativitie', 1635 edn, p.3.
38 Ibid., p.5.
39 Ibid., p.9.
40 Lancelot Andrewes: *Ninety-six Sermons*, 'Sermon 4 of the Nativitie', 1635 edn, p.28.
41 Lancelot Andrewes: *Ninety-six Sermons*, 'Sermon 3 of the Sending of the Holy Ghost', 1635 edn, p.623.

Chapter 13

Order: The Spirit's Gifts and the Relation of Existences

The perception, establishment and the living out of Order is a matter of the perception, establishment and the living out of that relation, the community of union, between God and humanity which Christ has forged out and through the Spirit has given. To the furtherance of this general *modus vivendi*, Christ has made available particular gifts by the Spirit. The most pertinent consideration here is that of sermon seven *Of the Sending of the Holy Ghost*. This was 'Preached before the Kings Maiestie at Green-Wich on the XII. of June, A.D.1614, being Whitsunday'.

The text (Psalm 68:18), Andrewes notes, begins with the ascending of Christ, 'Thou art gone up on high', and ends with the descending of the Holy Spirit, 'That God might dwell among us'. Here is a divine movement centring on the relation between the ascended Christ and the descended Spirit. It is, of course, a text from the old testament, but as Andrewes remarks, that it is Christ to whom in prophecy it refers, 'The Apostle is our warrant (Ephes.4.8.)'.[1] As to God dwelling among us, that this is the Holy Spirit is clear, he continues, from our Lord's own promise (John 14:17).

Moses, notes Andrewes, was a type of Christ. His particular ascension was of Mount Sinai where he received gifts, the Law, the Priesthood and the Ark of the Covenant above all to be the pledges of God's presence among his people. This was the significance of these gifts which Moses received. Likewise with Christ at his ascension; but the gifts he receives are qualitatively more than those given to Moses. Indeed, that which Christ receives is the source of all gifts: 'God, not by a wooden Arke, but by his owne Spirit came to dwell among them.'[2] Christ only ascended because he first descended. Andrewes compares and contrasts the descended and ascended states to heighten the condescension of Christ in the humility of his incarnation and atonement:

> *Christ*, in His *ascendant, going up; Christ, on high* is a good sight. A better sight to see Him so, *tanquam aquila in nubibus*, than *tanquam vermis in pulvere*; an *Eagle* in the clouds, than a *worme* in the dust, as a great while we did. To see a *cloud to receive Him*, than a *gravestone* to cover Him. Better, *leading Captivity*, than himselfe led *captive*: Better, *receiving gifts for men*, than receiving *wrong* from them. Yet, it is strange, *S.Paul (Ephes.4.)* commenting upon this *verse* (whereto we shall often have recourse;) as we are looking at *His going up on high*, pulls us backe, and tells us of His being here down below: *In that He ascended*, what is it (saith He) *but that He descended first*? A note, out of season, one would thinke. But, he best knew, what was proper, and pertinent; and that is, that *Christs going up, is ascensus post descentum*.
>
> And this, as it is for *His glory*: (For, when one hath beene *downe*, then to *get up*, is twice to get up. Far more, for *His glory*, than if He never had been *downe*. And, the lower

159

He hath been *downe*, the more glorious is His *getting up*. *Bis vincit qui victus vincit*; Being overcome, to overcome, is *twice* to overcome: For so, he overcomes his overcomers, and that is a double victory) As, for *His glory*; so, for *our good*. For, His being above, before He was below, is nothing to us. But being *below* first, and then, that He *went up*, that is it we hold by. As the *Sonne of God He came downe: As the Sonne of man, He went up*. If, as the *Sonne of man*; there is hope, that the *Sons of men* may doe the like. . . .

Keeping just correspondence betweene his *high*, and his *low*. That, was *ad ima terrae*, to the *lowest parts of the earth*, than which none lower, none beneath them. This was *ad summa Coeli*, the highest top of the heavens, than which none higher, none above them.[3]

It is the role of the Holy Spirit to make us like Christ by conjoining our being to his.

He that is thus *high* now, was once *low* enough. We to be as He was, before we be as He is. Descending, by *humility*; con-descending, by *charity*. For, he that so *descendeth* with Him, he it is, and none other, that shall *ascend* up after Him.[4]

So, by the Holy Spirit dwelling in our midst, we are given to participate in Christ's incarnation and atonement for us here that we might ascend and dwell with him hereafter.

Christ ascended in an estate different from that in which he descended. Andrewes notes that He came down as Son of God and ascended as Son of Man – He that has grasped our humanity and made it His own has ascended in and with that humanity which is now eternally His. Our humanity is writ into the very existence of the Triune God by the ascension of the Word made flesh. In that humanity Christ pleads for and makes intercession for us as we participate in all that Christ's humanity was and is and ever shall be, in its lowliness and in its glorified state. By the Holy Spirit given to us and dwelling with us, we are conjoined to that humility and that exaltation. The latter state cannot be reached without passing through the former, and it is to enable us so to pass that the Spirit is given, and with the Spirit Christ's gifts for us.

In this seventh sermon *Of the Sending of the Holy Ghost*, it is noteworthy how Andrewes uses the terms of contemporary military strategy to indicate the results of the victory of Christ, the nautical endeavours towards the geographical discoveries of his day and the prevalent commercial practice employing agents, to illustrate the passage and relation between heaven and earth, the ascended Christ and us:

He went not up till the battell fought, and the victorie gotten. For the next point is, *Captivitie is led captive*. So, no more for Him here to doe: *Consummatum est*. And after it was *consummatum est* for us, no reason but it should be *consummatum sum* with Him also.

But though all be done here, all is not there; there *above*, whither He is *gone*. There is still somewhat to be done for us. Wee have our cause there to bee handled against a false and slanderous adversarie (so *Job* found him.) By meanes of His being there *on high, habemus Advocatum* (saith Saint *John*) *we have an Advocate*, will see it take no harme. . . .

But as our case is (for the most part) wee rather stand in need of a good *High Priest*, to make *intercession*; than of a readie *Advocate* to put in a *plea* for us. And He is there likewise to that end: *on high* within the *sancta sanstorum*, as a *faithfull High Priest*, for ever to appeare, and make an *attonement* with God for our transgressions. Thus, there, all is well. . . .

By being there, He is the better able to helpe us: to helpe us against our enemies. For, in that He is *on high*, He hath the vantage of the *high ground*; and so able to annoy them, to *strike them downe*, and lay them flat. . . .

To helpe us against our wants. Wants, both *temporall*; (for, from *on high* He can *send downe a gracious raine upon His inheritance* to refresh it:) and *spirituall*; for from *on high*, He did send downe the *gifts* and *graces* of the *spirit*, the *dona dedit* of this *Feast*, and of this *Text*, both. Looke to the Text. He is so gone up, that *our enemies are His captives*: we shall not need to feare, they can goe no further than their chaine. And, though He be gone; *dona dedit*, He is ready to supply us, upon our need, with all *gifts* requisite. We shall not need to want: for, *no good thing will he with-hold from them, that have Ascensiones in corda*, that have their hearts upon Him and upon His *ascension*: that lift up their hearts to Him there. . . .

In that He is *ascended* into heaven, *Heaven* is to be *ascended to: by the new and living way that is prepared through the veile of His flesh*, a passage there lieth thither. They talke of *discoveries*, and much adoe is made of a *new passage* found out to this or that place: what say you to this discoverie *in altum*, this passage into the *land of the living*? Sure, it passes all. And this *discovery* is here: and upon this discovery, there is begunne a *commerce*, or *trade* of entercourse, betweene heaven and us. The commodities whereof, are the *gifts*: (we shall after deale with them.) And a kind of *agencie*: Christ being there, for us; and the *Spirit* here, for God; either *Agent* for other. It is the happiest newes, this, that ever came to mankind.[5]

This conversation and concourse between heaven and earth, God and humanity, is brought about by the Spirit bearing and distributing the gifts of Christ. The Spirit is the gift of gifts, the source of all gifts. Andrewes, in dealing with these gifts, begins first with this general gift of the Spirit himself. The insistences that the Holy Spirit is nothing less than God in all His Godness, dwelling with us, and that the Spirit is firmly the Spirit of the Word and that Word made flesh, are to be noted. To speak of all the gifts of Christ which he has to bestow by the Spirit

one hour-glasse will not serve, they bee so many. To recapitulate *Dona in Dona*, all in one: it is the *gift* of *gifts*, the *Gift* of the Holy Ghost, the proper *Gift* or *Misile* of this day. . . .

God it is, this *Gift*. The *Text* is direct: *This giving* is, to the end, God *may dwell with us*. That cannot bee, if *Hee* that is *given*, were not God. So then, *Man* Hee carried up to *Heaven*: God Hee sent downe to *earth*: Our flesh is there, with God; His *Spirit*, here, with us. *Felix captivitas*, wee said before; *Felix cambium*, may wee now say: A *happy captivity*, that; a *blessed exchange* for us, this.

This is but one: it is expressed plurally; *Dona*, many: There be many in it.[6]

The universality of the distribution of these gifts by the Spirit is then noted. All are given variously but not all to one person. They are measured out part by part to all – even to His human enemies – that all might do good with them. There is no one who is outwith 'the verge of Christs bountie, of Dona dedit hominibus'.[7] The manner of the Spirit's dwelling among humanity is then touched upon. The Spirit proceeding from the Father and the Son dwells with us now:

God, that is the whole *Trinitie*, by this *Person* of it . . .[8]

For, He Himselfe is *Love*, the essentiall *Love*, and *Love-knot* of the *undivided Trinitie*.[9]

Christ mediates the Holy Spirit still through himself, on earth and among us. In particular, Andrewes stresses that it is through Christ's Body and Blood that the Spirit is given to us, through that incarnate, dead, resurrected and ascended Body given to us in the eucharistic feast. Even here, after the historical event of Jesus of Nazareth, there is no activity of the Spirit independent of, and in isolation from, the incarnation and the atonement. While the general gifts of the Spirit are both universally dispersed and also given in a particular way in the Eucharist and, indeed, in baptism, yet both these general and particular gifts are firmly anchored in the Spirit's relation to the Word made flesh. They are essentially Christ's gifts administered by the Spirit, and because they are so administered they are called, by reference, the gifts of the Spirit.

The fact that the gifts are universally spread does not imply indiscriminate or haphazard action on the part of God. There is Order in that the gifts of the Spirit, whatever and for whomsoever they may be, are the gifts of Christ who has overcome the darkness and chaos of creation and established that Order which God wills in Himself. They are gifts of the Order of love for the establishing and exercise of love. They are gifts of *love, joy* and *peace*.

It is in the particular sacramental gifts that the 'Royall Exchange' is effected, the nature of all the gifts of Christ through the Spirit seen, and a living relation established whereby our existence is anchored in communion with the ascended existence of the Word made flesh and therefore in communion with the heavenly places and the very existence of the Triune God. Speaking of Christ's gifts, Andrewes continues:

> You shall observe: there ever was and will be, a neere alliance, betweene His *dona dedit hominibus*, and His *dona reliquit hominibus*; The *Gifts* He sent, and the *Gifts* He *left* us. He left us the *gifts* of *His* body and *bloud*. His *body broken*, and full of the characters of *love*, all over. His *bloud shed*, every drop whereof is a great drop of *Love*. To those which were sent, these which were left (*love, joy, peace*) have a speciall con-naturall reference, to breed and to maintaine each other. His *body*, the *Spirit* of *strength*; His *bloud*, the *Spirit* of *comfort*: Both, the *Spirit* of *Love*.
>
>   This *Spirit* (wee said) we are to procure, that it may *abide* with us, and be in *us*. And what is more intrinsecall in us, abideth surer, groweth faster to us, than what we eat and drinke?[10]

Here, with these sacramental seals and signs, we are at the very heart of the relation between humanity and God. They convey the substance of that relation – the very body and blood of the Word made flesh. As the heart is the life-giving organ of the whole body, so these particular sacramental gifts are the life-giving healthy growth of the whole body politic, both ecclesiastical and civil. Here the well-spring of life and the light in which we see light are given, substantially, for the nourishment, sustenance and enlightenment of all. They are therefore the concentration of the place – that is, the place which is the trysting place of God with us – where order may be perceived and strength, comfort and love given to advance it.

This order requires more than human endeavour of whatever excellence to uphold and observe it. It cannot be a question of mere human effort, for that is frail and transitory, however moral and honest. It necessitates another quality and dimension to begin, sustain and fulfil it. Humanistic philosophy cannot undergird and bear up all things in our existence in order. Andrewes says that this 'other' is available when

> we consider the *Spirit*, (as S. *Peter*: I Pet.4:10) *multiformem*; the *Spirit*, in his graces, or the graces of the *Spirit*, as of many kindes. Of many kindes; for, our wants and defects are many. Not to goe out of the Chapter: in the very words, He is called the *Spirit of truth*: and that is one kinde of grace, to cure us of *error*. In the XXVI Verse after, The *Spirit of holinesse*, which is His common name, which serveth to reduce us from a *morall* honest life, to a *holy*, and wherein the power of Religion doth appeare.[11]

This third sermon *Of the Sending of the Holy Ghost* reiterates throughout the inadequacy of human ability and comfort to sustain existence and the Spirit proceeding from the Father and the Son as that which gives us sure foundation and upholding. For example:

> He [Christ] will take order, we shall have supply of another [Comforter]: in absence of His body, the supply of His Spirit. That if we looke up, we have a *Comforter in heaven*, even Himselfe: and if we looke downe, we have a *Comforter on earth*, even His *Spirit*: and so are at anchor in both.
>
> For, as He doth in heaven, for us: So doth the *Spirit* on earth in us, frame our petitions and *make intercession for us, with sighes that cannot be expressed*. And as Christ is our *Witnesse in heaven*; so is the Spirit here on earth, *witnessing with our Spirits that we pertaine* to the adoption, and *are the children of God*. Evermore *in the midst of the sorrowes that are in our hearts* with His *comforts refreshing our soules*. Yet not filling them with false comforts; but (as Christs *Advocate* here on earth) soliciting us daily, and calling upon us, to looke to His *Commandements* and *keepe them*; wherein standeth much of our *comfort*, even in the *testimony of a good conscience*. And thus these two; this one, and this other; this second, and that first, yeeld plentifull supply to all our wants.
>
> . . . as for these . . . other *terrenae consolatiunculae*, pety poor comforts and solaces of the world: which God hath given us and we may use; but we must looke after *Paracletum alium, another* and another manner *Comforter*, when all is done. For, of these, it may be, we shall feele some comfort, while we be in health and meetly good estate, and in case not much to need it. But, let us come into their cases here, the *heart troubled*, the *minde oppressed*, the [human] Spirit wounded; and then, what earthly thing will there be, can minister any sound *comfort* to us? We must needs seeke for this *Paracletum alium* here, at any hand. . . . No other will doe it but this: that, when we have Him, we need looke no further.[12]

Andrewes also warns in Sermon 9 *Of the Sending of the Holy Ghost* of those who would confuse their human spirit with the Holy Spirit, fail to distinguish between both and think that they have within themselves the spiritual means to meet all needs and to stand sufficient.

> And are there not in the world somewhere, some such, as will *receive none*, admit of at no hand no other Holy Ghost but their owne *ghost*, and the *Idoll* of their owne conseit, the visione of their owne heads, the motions of their owne *spirits*; and if you hit not on that, that is there in their hearts, reject it, be it what it will: that makes their brests the *Sanctuary*; that (in effect) say with the old *Donatists*, *Quod volumus Sanctus est*, That, they will have *holy*, is *holy*, and nothing *else*? Men (as the *Apostle* speaks of them) *Causelesse puft up with their fleshly minde*?[13]

Andrewes's argument in this sermon is that the sacraments are the seals of the covenant between God and humanity, the binding together of Creator and creation in the order of their respective integrities. It is our necessitous duty to attend to them if we wish to so perceive and be strengthened in our callings and circumstances. For there we meet with God in the Holy Spirit sent by the Father in the promise of the Son, which Spirit will be with us throughout the days of our life and in every state wherein we find ourselves. There are blessings and gifts in life which provide us with but temporary, shallow comfort. But these are not enough to sustain the foundation of our existence and its proper relation to, and end in, God.

> Let us seeke for *another*, that through sicknesse, age and death, may abide with us to all eternitie, and make us abide with Him in endlesse joy and comfort. Such is this here, which Christ promised, and His Father sent this day: and which He will send, if Christ will aske: and Christ will aske, if (now we know the *Covenant* and see the *Condition*) we will seale to the deed.
>
> To a *Covenant*, there is nothing more requisite, than to put to the *Seale*. And we know the *Sacrament* is the *Seale* of the *new Covenant*, as it was of the *old*. Thus, by undertaking the *duty* He requireth, we are entitled to the *comfort* which here He promiseth. And, *doe this*, He would have us, as is plaine by His *Hoc facite*.[14]

The sacraments, and indeed preaching, are means by which the promises of Christ to send the Holy Ghost are evident. But these must not be thought of as purely mechanical means whose significance is divorced from that which they convey in themselves. That which they convey, the very presence and Person of Christ in and by the presence and Person of the Holy Spirit, is inseparable from, but distinct to, the means of conveyance, the water of baptism, the bread and wine of the communion, and the human words of the sermon.

Here in particular we are concerned with the relation between Christ, the Spirit and the sacraments. Andrewes has a passage in his third sermon *Of the Sending of the Holy Ghost* which sums this up and indicates his insistence on the Personal presence and majesty of the Holy Spirit. We may note the emphasis on the Holy Spirit in the Eucharist, for in Andrewes's thought, just as Christ gave Himself for us, so the Spirit is given to us by the Father at the behest of Christ, to comfort us and bring us to Him, the Word made flesh who has done all things necessary for our redemption in His body and blood. The Spirit therefore, is present and given to us in the sacrament: we are given Christ but by the Spirit whose work of comfort is to conjoin us to Christ and in Him to the life of the Triune God. This does not mean that the bread and the wine are conjoined to the Spirit, but that they are conjoined to the very body and blood of Christ by the Spirit whose presence conjoins the earthly Eucharist and its elements to the once and for all and sufficient consecration of our Lord of Himself upon the cross. It is in the conjoining work of the Spirit that our comfort lies – but it is the Personal work of the Spirit.

We are concerned here with a Christocentricity which does not stand alone as though the Word is independent and may be isolated from the Father and the Spirit. It is a Christocentricity which is conveyed as it only can be conveyed properly, through the Spirit by the will of the Father and the prayer of Christ to the Father. It is of import that Andrewes remarks in the following passage (preserving the one-ness in the distinction) that Christ is offered *for* us, and the Spirit offered *to* us. This passage is one instance of an emphasis throughout Andrewes's works on the anchoring of the Spirit in the Word and of the procession of the Spirit from the Son – Andrewes's strong advocacy of the *filioque* – yet without diminishing from the integrity of the Spirit. The Eucharist follows the parallel pattern of the incarnation, where, in the power of the Spirit the Word takes flesh.

Besides, it was one speciall end, why the *Sacrament* it selfe was ordained, our *comfort*; the Church so telleth us; we so heare it read, every time to us: *He hath ordained these Mysteries, as pledges of His love and favour, to our great and endlesse comfort* [Book of Common Prayer, Exhortation at the Time of the Celebration of the Communion]. *The Father shall give you the Comforter: Why*, He giveth Him, we see: *How*, He giveth Him, we see not [here again is Andrewes's and his contemporaries' refusal to pry into the how of God]. The meanes, for which, He giveth Him, is *Christ*: His entreaty by His *Word*, in *prayer*; by His *flesh* and *bloud* in *Sacrifice*: For, His *bloud speakes*; not, His *voice*, onely. These, the meanes *for which*: And the very same, the meanes, *by which*, He giveth the *Comforter*: by Christ the *Word*; and by Christs *body* and *bloud*, both. In *tongues* it came: but the *tongue* is not the instrument of *Speech* onely, but of *taste*, we all know. And, even that note hath not escaped the Ancient Divines; to shew, there is not onely comfort by *hearing the Word*, but we may also *taste of His goodnesse, how gracious He is*, and be *made drinke of the Spirit*. That not onely by the *letter* we *read*, and the *word* we heare; but by the *flesh* we eat, and the *bloud* we drinke at His table, we be made partakers of His *Spirit*, and of the comfort of it. By no more kindly way, passeth His Spirit than by His *flesh* and *bloud*, which are *Vehicula Spiritus*, the proper *carriages* to conveigh it. *Corpus aptavit sibi, ut Spiritum aptaret tibi*: Christ fitted *our body* to Him, that He might fit *His spirit* to *us*. For, so is the Spirit best fitted, made remeable, and best exhibited to us, who consist of both.

   This is sure: where His *flesh* and *bloud* are, they are not *exanimes*; spirit-lesse; they are not, or without life; His *Spirit* is with them. Therefore was it ordained, in those very elements, which have both of them a comfortable operation in the heart of man. One of them (*bread*) serving to *strengthen* it, or make it strong: and *comfort* commeth of *confortare*, which is to *make strong*. And the other (*wine*) to make it *cheerfull* or glad: and is therefore willed to be ministered to them that *mourne*, and are opprest with griefe. And all this, to shew that the same effect is wrought in the inward man, by the holy *Mysteries*, that is, in the outward, by the *Elements*: that there, the heart is *established by grace*, and our soule indued with *strength*, and our conscience made *light* and *cheerfull*, that it faint not, but evermore rejoyce in His holy comfort. To conclude: where shall we finde it, if not here, where, under one, we finde *Christ* our *Passe-over* offered for us, and the *Spirit* our *Pentecost* thus offered to us? Nothing remaineth but the *Father* Himselfe: And of Him, we are sure, too. *Filium in pretium dedit; Spiritum, in solatium; Se servat in praemium*. His *Sonne* He gave, to be our *price*; His *Spirit* to be our *comfort*: Himselfe He keepeth, to be our everlasting *reward*. Of which *reward* there, and *comfort* here, this day and ever may we be partakers, for him that was the price of both, *Jesus Christ*.[15]

Christ's body and blood are the vehicles of the Spirit, the seal of his promise to send the Spirit. Here again it is to be noted how firmly fixed is the Holy Spirit in the Word and what the Word has accomplished, yet to the preservation of the integrity of the Spirit and what the Spirit accomplishes. Pentecost cannot be divided from Christmas Day, Good Friday, Easter Day or Ascension Day – yet neither can these last be divided from Pentecost. The substance of these feasts is bestowed by the Spirit in that which is instituted as suitable for this bestowal in our creaturely existence – the preaching of the Word (the Word made audible) and the sacraments of the Word (the Word made visible). Just as the Holy Spirit overshadowed Mary at the incarnation, so he works in the sermon in which ordinary human words are used and in the sacraments in which ordinary earthly elements are used. Just as the Spirit was the mode of the Word made flesh, so here He is the mode whereby we are united to Christ – but He is so in all the integrity of His Being as the Personal Bond of Love within the Triune Being of God, His work *ad extra* corresponding to what He is *in se*.

This relation between Christ, the Spirit and prayer, preaching and the sacraments, is brought out further in the fifth sermon in *Of the Sending of the Holy Ghost*, in which Andrewes deals with the words of the sermon and the elements of the Eucharist and what they convey, or rather what the Spirit conveys in and with them. In the following passage it is clear that Andrewes is setting out the necessity of observing and taking together all the various parts of the Church's life, prayer, preaching and sacraments, as a whole, in order that that relation may be perceived fully and the fullness of our partaking of, and participating in, the Word made flesh through the Spirit, be just as full.

> . . . looke, how the *Breath* and the Voice *in naturalibus* goe together; even so doe the *Spirit* and the Word in the practice of *Religion*. The Holy Ghost is Christ's *Spirit*, and Christ is the Word. And of that *Word*, the *Word* that is preached to us, is an abstract. There must then be a nearenesse, and alliance, betweene the one and the other. And indeed (but by our default) the *Word* and the *Spirit* (saith *Esay*) *shall never faile, or ever part*; but one be received, when the other is. . . .
>
> And certaine it is that many sparkes kindled, for want of this, goe out againe straight: for, as fast as it is written in our hearts, it is wiped out againe: as fast as the *seed* is *sowne*, it is *picked up by the fowles* againe, and so our *receiving* is in vaine, the *Word* and the *Spirit* are severed, which else would keepe together.
>
> Lastly, as the *Word* and the *Spirit*; so the *flesh* and the *Spirit* goe together. Not *all flesh*, but *this flesh*, the *flesh* that was *conceived by the Holy Ghost*, this is never without the Holy Ghost, by whom it was *conceived*: so that, receive one and receive both. Ever with this *bloud*, there runneth still an *artery*, with plentie of *Spirit* in it: which maketh, that we eat there *escam spiritualem*, a spirituall meat; and that in that *Cup*, we be *made drinke of the Spirit*. There is not only *impositio manuum*, but after it, *positio in manus*; putting on of the hands, but putting it into our hands. Impositio manuum, putting on of the hands, in *Accepit panem et calicem*: And *positio in manus*; putting it into our hands, in *Accipite, edite, bibite*. And so, we in case, to receive body, blood, Spirit and all, if ourselves be not in fault.
>
> Now then, if we will invite the *Spirit* indeed; and if each of these, by it selfe in severall. be thus effectuall to procure it: put them all, and binde them all together, *Accipite verba*: take to you *words, Hose's words*, words of earnest *invocation*. *Suscipite infitum verbum*, receive, or take to you the *Word* (Saint *James* word) *grafted into you*, by the Office of *preaching*. *Accipite corpus, accipite sanguinem*; take the holy mysteries of His *body* and *bloud*, and the same, the holy arteries of His blessed Spirit. Take all these in one, (the attractive of *Prayer*; the *Word*, which is *Spirit* and *life*; the *bread of life*, and the *Cup* of *salvation*:) and is there not great hope, wee shall answere Saint *Pauls* question, as he would have it answered, *affirmative*? *Have ye received*? Yes; *we have received Him.*[16]

In setting all this out, Andrewes is concerned with dynamic relations – the interaction of existences and the taking up of created entities by the Word and Spirit in the whole lively and life-giving mode of redemption. In the use of his language there is also interaction between the themes of creation, incarnation and re-creation, and the attendant insistence that the Spirit is the same Spirit who bestows order on creation, who brings about the *oikonomia* of the incarnation, who gives new dimension and meaning to ordinary things, words, water, bread, wine, causing them to bear witness to the order of the new creation breaking in to the old by His presence. Here is the source of all true order and the place where natural law is seen to be anchored in the very relation between Creator and creature.

This new order breaking in is seen in emphatic terms by Andrewes when he deals with the sacrament of baptism. This is done immediately, as has been instanced before, in Sermon 8 *Of the Sending of the Holy Ghost*, preached on the text of Luke 3:21, 22, by Andrewes's juxtaposition of Christ's baptism, creation, the old and the new testaments, heaven, earth and the involvement of the three Persons of the Trinity.

> To looke into the Text, there is no man but at the first blush will conceive that there is some great matter in hand. First, by the *opening of heaven*: for, that *opens* not, for a small purpose. Then, by the solemne presence of so great Estates at it: for, here is the whole *Trinitie* in person. The *Son in the water*, the *Holy Ghost in the dove, the Father in the voice.* This was never so before, but once: Never but twice, in all; in all the Bible. Once in the Old Testament, and once in the New. In the Old, at the *creation*, the beginning of *Genesis*. There finde we *God*, and the *Word* with *God* creating, and the *Spirit of God moving upon the face of the waters.* And now here againe, at *Christs christening* in the new.
>
> *The faces of the Cherubins are one towards the other*: (that is) there is a mutuall correspondence betweene these two. That, was at the *creation*: this, a *creation* too; *If any be in Christ, he is a new creature of this new creation.* That was the *Genesis*, (that is) the *generation* of the World: this . . . the *regeneration*, or spirituall *new birth*, whereby we be borne againe the *Sonnes of God*. And better not borne at all, than not so *borne againe*.
>
> This then, being every way as great; (indeed, the greater of the twaine) meet it was, they all should present themselves at this, no lesse than at that; and every one have His part in it (as wee see, they have.) All (I say:) seeing the Commission for *Baptisme* was to runne in all their Names, and it selfe ever to be ministered accordingly.[17]

Sermon 13 in *Of the Sending of the Holy Ghost* describes baptism as 'a fountain never to be drawn dry'.[18] This does not imply that baptism, like the Eucharist, may be repeated again and again. It is a sacrament which is administered but once to each person and not again. This description of baptism merely implies how it is given to the church for all time. It is also given for all people.

The baptism by John in the Jordan was for all people. At the beginning of Sermon 8, *Of the Sending of the Holy Ghost*, Andrewes draws out the significance of John's baptism for Christ and people. It is a baptism into repentance, and all the people required that. The need and stain of humanity is even from the womb, for from the womb all humanity is *baptized* into frailty and mortality; another baptism is required to counteract that. Not even the supposedly righteous escape this necessity, for this claimed righteousness is unclean and polluted:

not a childe a day old, but needs *baptismus lavacri*, if it bee but for *baptismus uteri*; the baptisme of the Church, if it be but for the baptisme, it had in the wombe. Let the people then be baptized in God's name; good and bad, men and children and all.[19]

Andrewes emphasizes that the reason for Christ's baptism was his identification with those who stand in need of repentance. Not that He required repentance who did no sin, but He had come to take their needy estate to Himself, being made sin for us:

> One might well aske, Why did not the *Baptist* repell Him finally? Not say: *I have need to be baptized of thee*, (that is) *Thou hast no need to be baptized of me*: that was too faint; that, was not enough: But, Thou hast no need to be *baptized* at all. Yea, one might well aske the *water* (with the *Psalmist*;) *Why it fled not*; and *Jordan, why it was not driven backe*, at this *baptisme*?
>   Yet the *Verse* is plaine: that, *with the People, Christ also was baptized.*
>   How *came this to passe*? Why *baptized*? Why *with the People*?[20]

This was not, Andrewes notes, merely to give an example of humility, though certainly great humility is here. There is in action that which is more profound than example, concerning the relation of Christ as the Word made flesh, to Adamic humanity. This Andrewes sets out in terms of Irenaeus's doctrine of recapitulation, and in so doing sets out a survey of the substance of the doctrine of baptism.

> To shew you, how this *comes to passe*; we are to consider Christ, as having two capacities (as they terme them.) So are we to consider Him (the second *Adam*:) for so doe we the first *Adam*: as a *person* of himselfe; and, as the *Author of a Race or Head of a Society*. And, even so doe we, Christ: Either as *totum integrale*, a person entire (they call it a *body naturall*;) or, as *pars communitatis* (which they call a *body politike*) in conjunction, and with reference to others: Which others are His *Church*; which *Church*, is His *body*. They His *body* and He their *Head* (so told us often, by the *Apostle*.) And, by *Himselfe* considered, He is *Unigenitus*, the only begotten, hath never a brother: so, as together *with the people*, He is *Primogenitus inter multos*, the first begotten among many brethren. To apply this, to our purpose. Take Christ by *Himselfe*, as severed from us; and no reason in the world, to *baptize* Him. He needed it not. Needed it not? Nay, take Him so; *Jordan* had more need come to Him, than He to *Jordan*, to bee cleansed. *Lavit aquas ipsum, non aquae ipsum*, the waters were *baptized* by Him, they *baptized* Him not: He went into them, *Ut aquae nos purgaturae prius per Ipsum purgarentur* (it is *Epiphanius*: In Anchorata) that they which should cleanse us, might by Him first be cleansed. It is certaine; so, He received no cleannesse, no vertue; but vertue He gave, to *Jordan*, to the waters, to the Sacrament it selfe.
>   But then, take Him the other way, as in conjunction *cum populo*, they and Hee *one bodie*, and the case is altered. For, if He be so *cum populo*, with them, as He be one of them. . . .
>   But if we looke a little further, then we shall finde greater reason yet. A part He is; and parts there be, that in some case undertake for the whole; as the arme, to bee let bloud, for all the body. And it *came to passe*, that such a part He was; Hee undertook for us. For, in His *baptisme* He put us on; as we *put Him on*, in ours. Take Him then, not only as *cum populo*, but as *pro populo*; not only, as *nobiscum*, but as *pro nobis*: Put Him in the case, the *Prophet* doth, *Posuit super Ipsum iniquitates omnium nostrum*, put upon Him the *transgressions of us all*: Put Him as the *Apostle* puts Him, *Factus est peccatum pro*

nobis, make Him *sinne, for us*; put all our sinnes upon Him; and then, it *will come to passe*, He will neede *baptizing*: He will need that, for me and thee, that for Himselfe He needed not, and *baptisme* in that case, may well be administered unto Him.[21]

We may notice how Andrewes sets baptism in the context of the active and passive obedience of Christ, His submitting to baptism by John, yet His cutting forward towards the baptism with which He is fully baptized, towards His cross and passion. His argument is that our Lord, identified as He is with the vast multitude of the human race in its sin and therefore, because of His solidarity with it, standing thus in need of baptism, has a baptism to be accomplished which alone can cleanse this race – a baptism which no water can achieve. His baptism in the Jordan was but a 'foule baptisme', a baptism of the human need of repentance. What baptism then to fulfil the positive action of putting humanity right with God and deal with sin at its root?

> A whole River too little, in that case. For, being first *baptized* (as I may say) in so many millions of sinnes (in so foule a *puddle*;) well might He then be *baptized*, if it were but to wash away that His former *foule baptisme*. . . .
>
> How *Jordan* or any water could doe this; *wash* away *sinne*? To cleare it shortly; the truth is, it could not. It is no *water*-worke, without somewhat put to it, to help it scoure. But, nothing on Earth: No, not if you put to it *Nitre, much Sope, Fullers-earth, the hearbe borith* (say the Prophets) all will not doe; it will not off, so. Therefore, this of His in *Jordan* did not, could not doe the feat, otherwise, than in the vertue of another to follow. For, after this was past, *Hee spake of another baptisme, He was to be baptized with* . . . that was *baptismus sanguinis*. For, *without bloud*, without the mixture of that, *there is no doing away sinne*.[22]

John's baptism is of the ordinance of God: but there is a higher ordinance of which this baptism in the Jordan is but the pledge and preparative, Christ's own baptism.

> And so was He *baptized*. And He had *trinam mersionem*: One in *Gethsemane*, One in *Gabbatha*, and a third in *Golgotha*. In *Gethsemane*, in His *sweat of bloud*. In *Gabbatha, in the bloud*, that came from the *scourges* and *thornes*: and in *Golgotha*, that which came from the *nailes* and the *speare*. Specially, the *speare*: There, met the two streames, of *water and bloud*, the true *Jordan*, the bath or *laver*, wherein we are *purged from all our sinnes*. No sinne, of so deepe a die, but this will command it, and fetch it out. This in *Jordan*, here, now, was but an undertaking of that, then; and in vertue of that, doth all our *water-baptisme* worke. And therefore, are wee *baptized* into it: not into His *water-baptisme*, but into His *Crosse-baptisme*; not into His *baptisme*, but into His *death*. So many as are baptized, are baptized into His death: It is the *Apostle, Rom.VI.3*.[23]

There is, at work here in Andrewes's thought, a multi-dimensional aspect to Christian baptism. The water with which we are baptized is itself baptized by Christ in His passion and death. The water, as the Jordan, signifies our need of repentance – the recognition of our frailty and mortality. But much more is required – the overturning of the human estate as that which is lost into that which is found and restored. Hence, Christ gives 'vertue . . . to the sacrament itself', and to the signs used in the sacrament. Our baptism has to be baptized in His. This, in the sacrament of baptism is the work and estate of the Holy Spirit. Through this baptism of ours, the sign of our need for repentance as we stand judged, we are brought by the Spirit into that deeper and effective baptism, which is Christ's sacrifice of Himself on the cross. As He has *put us on* in our need, so we *put him on* in the fulfilment of that need. The water of our baptism becomes through the operation of the Spirit, the water and blood which is the finale of His Self-sacrifice on the cross. By the presence of the Holy Spirit, the Person of Christ stands behind, and is operative in, our baptism, even to the hallowing of the very element of baptism.

There is a dynamic interaction between the created element of water and our existence. But this is only so because all that Christ has accomplished for us is brought to bear in the lively and life-giving presence and action of the Holy Spirit lifting up the element of water and our existence into the cleansing stream of Christ's body on the cross.

This is taken up by Andrewes in the way in which he combines mention of the waters over which the Spirit hovered at creation bringing order, the waters whereby God's judgement came on the earth and which became the saving waters on which Noah's ark floated, and the waters of the Jordan in which Christ was baptized and which pointed to much more. The Spirit brings order out of the waters, the ark out of the flood, the saving sacrifice of Christ out of the waters of Jordan. The interplay in Andrewes's presentation of this is on the transforming work of the Spirit, so that

> The element, whereof all were made, and wherewith all were *destroyed* after; that, with the same, all should be saved again: the *water* it selfe, now becoming *the Arke*; the *drowning water*, the *saving Arke*, as St. *Peter* noteth. That, as then, by *His moving on the waters*, He put them into a life and heat to bring forth: so now, by His comming downe upon them, He should impregnate them to a better birth. That, as His Title is, the *Lord and giver of life*, Hee might be the *Giver of true life* (that is) *eternall life*.[24]

By the Holy Spirit bearing upon the very elements of creation He makes them the mode of our participation in all that Christ has accomplished, and our communion with Christ. These are His gifts – the transformation of these things to serve this end among all the relativities and contingencies of our temporal/spatial existence. They are, in their created realities, the things which the Holy Spirit uses to effect the 'Royall Exchange'. All the qualities and 'vertues' of Christ are administered to us, and we made to partake of them, by the Spirit. They are contained, all these 'vertues' such as '*peaceable*, to love *singlenesse* in *meaning, speaking* and *dealing*, to *suffer harme*, but to *doe* none. *Peace, sincerity, patience*, and *innocency*, as 'the *silver feathers* of this *Dove*', in the sacraments. For 'They be vertues, and (which is more) *virtutes baptismales*, the very *vertues of our baptism*.'[25]

The gifts of the Spirit are centred on those signs and seals which have been ordained to unite us to Christ, and beyond that, on Christ Himself who has procured these gifts for us and dispenses them in the relation which He bears to the Holy Spirit. There is unitary thought here in Andrewes's mind, where all things for our creation, redemption, upholding and fulfilment rest on the relations of the Triune God *in se* and in these self-same relations in His work *ad extra*. They rest on the reality of the existence of God in relation to the reality of the creation which He has made and redeemed. There perception and reception is not by a mystical escaping of created realities, but by the acceptance that true reality lies in the fact that God has bound His creation to himself by Word and Spirit and operates in that medium. There is *palingenesis* in the midst of *genesis*, and the perception of true order lies in that recognition. Baptism is 'with the *bloud* of Christ, by the *hand* of the Holy Ghost . . . without which [water] is but *a naked, a poore, and a dead element'*.[26]

But this as a principle, while applied properly and particularly to the sacraments, is nevertheless a perception spread throughout Andrewes's sermons regarding a more general application to the whole of creation, re-created as it is in and by the Word made flesh. This neither disparages the created entities by treating them as being merely pointers beyond themselves to another truth lying afar, nor does it destroy the integrity of created entities as they are in themselves, with their own place and significance. It does point to the truth that what they are in themselves, and what they are truly in themselves, is held by them because of the relation they are in, through that re-creation and by the hand of the Spirit, with their Creator. Herein order lies and what is truly natural law perceivable.

Andrewes does not flee reality in any sort of false mysticism. Rather, he sees truth anchored firmly in the existences and realities of the temporal/spatial dimension, their whole being bearing witness with and to the 'bloud of Christ by the hand of the Spirit'. There is indeed *genesis* and there is indeed *palingenesis – and we are at anchor in both*, as surely as the Word was made flesh and the Spirit inhabits with us.

Notes

1   Lancelot Andrewes: *Ninety-six Sermons*, 'Sermon 7 of the Sending of the Holy Ghost', 1635 edn, p.662.
2   Ibid., p.663.
3   Ibid., p.664.
4   Ibid.
5   Ibid., p.665.
6   Ibid., p.669.
7   Ibid., p.670.
8   Ibid., p.671.
9   Ibid., p.672.
10   Ibid., p.672.
11   Lancelot Andrewes: *Ninety-six Sermons*, 'Sermon 3 of the Sending of the Holy Ghost', 1635 edn, p.623.
12   Ibid., p.625.
13   Lancelot Andrewes: *Ninety-six Sermons*, 'Sermon 9 of the Sending of the Holy Ghost', 1635 edn, p.694.
14   Lancelot Andrewes: *Ninety-six Sermons*, 'Sermon 3 of the Sending of the Holy Ghost', 1635 edn, p.626.
15   Ibid., pp.626f.
16   Lancelot Andrewes: *Ninety-six Sermons*, 'Sermon 5 of the Sending of the Holy Ghost', 1635 edn, pp.648f.
17   Lancelot Andrewes: *Ninety-six Sermons*, 'Sermon 8 of the Sending of the Holy Ghost', 1635 edn, p.675.
18   Lancelot Andrewes: *Ninety-six Sermons*, 'Sermon 13 of the Sending of the Holy Ghost', 1635 edn, p.738.

19   Lancelot Andrewes: *Ninety-six Sermons*, 'Sermon 8 of the Sending of the Holy Ghost',
     1635 edn, p.676.
20   Ibid., p.676.
21   Ibid., p.677.
22   Ibid., pp.677f.
23   Ibid., p.678.
24   Ibid., p.680.
25   Ibid., p.681.
26   Ibid., p.679.

Epilogue

This study has sought to interpret the Laudian mind as it applied itself to a variety of circumstances with which it found itself confronted. One of the problems immediate to such a study is the way in which the seventeenth-century divines expressed themselves. It was noted at the outset that their unsystematic treatment of theology nevertheless was born out of their determination not to reduce the truth of God to a system, but yet that such an approach let the order of God be shown in its own terms and not compromised by definitive statements about it. They distinguished between Truth itself, and statements about Truth. As already stated, I have therefore taken the liberty of quoting sometimes at length from their works. This I deem to be the best way to demonstrate the points that various writers were trying to make. There is a temptation to merely pick out their pithy sayings, for, generally, they were masters of the short but telling statement. But this can be to wrest such from their contexts, and rob them of the necessary background which not only shows them in their proper sharp significance, but also tears them from the matrix of the process of thought in which they were nurtured.

I have sought to show that the concept of 'order' was perhaps the foremost concept which formed their theological method, content and expression. 'Order' is a word held in much suspicion. It is commonly construed as 'regulation', that which is imposed upon lives and liberties, and therefore that which is questionable and unacceptable. This general attitude, however, is misinformed – at least as far as the theological concept of order is concerned, and certainly as that concept is expressed in the theology of the Laudian Divines.

'Order' theologically understood, is not a hard and fast set of rules. A distillation of that theology may suggest that the Laudians saw it as a guiding principle, corresponding to the rationality which God is eternally in Himself, and applied to the understanding of creation and of humanity in the light of God's Self-revelation in Jesus Christ.

It is the declaration of Who the Creator is. It is the proclamation that He is the Father, the householder of all creation, His great household. Following from that, it is also the declaration that humanity and all creation lives and moves and has its being in relation to Him who brought it into being out of nothing by His Word, sustains and gathers it together by that same Word even when that Word was made flesh, and will gather it up in the declaration of what it really is in His decree by that same Word in open disclosure.

The Laudians – even Laud himself in his zeal for uniformity – never attempted to reduce the concept of order to any programme of regulations, statutes or canons. Since it is primarily the declaration of that order which God is in Himself, and therefore that which defies all human attempts to master it and contain it within statements about it, it can only be a matter, from humanity's side, of a constant striving to exist and act in correspondence with that order which God has so revealed, and which He will openly disclose.

Unfortunately, as the Laudians saw in their troubled period, all those engaged in theology have not always seen order in this light. From time to time, and certainly then with the extreme elements of Puritanism, theology has either tried to reduce it to a set of rules, or, having given up the struggle to achieve that, it has looked elsewhere to deduce what order is so that it can produce such a set of rules, to justify its religious dimension in the face of other competing claims and yet still pay lip service to that Lordly revelation. When it has looked elsewhere, it has done so in realms of cultural norms, political manifestos, social programmes, and in what is interpreted in the process of social evolution to be 'justice', 'equality' and 'rights'.

Theology, properly, the Laudians seem agreed, sees order in terms of God's Self-revelation. 'Order' is there – the order which God is and according to which He acts, and the order which He has decreed that creation should be if it is His creation. When this concept has been interpreted either as the imposition of mechanistic laws, or has been rejected – perhaps unconsciously – as the source of all order, is because Christ has been side-stepped as the essential key to the opening of an understanding of order, and has been replaced by what can only be described as an essentially humanist interpretation of creation and mankind out of a superficial analysis of surface appearances.

These divines saw that there was a continually besetting tendency to base understanding on what it can see, understand and control. Order, therefore, could become the set of rules and principles which is seen to be most expedient. Since the expediency of one person or party is not necessarily the expediency of another, order has been brought down into the debate, argument and strife of relative and competitive claims. This is why the concept of order can become debased – and, indeed, it would be the Laudian claim that it had become so ill-formed in the minds of those factions showing either Puritanical or Jesuitical tendencies.

Since this debased and alien concept of order stems from the relativities of human endeavour alone, it is subject to the criticism of those who think differently out of these relativities. It, in turn, becomes something which is to be rejected, reinterpreted and manipulated, if it does not suit a particular and opposing point of view which has been arrived at out of the same relativities. The proliferation of Puritan sects in the seventeenth-century, each with its own particular emphases on the varying decrees of God, exhibit this only too well.

The attempt to impose order by civil power on the basis of this relative understanding is resented by those who have come to a different view of things. The law – that is governmental expression of an understanding of order – and therefore the concept of order, is then brought into disrepute because it can be criticized from an equally valid but opposing point of view, from within the standards which give validity in this area of human endeavour. That the New Model Army was, in the last resort, the means by which Oliver Cromwell ruled, is a comment on this.

Such instability of society is always because law and the ordering of society have become detached from any stable equilibrium. The Laudians emphasized that the point on which all true order rests is that time and place where God reveals Himself in all His Godness and in His concern and love for creation and humanity. That time and place is the time and place of Jesus Christ. In Him, in His Godness as the eternal Son of God by whom all things are created, and in His taking upon Himself the realities of creation in becoming a son of man bearing all the burden which the sons and daughters of men have made for themselves in their self-orientated interpretation and actions in and to creation, the work of re-ordering is accomplished. In Him, the only true order is established, and natural law – mankind's Amen to that order – becomes a valuable possibility.

Here we are faced with the exclusive and yet universally sweeping claim of Caroline theology. This claim is narrow, in the sense it pin-points Christ as that fulcrum on which all order rests. Yet it is generously cosmic in that it does not exclude anything – visible or invisible, man's mind, and that which lies beyond man's capabilities of understanding, the whole of creation – within this Christ-centred concentration.

Yet our understanding of natural law as a response to what we have learnt from Christ will always be a *possibility*. It will never become a sufficient set of codified rules. Christ confronts us in all the mystery of Godness taking Himself human-ness. This is an act of God involving His being – as all acts of God do. But this is the central act of God, on which all His other actions are anchored. For here He gives Himself totally, to which giving all His other acts are a witness, as the faithful God who will not let His creation destroy itself.

He confronts us in this act as the Lord of all creation, and therefore as that which cannot be satisfactorily explained from within the relativities of creation and contained in the measures of the workings of the human mind. On the contrary, He informs all that, and all endeavours to reach an understanding of order have to be brought in humility and awe before this mystery and laid in its controlling context. That is why our response to this is a matter of continual striving and reformation. It has to be referred back, again and again, to that central and formative fact of the Word made flesh.

The desire of so many who have enriched Christian teaching and writing – in this country, the witness of a Bede, Grosseteste, John Duns Scotus and so many among the sixteenth- and early seventeenth-century Anglican divines, to do exactly this, given the limitations of their particular circumstances, is something which we have lost or ignored in the relative circumstances of our days. This is because we live under the arrogant shadow of eighteenth-century rationalism which had its roots in the late-seventeenth-century's love affair with a romantic classicism in which a barren interpretation of Greek and Latin values were elevated into mechanistic idealisms.

The principle propounded by Jeremy Bentham in the eighteenth century of 'the happiness of society' as the governing law of humanity's collective endeavour has become the touchstone on which all things are valued. This is supremely a human orientated law. Who determines that 'happiness'? Invariably those who have the ability to see to their own interests. The weakest go to the wall.

Perhaps the best comment on this is the fact that statute law has increasingly usurped common law (and therefore natural law on which common law rests). Issues of fundamental significance to human existence and quality of life are wrested from where they properly belong in common law, and are made subject to the ever-increasing and ever-increasingly complex making and passing of statutes. Such proliferation of the law can only bring the law into disrepute, not only because such issues are made the victims of political fashion, but because it becomes increasingly difficult to enforce the law. Andrewes hinted at this when he complained 'Westminster-Hall Laws . . . like cobwebs', as did Francis Bacon in his *A Proposition to His Majesty Touching the Compiling and Amendment of the Laws of England*[1] and his *An Expostulation to Lord Chief Justice Coke*.[2] Later Benthamite dictum merely made fast the practice against which such protests were being made in the Jacobean period.

Not only in law, but in science also, the same trend has been seen. The Newtonian idea of a universe operating according to absolute principles whereby all that was inexplicable was accorded to the intervention of God, who otherwise had no interaction with creation, has meant that God has been pushed out as scientific discovery and explanation increases. This has enhanced the notion that mankind will and can discover for itself the perfect order, given time and mental development. However, Newtonian theories have been superseded by all the development in the realm of science since Clerk Maxwell and Einstein. These later theories are approximated by so much of the theological outlook of the Laudians, regarding the ordering of the whole of creation in all its fields and dimensions, and the awe and wonder, rather than surface idealization, and attempts at manipulation and control, which recognition of this, in the light of the relation of Creator to creation, evokes. In a sense, the Laudians were much more allied to the thought forms and outlook of the present pure scientists than to present technologists.

That all order rests in and springs from Jesus Christ is an assertion which depends on a much neglected doctrine. That doctrine is the doctrine of Recapitulation. It was this doctrine, of which Irenaeus was the great exponent, which lies behind so much of Laudian theology. We may summarize and tease out the fabric of this doctrine, as it lies in Laudian thought.

It meant, basically, bringing all things to a head. Christ is the recapitulation of all creation. But He is this in a singular way. He is, with respect to His divinity, the One by whom all things were made. Creation is brought into existence by Him, at the decree of the Father and in the power of the Holy Spirit, out of nothing. Creation is a matter of *grace*. God has no compulsion from within to create – He is all sufficiency, companionship and love within Himself. Nor has He any compulsion from without to create. He does not need anything else to justify Himself or fulfil Himself – He is all majesty, dominion and power within Himself. He creates as a matter of sheer overflowing love. He creates in order to share His love and His glory with an entity other than Himself.

All creation, therefore, is *contingent* upon God. This contingency is twofold. It is, first, contingency *to* God. It depends upon Him for its very existence – its beginning, its continuance, and its fulfilment. It is, secondly, contingency *from* God. God creates that which is qualitively different from Him. He is eternal; creation is temporal. He is infinite, creation is limited. Creation is a matter of time and things. It has its own nature and identity which are different from the nature and identity of God. Yet this nature and identity of creation depend on its relation with God. It can only have its own nature and identity as long as it is God's creation. Contingency *to* and contingency *from* have to be held in exact balance, and in acknowledgement. From His side, God acknowledges that He is the God of creation and that creation is His, by entering and taking to Himself its realities of time and things at the Incarnation.

Here we have a profound bracketing together of Creator, humanity and creation. Before this we can only have a sense of awe and humility – and a sense of the necessity to strive in correspondence with this overwhelming Truth in all that we are and all that we do. Such a striving can only be our grateful 'Amen' to this grace of God. It will not be the self-assured, and therefore self-seeking, attempt to codify everything legalistically, as if we could round off God and the decrees of God satisfactorily.

This 'Amen' of ours will be a matter of reverence and love and wonder for God the Creator and Re-Creator and for the humanity of God and the whole creation of God. It will take very seriously God's creative decree that humanity is made in His image, and that humanity has an estate and vocation from Him concerning the relation between Creator and creation, eternity and time. Humanity has a unique dignity and a high calling.

If anything, this is the essence of the Laudian attitude, and it coloured not only the great panorama of their theological endeavour, but they sought as far as they could to let it permeate their daily round, concourse and conduct. That, at least, is what they earnestly laid before their hearers and readers.

Notes

1   Francis Bacon: *A Proposition to His Majesty*, 1778 edn, Vol.II, pp.546ff.
2   Francis Bacon: *An Expostulation to Lord Chief Justice Coke*, 1778 edn, Vol.III, pp.234ff.

Appendix A

Principal Seventeenth-century Authors Quoted

Lancelot Andrewes (1555–1626)

Educated at Merchant Taylors' School and Pembroke Hall, Cambridge, being elected Fellow in 1576, Catechist in 1580. From 1589 he held the mastership of Pembroke Hall and the Vicarage of St Giles, Cripplegate, with which a Prebendal Stall at St Paul's was associated. He was offered the Bishoprics of Salisbury and Ely by Elizabeth I, but demonstrated that independence of mind characteristic of career, by refusing them because of his disquiet concerning the Crown's appropriation of certain revenues of these Dioceses. However in 1601 he became Dean of Westminster, and in 1604 was a guiding figure in the Hampton Court Conference, and a translator in the production of the Authorized Version of the Bible which resulted from this Conference. During the reign of James VI and I he was advanced rapidly, being appointed Bishop of Chichester (1605), Ely (1609) and Winchester (1619). The encouragement of scholarship was one of his principal interests, and he numbered among his friends not only the significant academic figures of his day in England, but also notable names abroad – I. Casaubon, P. Du Moulin and H. Grotius. His theological status greatly influenced the settlement of the Anglican expression of theological method and content, Scripture, Tradition and Reason in their relatedness being thoroughly implicit in all his sermons and works.

Francis Bacon (1561–1626)

He was educated at Trinity College, Cambridge, entering in 1573, and was admitted to Gray's Inn in 1576. Although Elizabeth I held him in high regard as her 'learned counsel', he advanced in his career under James VI and I. In 1607 he became Solicitor-General, Clerk of the Star Chamber in 1608, Attorney-General in 1613, Lord Keeper in 1617, and Lord Chancellor and Viscount St Albans in 1618. His championship of Buckingham probably contributed to the downfall of his career. At the instigation of Sir Edward Coke a Parliamentary Inquiry looked into abuses in the Courts of Justice, and Bacon was accused of bribery and corruption, being disgraced in 1621 and retiring into private life. To a great extent he was a scapegoat and the victim of Coke's long-standing vendetta against him. His academic interests were wide, his knowledge wide-ranging. His main contribution to thought was his insistence on objective reasoning in every area of learning and in every discipline of knowledge. This was in accord with the theological emphasis of the day as expressed by many of the Anglican Divines, and his application of objective thinking in theology to all other manner of disciplines was a notable contribution of the time.

John Hales (1584–1656)

Educated at Bath Grammar School and at Corpus Christi College, Oxford, taking his degree in 1603 and being elected Fellow of Merton in 1605. He was public lecturer in Greek from 1612, probably assisting in the preparation of Henry Saville's publication of eight folio volumes of the works of St Chrysostom. As Chaplain to the Ambassador to Holland, Sir Dudley Carleton, he was present at the Synod of Dort in 1618 – the proceedings of which did not appeal to his generosity of mind. This breadth and generosity is reflected in his tract *Schism and Schismatics* first published in 1642. His example and academic influence did much to encourage a like generosity of mind in many of his contemporaries.

George Herbert (1593–1633)

Educated at Westminster School and Trinity College, Cambridge. Elected Fellow in 1614, he was appointed Public Orator of Cambridge University in 1620. A friend of Nicholas Ferrar, he was persuaded by him to study theology, and in 1630 was ordained priest and presented to the living of Fugglestone with Bemerton, near Salisbury, by William Laud. His ability in things musical and his classical training, as well as his theological insight, lay behind his poetic expression and work. Often labelled a 'mystic', Herbert in fact was thoroughly orthodox and down to earth in his theological activity, but expressed himself in a singular use of imagery in simple language in his devotional poetry. His piety and gentleness were influential in shaping so much of the Anglican attitudes of the day.

Richard Hooker (*c*.1554–1600)

Admitted to Corpus Christi College, Oxford, becoming a Fellow in 1577 and being appointed deputy Professor of Hebrew in 1579. On his marriage he had to relinquish his Fellowship and in 1584 became Rector of Drayton Beauchamp. His subsequent appointments were that of Master of the Temple (1585), Rector of Boscombe, Wiltshire (1591) and Rector of Bishopsbourne, Kent (1595). Izaac Walton in his *Lives* notes the unhappiness of Hooker's marriage. Hooker's *Treatise on the Laws of Ecclesiastical Polity* became the standard work for the succeeding Divines. They developed his three categories of Scripture, Tradition and Reason, seeing in them a relation as the joint witnesses to Christ and bound by Him as their common 'scope', in a way which is not found explicit in Hooker's work. He roundly attacked the Puritan faction for their insistence on the mechanical literalism and therefore infallibility of the Scriptures. Behind this lay his masterly observations on the role and significance of Natural Law, as expressing in the created dimension a correspondence to the nature of God. It is God Himself who is the authority, and the whole of Natural Law, as expressed in Scripure, in Tradition and by Reason, is the supreme authority for the interpretation of all things – including Scripture. As the foremost apologist of the Elizabethan Settlement of 1559, Hooker was the guiding influence of later theology which used his work as a foundation and developed it into the peculiar ethos of the Laudian Tradition.

William Laud (1573–1645)

Educated at St John's College, Oxford, becoming Fellow in 1593 and President in 1611. This last position he resigned in 1616 on his elevation to the See of St David's, having been also Dean of Gloucester from 1616. Translated to Bath and Wells in 1626 he was then moved to the See of London in 1628, and appointed Chancellor of Oxford in 1629. His Chancellorship was noted for its reforms within the University and the Statutes he revised, ensuring discipline and the encouragement of worthy scholarship. In 1633 he was appointed Archbishop of Canterbury. His scholarship was notable and used effectively – perhaps too effectively – against the Puritans, whom he saw as the worst enemies of that uniformity which was the hedge of true doctrine. After his abortive attempts to enforce a new Liturgy on the Scottish Church, his downfall began. The new Canons he attempted to introduce in the Convocation of 1640 brought ridicule upon him for the formula that there should be an oath swearing that there should never be altered the 'government of this Church by Archbishops, deans and archdeacons, etc.' (known as the 'etcetera oath') had to be suspended by order of the King. His illegal imprisonment and trial and eventual execution showed the mettle and determination of the Commons to overcome all obstacles (even to browbeating the House of Lords) to attain their objectives. His influence with regard to uniformity, decency and reverence in worship, long characterized the Church of England, and was still a basic attitude held by those responsible for Church affairs after the Restoration.

Francis Mason (1556–1621)

Educated at Oriel College, but with connections with Merton and Brasenose. He was noted for his defence of Anglicanism against Roman Catholic claims, particularly over the validity of bishops' consecrations, which he argued in his *Of the Consecrations of Bishops in the Church of England*, published in 1613. This earned him the title *Vindex Ecclesiae Anglicanae*. He exhibits in his works a broadmindedness towards all the emphases within the Church of England, but deplored the extremes of some Puritan parties.

Robert Sanderson (1587–1663)

Educated at Rotherham Grammar school and Lincoln College, Oxford, becoming a Fellow of that College in 1606 and Regius Professor of Divinity in 1642. He enjoyed the favour of William Laud and was appointed Chaplain to the King in 1631. He was removed from the Regius Chair during the Civil War, but was reinstated at the Restoration, becoming Bishop of Lincoln soon afterwards. He much influenced the Savoy Conference of 1661, and was the drafter of the Preface to the *Book of Common Prayer* of 1662. His mind was both theologically able and acute in legal matters. In all his works he exhibits that generosity of mind which expresses itself in the irenic tone of the Preface to the 1662 prayer book.

John Swan

It is necessary to append separately (see Appendix B) an examination of the problems surrounding the authorship of books attributed to this name. John Swan was a theologian who undeservedly is given no great prominence – indeed any mention at all – in works on seventeenth-century Anglicanism.

Francis White (*c*.1564–1638)

Educated at Gonville and Gaius College, Cambridge. Ordained in 1588, he was Incumbent of several Livings before being appointed Dean of Carlisle in 1622. Thereafter he was Bishop of Carlisle (1626), of Norwich (1629) and of Ely (1631). White was a noted apologist for Anglicanism over against Roman claims, and assisted William Laud in his disputation with the Jesuit, Fisher. His works show an appreciation of the Anglican theological method, and an ability to put that into practice in his defence of Anglicanism and its claims. He was equally an opponent of Puritan tendencies, particularly of the Sabbatarian emphases which were becoming more prevalent and insistent in his day. His final publications were *A Treatise of the Sabbath Day* (1635) dedicated to William Laud, and a reply to the work published by Richard Byfield the Puritan against that treatise, entitled *An Examination and Confutation of . . . a Briefe Answer to a late Treatise of the Sabbath Day* (1637).

Appendix B

Note on John Swan

The authorship of *Speculum Mundi* and other works attributed to him.

There is some confusion as to books attributed to John Swann *in The British Library Catalogue, Lowndes: The Bibliographer's Manual* (1864) the *Short Title Catalogue* (Pollard and Redgrave, revised Katherine Pantzer, 1976) and *Wing* (revised edition, ed. J. Morrison *et al.*, 1988). The attribution of all works to the John Swan, or Swann, elder or younger, both being Incumbents of Sawston in the County of Cambridge, Diocese of Ely, is found there. To clarify the issue, it is necessary to note that there were a number of seventeenth-century Incumbents who shared this name.

In Venn's *Alumni Cantabrigienses* (Cambridge, 1922–54) there is an entry for:

SWANNE, JOHN. Matric. sizar from TRINITY, Michs. 1587; Scholar, 1593; B.A. 1593–4; M.A. 1597. V. of Sawston, Cambs., 1600–1639. Married Sarah Adams, of Gt Shelford, in 1604. Buried, Nov. 19, 1639, at Sawston. Probably father of John (1622) and perhaps of Thomas (1622).

This John Swan (the spelling used in the Parish Registers of Sawston) was obviously held in great regard. In the will of John Jefferie, a yeoman (cited *in St Mary's Sawston 970–1800* by F. Bywaters), made on 20 September 1624, after various bequests to the poor of the Parish, there is an item regarding the Incumbent which directs that £5 'be paid unto Him within one month after my decease by my Executors, he preaching at my buriall'. Again, the deed of gift of Elizabeth Wakelin, dated January 27th, 1636 (cited in *St Mary's Sawston 970–1800* by F. Bywaters), makes note of

the great zeal and good will which she beareth to John Swan the Vicar now being, and for the better maintenance of him the said John Swan and his successors, and for the better enabling him and them in his and their hospitality and studies and to live and reside in the said town of Sawston where there is now no dwelling house belonging to the said Vicarage, and again for the great zeal which she hath to the poor people,

granted a dwelling house and one and a half acres of land to the Vicar, on condition of his residency there and his payment of 40 shillings to the poor on the anniversary of her death each year, and his preaching a sermon on that day.

This John Swan seems to have ministered faithfully to his people, and in the Visitation of 1622 (Ely Diocesan Archives – Bishops' Records in Cambridge University Library: Parochial Records in Cambridge Record Office, Shire Hall, Cambridge) he is reported as having 'done all things according as is required'. Of this second John Swann, Venn enters:

SWANN, JOHN. Matric. sizar from TRINITY, Easter 1622. Probably s. of John (1587). B.A. 1625–6; M.A. 1629. Ord. deacon (Peterb.) Dec. 2; priest Dec. 3, 1629. Minister of Duxford St. Peter, Cambs. 1630. V. of Sawston, 1641–60; again presented, 1664–9. V. of Whittlesford, 1647–69. Buried at Sawston, Mar. 17, 1670–1

Here there is a considerable discrepancy with Parish and Diocesan Records (Ely Diocesan Archives) in the matter of the second John Swann's appointments. The archives and Venn agree that this John Swann was priested the day after he was made Deacon. He then became Minister of Duxford St Peter in 1630, and Vicar of Whittlesford from 1647 to 1669. The parish records, however, claim that he became Vicar of Sawston, presumably in plurality with Whittlesford, at the Restoration of the Monarchy in 1660 – not 1641 as Venn notes. It is not without significance that the corner of the river at the end of Common Lane in Sawston is known as Swan's Corner. The parish history by the Reverend Ronald Bircham, sometime Vicar of Sawston, claims that it was so called in local tradition because it was the place where John Swan crossed the river coming from Whittlesford (R. Bircham: *St Mary's, Sawston: a History 970–1800*, 1981).

Venn would appear to be mistaken with regard to this John Swann being Vicar of Sawston from 1641, for it is clear from both diocesan and parish records (Ely Diocesan Archives) that on the death of the first John Swann, one John Gates, a Master of Arts of Corpus Christi College, Cambridge, was presented with the Living of Sawston by John Byatt and his wife, Elizabeth Greenhill or Greenell. The Greenells were the Patrons of the Living. The only other note concerning this incumbency is that in 1643 William Dowsing, the militant Puritan iconoclast, visited Sawston on 19 March and broke down

> the five superstitious Inscriptions 'Orate pro animabus' and 'cuius animae propitietur Deaus' and 'Pray for the Soules,' and a Crucifix in the Chancell, and some sixteen superstitious pictures.

These had been tolerated by the first John Swann, which fact takes him out of the category of the Puritan minded. These records also state that in 1645 a Master of Arts of St Catherine's College, Cambridge, was presented. In the survey of 1650, this person is described 'an able preaching minister, and a very deserving man'. This description, and his removal at the Restoration would seem to indicate where his sympathies lay.

In 1660, according to these Records (Ely Diocesan Archives) John Swann was presented with the Vicarage of Sawston. He seems to have resigned in 1662. The reason for this is not clear, but there does seem to have been a matter of considerable concern that the Chancel steps, which had been levelled between the Visitations of 1638 and 1665, were to be raised again. That they were not so dealt with until at least after 1665 is clear. John Swann was re-presented in 1664 and remained as Incumbent until 1669. It may well be that he instigated the reinstatement of a raised Chancel, and came up against the echoes of Puritan minded opposition. The intervening Incumbency between 1662 and 1664 was filled by William Stukeley, MA of Magdalene College, Cambridge. He left abruptly. There may have been two factions in the Parish – one Puritan minded, one thinking back to the days of the first John Swann – between which both this John Swann and William Stukeley fell, the one supporting one, the other the opposing party. That one won the day perhaps reflects the success of John Swann. All this, of course, can only be conjecture, but this is the only issue of note which could possibly explain these comings and goings of Incumbents.

There is no doubt, despite Venn's proviso, that the second John Swann was the son of the first Incumbent of Sawston of the same name. He was so baptized in Sawston Church, and in 1634 married Frances Rudland at Sawston on 21 June 1634, probably by his father. She died on 6 December 1667.

From all this, we have an impression of the second John Swann as a man in the same tradition as his father – a moderate churchman, well educated and principled. This is borne out by the sources he uses in some of the books attributed to him. There is a knowledge of the classical Greek and Latin philosophers and mathematicians, an appeal to the Fathers of the early Church to an extent which no Puritan would accord such a source of authority, and a handling of the scriptures more reminiscent of Andrewes's paradigmatic method – or even that of his contemporary John Hales – than of any of the accepted Puritan inclined interpretations.

A note in the papers of Bishop Simon Patrick, Bishop of Ely, 1691–1707, decisively attributes the authorship of *Speculum Mundi* to the second John Swann. The dedicatory notice in the second edition (1643) would make this so, particularly as it mentions 'continuing the Dedication of this unworthy Work ... to James, Duke of Richmond and Lenox', which, had the first John Swann been the author, would have necessitated different wording after his death in 1639. On the basis of his theological methodology (the appeal to scripture used in a paradigmatic way, the appeal to the Fathers, the appeal to classical authors' works, and the appeal to contemporary comentators on Genesis, both in France and England) his interest in chronology and mathematics, and his style (his development of an argument by precise steps and divisions, and his employment at significant parts of his argument of rhetorical questions), it is possible to be clear as to which books promiscuously attributed to him by the *Short Title Catalogue*, by *Lowndes* and by *Wing*, are indeed of his authorship. These are:

1   Speculum Mundi, or a Glasse representing the face of the world; shewing both that it did begin, and must end: The manner How and time When being largely examined. Whereunto is Joyned an Hexameron, or a serious discorse of the causes, continuance, and qualities of things in Nature; occasioned as matter pertinent to the work done in the six dayes of the Worlds creation. The second Edition enlarged. Printed by Roger Daniel, Printer to the Universitie of Cambridge. Anno Dom. 1643. First edition, 1635, later editions and reprintings, 1643, 1644, 1665, 1670, 1698. (Wing rev. S6238 etc, STC rev.23516).

2   The Signs of Heaven. Or a Sermon on Jeremiah x.2, preached on the day before that Great Eclipse of the Sun, which was on the Nine and Twentieth day of March in the year of our Lord God 1652 and year of the world 5656. By John Swan, Minister of God's Word, London 1652. The text from Jeremiah reads 'Thus says the Lord: Learn not the way of the Nations, nor be dismayed at the signs of the heavens because the Nations are dismayed at them, for the customs of the peoples are false'. (Wing rev. S6237).

3   Calamus Mensurans: The Measuring Reed or the Standard of Time. 1653. By

the author of Speculum Mundi. Printed for John Williams. London 1653. (Wing rev. S6235).

4   An Ephemeris or Almanack for the year of our Lord (years from 1657–1661), Being the first after Leap Year and from the world's Creation 5664. Calculated properly for the meridian of Ickleton in Cambridge-shire, where the Pole-Artick is elevated above the Horizon 52 degrees and 9 minutes. But may indifferently serve for any other place within this Nation. by John Swan, Cambridge. John Field, printer to the Universitie, (1657–1661. (Wing rev. A2465 etc).

5   Profano-Mastix, or a briefe and necessarie Direction concerning the respect which wee Owe to God, and His House, London, 1639. (STC rev. 23513).

The thing of interest to note is that in both the *Almanack* and *The Signs of Heaven*, Swan has reviewed his dating of the creation of the world as he states it in *Speculum Mundi*. There he writes concerning the first day of creation: 'So that the 17 of April seems to me to be the first day of the worlds Creation, 3948 years before the beginning of the common Aera of Christs birth' (Chapter 2, p.36). In both the later works, he rather agrees with Archbishop Ussher's calculation of 4004 years before the birth of Christ. Ussher published his ideas on the matter in his *Annales Veteris et Novi Testamenti*, between 1650 and 1654. Had he kept to his former calculations, Swan would have written in *The Signs of Heaven* and the *Almanack*, 5600 and 5609 respectively for his dating of the year of the world.

These four works are, on the bases of the above criteria, the only books which can be attributed undoubtedly to this John Swan, the younger, of Sawston.

There is, however, also a third John Swan, Swann, or Swain (variously) who was Rector of Burwash in the County of Sussex, Diocese of Chichester. From the dedication in *Speculum Mundi* to 'James, Duke of Richmond and Lenox', the suspicion arises that this work might be attributable to this John Swann. The reason here is that for a considerable time, the Dukes of Richmond had been Patrons of Burwash. However, the Diocesan Records for Chichester have very little pre-1670 information. George Hennessy's *Clergy Lists of the Diocese of Chichester*, 1900, indicates a Duke of Richmond as Patron of Burwash in the fifteenth century, an Ashburnham in the sixteenth, but nothing for the seventeenth. The evidence for the authorship of the younger John Swann of Sawston is clear, however, but it is intriguing that the dedication should be so rendered, particularly with the estates of the Richmond and Lennox family being in the area of the Parish of Burwash. The only possible reason could be a conjectural cultural interest of the then Duke in things mathematical or astronomical – a not uncommon interest among the seventeenth century nobility since they could afford astronomical instruments.

John Swann, Rector of Burwash, was a graduate of The Queen's College, Oxford. Foster notes that he first matriculated from Christ Church in 1607, but entered Queen's as a Commoner (also according to the College Entrance Book), in Christmas (Hilary) Term 1607/8, graduating BA on 23 October 1611, MA on 6 July, 1615. It is perhaps significant that this Swann became Rector of Burwash at the same time that Brian Duppa, who had been Dean of Christ Church when Swann matriculated (graduated?), became Bishop of Chichester. This significance lies in Duppa's fervent royalist sympathies.

One of the books attributed to John Swann the younger of Sawston by the *Short Title Catalogue* is

> Redde Debitum. Or a Discourse in defence of three chiefe Fatherhoods, grounded upon a Text dilated to the Latitude of the Fift Commandment; and is grounded thereupon because 'twas first intended for the Pulpit, and should have been concluded in one or two Sermons, but is extended since to a larger Tract; and written Chiefely in confutation of all disobedient and factious kinde of People, who are enemies both to the Church, and State. By John Swan. London, Printed by I.D. for John Williams, at the Signe of the Crane, in St. Pauls Church-yard. 1640. (STC rev. 23514).

The only link with this book and the books which have been definitely attributed to John Swan of Sawston, above, is that it is printed, as was *Calamus Mensurans* later, for John Williams, London. However, the style and content of *Redde Debitum* bears no resemblance to the form and substance of those other works. The subject matter was dear to the heart of high church royalists – the Fatherhood of God in its relation to the Fatherhood of the Monarch and the Fatherhood exercised by spiritual fathers-in-God within the Church. There is no such interest in the works of John Swann the younger of Sawston. He is more concerned with the broad sweep of the doctrines of Creation and the Incarnation affecting existence and the cosmic ordering of things, than with doctrine which is harnessed to the – albeit necessary – dimension of national politics and ecclesiology.

Moreover, the style is different. There is, in *Redde Debitum*, a use of judgemental phraseology to give weight to an argument, which is totally lacking in, for example, *Speculum Mundi*. Also, in the latter work, there is no hint of any attempt to comment on affairs of state, Church and society in this way, which would have been the case had the author also been the author of *Redde Debitum*, order in creation as it is outlined in *Speculum Mundi* lending itself to a development of argument in favour of national and social order. But in *Redde Debitum*, there is no recourse to such a development of thought as is found in *Speculum Mundi*. The same holds true of *Profano-Mastix* compared with *Speculum Mundi*.

Again, a partisan spirit, notably lacking in *Speculum Mundi*, is clearly stated in *Redde Debitum* and *Profano-Mastix*. Criticism of the Puritan faction abounds. The sources appealed to – the Bible and the Fathers – are used in a different way. In *Redde Debitum*, the cause of Royal Fatherhood is known, the end is clear, and scriptural and Patristic are used rather as evidences to support a conclusion already reached, rather than the meticulous use of sources to reach a conclusion as is found in the other works of John Swan of Sawston. Neither are the same contemporary sources cited. The King's own works are the mainstay of this work in this respect. The unlikelihood of three such diverse works being published by the same author within such a short space (for the seventeenth century) of each other is also considerable.

The most likely author of *Redde Debitum* and *Profano-Mastix* (the grounds for saying this of this latter are again, style and content) is John Swan, Rector of Burwash. He was removed in 1658 from his Benefice, and an intruded Minister, Wail Attersole, took over. This John Swan was clearly not acceptable to the Puritans. (see J. Foster: *Alumni Oxomienses*).

One other work attributed in the *Short Title Catalogue* to John Swan of Sawston has to be considered here. This is: *A True and Briefe Report of Mary Glover's Vexation, and of her deliverance by meanes of fastinge and prayer*, by John Swan, student in Divinitie, 1603 (STC rev. 23517). This narrates an exorcism in which a number of clergy took part. Mary Glover was supposedly bewitched by one Elizabeth Jackson, and the author outlines the case and subsequent happenings. There are two reasons for doubting the attributed authorship. The first is the content and style. Neither the subject matter nor the obsession with witchcraft – clearly a Puritan tendency in the way it is expressed here (despite the dedication to the King, who, in any case had taken an interest in the case of Elizabeth Jackson) – are hallmarks of John Swan the younger of Sawston. There is nothing remotely resembling the way in which Swan of Sawston thought, had interest or wrote. Nor could this be attributed to his father, to whom the date would be more appropriate. The case against attributing this work either to the father or the son is the title accorded to this John Swan – 'Student in Divinity'. This is possibly a Lambeth licence of status, but it would be a curious description to use if it were the older John Swan who was the author, a graduate and an Incumbent. The case was heard in London, the happening having occurred there, and the whole description implies that it was a body of local ministers which was concerned in it. From the dates of his matriculation, graduation and ordination, the date of birth for John Swan the younger would have been 1604. This rules out any possibility that he was the author of this work. The same disbarrment through age is applicable to John Swan of Burwash.

We are therefore left with what is more than a probability; that there were four John Swans of this period – John Swan the elder, Incumbent of Sawston; his son John Swan the younger, also Incumbent of the same benefice and author of the four books listed above; John Swan, Vicar of Burwash and author of *Redde Debitum* and *Profano-Mastix*; and John Swan, a licentiate of London (although there are no references to him in the London Diocesan Records, not surprisingly in view of his comparitively insignificant status, there being not a few Students in Divinity), author of the work on Mary Glover's case. This being so, it can only be concluded that the *Short Title Catalogue* requires correction in the matter of attributions to John Swan.

This note on John Swan was published in *Notes and Queries*, Volume 41 (new series), No. 2 (1994), pp.161–5 and is reproduced here by permission of Oxford University Press.

Bibliography

Andrewes, Lancelot, *Ninety-six Sermons*, 1635 edn.

Andrewes, Lancelot, *Oposcula* (Collected Works), L.A.C.T. edn.

Andrewes, Lancelot, *Preces Privatae*, Oxford edn, 1675.

Andrewes, Lancelot, *Preces Privatae*, trans. F. Brightman, 1908.

Athanasius, St, *Works* (*Nicene and Post Nicene Fathers*), Vol. IV, Edinburgh edn, reprinted Eerdmans, 1980.

Bacon, Francis, *Collected Works*, printed by J. Rivington, London, 1778 (Five Vols).

Barlowe, Sir William, *The Sum of the Conference*, 1625 edn.

Barth, K., *Church Dogmatics*, Volume I, part 2, T. and T. Clark, 1956, Volume III, parts 1, 2, 3 and 4, T. and T. Clark, 1958–1961.

Barth, K. *Fides Quaerens Intellectum*, 1931.

Basil, St, *Hexaemeron* (*Works*), Edinburgh edn, reprinted Eerdmans, 1983.

Bingham, M., *Scotland under Mary Stuart*, Allen and Unwin, 1971.

Bourne, E.C.E., *The Anglicanism of William Laud*, 1947.

Brookes, P., *Thomas Cranmer's Doctrine of the Eucharist*, Macmillan, 1965.

Browne, Sir Thomas, *Religio Medici*, 1642 edn.

Cadoux, J.C., *The Early Church and the World*, T. and T. Clark, 1925.

Calvin, John, *Sermons from Job*, trans. by L. Nixon, Baker, 1952.

Calvin, John, *On God and Political Duty*, trans. by J.T. McNeill, Bobs-Merrill Co., 1956.

Calvin, John, *Commentaries*, Oliver and Boyd, 1959 and various years.

Calvin, John, *De Aeterna Praedestione* (*Concerning the Eternal Predestination of God*), trans. J.K. Reid, James Clarke & Co., 1961.

Calvin, John, *Concerning Scandals*, trans. by J.W. Fraser, St Andrew Press, 1978.

Calvin, John, *Institutes of the Christian Religion*, trans. H. Beveridge, Eerdmans, 1979.

Chrimes, S.B., *English Constitutional History*, Oxford University Press, 1967.

Clarendon, *History of the Rebellion and Civil Wars in England*, 1704 edn.

Clarke, F.A., *Life of Thomas Ken*, 1896.

Cyprian, St, *De Catholicae Ecclesiae Unitate*.

Dacre, Lord (H.R. Trevor-Roper), *Archbishop Laud*, Oxford University Press, 1940.

Davies, G., *The Early Stuarts* (in the Oxford History of England), Oxford University Press, 1934

Dick, O.L. (ed.), *Aubrey's Brief Lives*.

Dictionary of National Biography, 1893.

Diocesan Records, Chichester; Ely; London; Winchester.

Donaldson, G., *Scotland: James V to James VII*, Edinburgh, 1970.

Duckett, E.S., *Anglo-Saxon Saints and Scholars*, New York, 1948.

Duke, A., 'The Face of Popular Religious Dissent in the Law Countries, 1520–1530', *Journal of Ecclesiastical History*, Vol. XXVI, no.1.

Eliot, T.S., *For Lancelot Andrewes: Essays on Style and Order*, Oxford University Press, 1928

Elton, G.R., *England under the Tudors*, Cambridge, 1955.

Elton, G.R. (ed.), *The Tudor Constitution, Documents and Commentary*, Cambridge University Press, 1960.

Frere, W.H., *A History of the English Church*, Vol. V, *Elizabeth and James I*, Macmillan, 1911.

Harington, Sir J., *A Briefe View of the State of the Church of England*, 1653 edn.

Henry, D.P., *The Logic of St Anselm*, Oxford University Press, 1967.

Herbert, George, *Priest to the Temple*, 1701 edn.

Higham, F., *Lancelot Andrewes*, SPCK, 1951.

Hill, C., *Economic Problems of the Church from Archbishop Whitgift to the Long Parliament*, Oxford University Press, 1956.

Hill, C., *Puritanism and Revolution*, Secker and Warburg, 1958.

Hill, C., *Society and Puritanism in Pre-Revolutionary England*, London, 1964.

Hill, C., *Change and Continuity in Seventeenth Century England*, Weidenfeld and Nicolson, 1979.

Hollings, M., *Europe in Renaissance and Reformation*, Methuen, 1948.

Hooker, Richard, *The Laws of Ecclesiastical Polity*, ed. Keble, 1836 edn.

Irenaeus, St., *Works* (*Ante-Nicene Fathers*, Edinburgh edn, reprinted Eerdmans, 1981).

Isaacson, H., *An Exact Narration of the Life and Death of Lancelot Andrewes*, 1650 edn.

Kenyon, J.P., *The Stuart Constitution*, Cambridge University Press, 1966.

Kenyon, J.P., *Stuart England*, Cambridge University Press, 1978.

Laud, W., A Relation of the Conference betweene William Laud then Lrd. Bishop of St. Davids, Now Lord Archbishop of Canterbury and Mr. Fisher the Jesuit, London, Printed by Richard Badger, 1639.

Laud, William, *Sermons*, ed. J.W. Hatherell, London, 1829.

Laud, William, *A Summary of His Devotions*, ed. J.H. Parker, Oxford, 1838.

Laud, William, *Private Devotions*, ed. J.H. Parker, Oxford, 1888.

Lawson, J.P., *The Life and Times of William Laud, D.D.*: Vol.I and Vol.II, C.J.G. and F. Rivington, 1829.

McAdoo, H.R., *The Spirit of Anglicanism*, A. & C. Black, 1965.

McEvoy, J., *The Philosophy of Robert Grosseteste*, Clarendon, 1986.

McIntyre, J., *St. Anselm and His Critics*, T. and T. Clark, 1954.

MacKenzie, I.M., Unpublished MTh Thesis, 'The Doctrine of the Holy Spirit in the Works of Lancelot Andrewes', Edinburgh University, 1970.

McKinney, R.W.A. (ed.), *Creation, Christ and Culture, Studies in Honour of H. F. Torrance*, T. and T. Clark, 1976.

MacLeane, D., *Lancelot Andrewes*, George Allen and Sons, 1910.

Mason, F., *The Authoritie of the Church in Making Canons and Constitutions Concerning Things Indifferent*, 1607 edn.

Medley, D.J.. *English Constitutional History*, B.H. Blackwell, 1898.

Milton, John, *New Forcers of Conscience under the Long Parliament*, from Poems Upon Several Occasions, 1673.

Moorman, J.R.H., *A History of the Church in England*, A. & C. Black, 1953.

More, P.L. and Cross, F.L., *Anglicanism*, SPCK, 1951.

O'Donovan, O., *On the Thirty Nine Articles*, Paternoster Press, 1986.

Ottley, R.L., *Lancelot Andrewes*, Methuen, 1905.

Oxford Dictionary of the Christian Church (2nd edn), Oxford University Press, 1974.

Palmer, G.H., *A Herbert Bibliography*, Cambridge University Press, 1911.

Parish Records: St Giles-in-the-Fields, London; Sawston, Ely.

Parker, T.H.L., *The Doctrine of the Knowledge of God: A Study in the Theology of John Calvin*, Oliver and Boyd, 1952.

Parker, T.H.L., *John Calvin*, J.M.Dent and Sons, 1975.

Pearson, John, *The Golden Remains of the Ever Memorable John Hales*, 1659 edn.

Relton, H.M., *Religion and the State*, Unicorn Press, 1937.

Rowse, A.L., *Reflections on the Puritan Revolution*, Methuen, 1986.

Russell, A.T., *Memoirs of the Life and Works of Lancelot Andrewes*, 1860.

Sander, N., *Rise and Growth of the Anglican Schism*, Burns and Oates, 1877.

Sanderson, Robert, *Sermons Preached*, 1627 edn.

Smith, D.N., *Seventeenth Century Characters*, Clarendon, 1918, reprinted 1950.

Southern, R., Robert Grosseteste: *The Growth of an English Mind in Medieval Europe*, Clarendon, 1988.

Southey, R., *The Book of the Church*, John Murray, 1837.

Stone, Lawrence, *The Causes of the English Revolution 1529–1642*, Routledge, Keegan and Paul, 1972.

Story, G.M., *Lancelot Andrewes: Sermons*, Clarendon, 1967.

Streatfield, F., *The State Prayers and Other variations in the Book of Common Prayer*, A.R. Mowbray, 1950.

Swete, H.B., *Church Services and Service Books Before the Reformation*, SPCK, 1896.

Sykes, N., *The Crisis of the Reformation*, Geoffrey Bles, 1938.

Sykes, N., *Old Priest and New Presbyter*, Cambridge University Press, 1957.

Tanner, J.R., *Constitutional Documents of the Reign of James I*, Cambridge University Press, 1930.

Tawney, R.H., *Religion and the Rise of Capitalism*, Penguin edn, 1938.

Tawney, R.H., *The Rise of the Gentry*, 1941.

Tertullian, *Works* (*Ante-Nicene Fathers*, Edinburgh edn, reprinted Eerdmans, 1980, 1982).

Thomas, Edward, *Oxford*, Hutchinson, re-published 1983.

Tillyard, E.M.W., *The Elizabethan World Picture*, Chatto and Windus, 1960.

Torrance, T.F., *Kingdom and Church*, Oliver and Boyd, 1956.

Torrance, T.F., *Conflict and Agreement in the Church*, Vols. I and II, Lutterworth, Vol.I, 1959, Vol.II, 1960.

Torrance, T.F., *Theology in Reconstruction*: SCM, 1965.

Torrance, T.F., *Space, Time and Incarnation*, Oxford University Press, 1969.

Torrance, T.F., *Theological Science*, Oxford University Press, 1969.

Torrance, T.F., *God and Rationality*, Oxford University Press, 1971

Torrance, T.F., *Theology in Reconciliation*, Geoffrey Chapman, 1975.

Torrance, T.F., *Space, Time and Resurrection*, Handsel Press, 1976.

Torrance, T.F., *Christian Theology and Scientific Culture*, Christian Journals, 1980.

Torrance, T.F., *The Ground and Grammar of Theology*, Christian Journals, 1980.

Torrance, T.F., *Divine and Contingent Order*, Oxford University Press, 1981.

Torrance, T.F., *Transformation and Convergence in the Frame of Knowledge*, Christian Journals, 1984.

Torrance, T.F., *The Christian Frame of Mind*, Handsel Press, 1985.

Torrance, T.F., *The Trinitarian Faith*, T. and T. Clark, 1988.

Trevor-Roper, H.R. (Lord Dacre) *Archbishop Laud* (2nd edn, 1962).

Wakeman, H.O., *An Introduction to the History of the Church of England*, Rivingtons, 1904.

Walton, I., *The Lives*, Rivington, London, 1840 edn.

Wedgewood, C.V., *The Trial of Charles I*, The Reprint Society, London, 1966.

Welsby, P., *Lancelot Andrewes, 1555–1626*, SPCK, 1958.

White, A., *Lancelot Andrewes and His Private Devotions*, 1896.

White, Francis, *A Treatise of the Sabbath Day, Containing a Defence of the Orthodoxal Doctrine of the Church of England against Sabbatarian Novelty*, 1635 edn.

Index